T0330365

Innovation, Growth, and Succession in Asian Family Enterprises

THE JOHNS HOPKINS UNIVERSITY SERIES ON ENTREPRENEURSHIP

Series Editor: Phillip H. Phan, *The Johns Hopkins University, USA*

From its inception more than 130 years ago, The Johns Hopkins University has led the world in scientific discovery and innovation. Starting with the Master of Science in Management Science in 1916, the university has focused its lens on bringing the most up-to-date concepts to business education. In 2007, the university established the Johns Hopkins Carey Business School to transform business education through a uniquely humanistic, integrated approach to research. This series continues the tradition of discovery and innovation by bringing the best research in technological entrepreneurship and management in the form of book-length original contributions and edited volumes on topics of contemporary interest and theoretical significance.

Titles in the series include:

Innovation, Growth, and Succession in Asian Family Enterprises

Edited by

Hung-bin Ding

Associate Professor, Department of Management and International Business, Sellinger School of Business and Management, Loyola University, Maryland, USA

Hsi-Mei Chung

Professor, Department of Business Administration, I-Shou University, Taiwan

Andy Yu

Associate Professor of Management, Management Department, University of Wisconsin-Whitewater, USA

Phillip H. Phan

Alonzo and Virginia Decker Professor, The Carey Business School, The Johns Hopkins University, USA

THE JOHNS HOPKINS UNIVERSITY SERIES ON ENTREPRENEURSHIP

Edward Elgar
PUBLISHING

Cheltenham, UK • Northampton, MA, USA

Published by
Edward Elgar Publishing Limited
The Lypiatts
15 Lansdown Road
Cheltenham
Glos GL50 2JA
UK

Edward Elgar Publishing, Inc.
William Pratt House
9 Dewey Court
Northampton
Massachusetts 01060
USA

A catalogue record for this book
is available from the British Library

Library of Congress Control Number: 2020952036

This book is available electronically in the **Elgar**online
Business subject collection
http://dx.doi.org/10.4337/9781839104336

ISBN 978 1 83910 432 9 (cased)
ISBN 978 1 83910 433 6 (eBook)

Printed and bound by CPI Group (UK) Ltd, Croydon, CR0 4YY

Contents

Figures

Contributors

Soroush Aslani is Associate Professor of Management at the University of Wisconsin-Whitewater. He received his PhD degree in Organizational Behavior from Northwestern University in Evanston, Illinois, USA. His research is primarily in the area of cross-cultural management, cross-cultural negotiations, and social movements. In particular, he studies the impact of culture on motives, emotions, and strategies of people in conflict situations.

Katalien Bollen is affiliated to research group Occupational and Organizational Psychology and Professional Learning at KU Leuven, Belgium. Her research focuses on conflict management, mediation, leadership, and coaching in both family and non-family businesses. Katalien also acts as consultant and mediator.

Donella Caspersz is Senior Lecturer and Director of United Nations Principles for Responsible Management Education at the University of Western Australia's Business School. Donella is also Academic Advisor on the Board of Family Business Australia, Western Australia and co-convenes the annual Asia-Pacific Family Business Symposium. She researches in the area of family business studies, and human resource management and employment relations. Donella publishes extensively with her research in family business focusing on how non-financial factors influence operations and management in a family business.

Artemis Chang is Associate Professor at QUT Business School and Principal Supervisor of the Australian Taiwanese Chamber of Commerce – Queensland Chapter. Artemis is a first-generation migrant from Taiwan and is currently researching immigrant entrepreneurship activities in Australia. Artemis is a process researcher, focusing on the influence of time and context. She has published in journals such as *Academy of Management Journal*, *Asia Pacific Journal of Management*, *European Management Review*, *International Journal of HRM*, and *International Journal of Project Management*.

Hsi-Mei Chung is Professor of the Department of Business Administration, I-Shou University, Taiwan. She has served as Global Board Member for the STEP Project for Family Enterprising (2014–16), 2015 and 2016 International Family Enterprise Research Academy (IFERA) Best PhD Research Proposal

Award Jury Chair, and Program Co-Chair of the 2017 IFERA Global Conference in Taiwan. She has published over 60 academic articles, book chapters, and magazine articles. Hsi-Mei aims to push the long-lasting plan of family businesses and keeps good collaborative relationships with multiple research and practical institutions.

Hung-bin Ding is Associate Professor of Entrepreneurship and Strategic Management. He is also Chair of the Department of Management and International Business in the Sellinger School of Business and Management at Loyola University, Maryland, USA. He received his PhD in Management from the Rensselaer Polytechnic Institute. Hung-bin's research interests are in the areas of family business, family office, entrepreneurship, and corporate social responsibility (CSR). His recent research projects focus on family offices and CSR in family businesses.

Komala Inggarwati Efendy is Senior Lecturer in the Faculty of Economics and Business at Satya Wacana Christian University, Indonesia. Komala heads the Centre for Family Business Studies, which seeks to promote the study of family businesses particularly in Indonesia and disseminate the results to academic communities of interest, family business owners and practitioners, and other interested groups. She has been an instructor in numerous entrepreneurship training programs for university students and for micro, small, and medium enterprises.

Martin C. Euwema is Full Professor in Organizational Psychology at KU Leuven, Belgium, Co-Director of the Leuven Center for Collaborative Management, and Chair of the research group Occupational and Organizational Psychology and Professional Learning. He is past president of the International Association for Conflict Management. Martin's interests are conflict management and mediation, organizational change, and (international) leadership. He has wide experience as a consultant and mediator.

Stone Han received his PhD in management from I-Shou University, Taiwan. His research interests include cross-national studies, institutional theory, strategic management and family business.

Min-ping Kang is Associate Professor in the Graduate Institute of Global Business and Strategy at National Taiwan Normal University. Her research, drawing largely on transaction cost, resource-based, and learning perspectives, examines interorganizational relationships, managerial resources, and firm growth, and has been published in journals such as *Strategic Management Journal*, *Management Decision*, and *NTU Management Review*. Her current research focuses on the roles of female family members in family business.

Rong Pei is Full Professor at the School of Management and Economics, Beijing Institute of Technology (BIT) in China and Director of the Joint Research Center for Sino-Foreign Family Business at BIT. She is also the dissertation evaluation expert in the academic papers expert database of the Chinese National Education Commission, and the special expert at the *Journal of China Family Business Review*. Rong's research interests include management communication, social networking and *guanxi*, family businesses, and entrepreneurship. She has rich practical experience as a management consultant.

Phillip H. Phan holds a joint appointment in medicine at the Johns Hopkins University School of Medicine. His research focuses on the processes and barriers to the successful innovation of devices, therapies, services, and processes. Phillip is the Alonzo and Virginia Decker Professor of Strategy and Entrepreneurship in the Carey Business School at the Johns Hopkins University. He received his BBA from the University of Hawaii and his PhD from the University of Washington, USA. He joined the Carey Business School faculty in 2008.

Henry Shi is Senior Lecturer in Family Business and Entrepreneurship at the University of Adelaide. He has a PhD in Management from the University of Auckland. His research focuses on the strategic management and entrepreneurial undertakings of family firms and their interplay with the socio-economic context. His work has been published in multiple scholarly journals, including the *Journal of Small Business Management*, *Journal of Business Ethics*, *Long Range Planning*, and *International Journal of Entrepreneurial Behaviour and Research*.

Dina L. Taylor is Assistant Dean of Administration for the College of Architecture, Design, and the Arts at the University of Illinois in Chicago, USA. She received her Doctor of Business Administration in Management and Entrepreneurship from the University of Wisconsin-Whitewater. Her current research focuses on long-term orientation, entrepreneurial orientation, firm performance, family businesses, and small and medium-sized enterprises.

Salvatore Tomaselli is Associate Professor of Business Administration at the Università di Palermo, Italy and Visiting Professor of Entrepreneurship and Family Business at Zagreb University, Croatia. He was visiting professor of family business strategy and governance at the Beijing Institute of Technology, China in 2015. Salvatore is a founding member and fellow of IFERA and his research on family businesses focuses on strategy and governance, ethics, education, agreements, integrating family and business perspectives, and family-in-business model design. He is a member of the Real Academia Europea de Doctores, Barcelona, Spain.

Yong Wang is Professor of Family Business and Entrepreneurship at the University of Wolverhampton, UK. He previously served at IFERA as the board director and was elected as fellow in 2018. He is also Associate Editor for the *Journal of Small Business Management*. His research interests include family business, entrepreneurship, and business performance. His publications have appeared in journals such as the *Journal of Small Business Management*, *Journal of Strategic Information System*, *Journal of Family Business Strategy*, and *International Journal of Entrepreneurial Behaviour and Research.*

Ran Michelle Ye is currently Visiting Professor in the Faculty of Psychology and Educational Science at KU Leuven, Belgium. Michelle's academic research explores the individual's leadership behavior (managerial coaching), diversity in organizations, workplace generational differences, innovation ecosystems, and family business. Her research activities have equipped her with the latest research results and profound theories in areas in which she has hands-on working experience. She has published in several international peer-reviewed journals and presented her research at high-level international conferences.

Andy Yu is Associate Professor of Management in the College of Business and Economics at the University of Wisconsin-Whitewater. He received his PhD from Texas Tech University. His work has appeared in *Family Business Review*, *International Small Business Journal*, *Advances in Entrepreneurship*, *Firm Emergence and Growth*, *Journal of Small Business and Entrepreneurship*, and *Asian Business and Management*. He also co-edited *The Landscape of Family Business* (2013). His research interests include entrepreneurship, family business, and strategy.

Dexi Zheng is Director of Operations for DM Hoffbeck, PLLC, a public accounting firm. He has a Doctor of Business Administration from the University of Wisconsin-Whitewater with an emphasis on entrepreneurship. His research interests include entrepreneurial orientation, market orientation, small and medium-sized enterprises, family businesses, and computer-aided text analysis.

Feihu Zheng is Associate Professor in the International Economics Department of Business School, Beijing Normal University (BNU). He is also Executive Director of the International Industrial Cooperation and Innovation Center of BNU and was Visiting Scholar for Haas, University of California Berkeley in 2012. His research interests include family firm governance, open innovation, and multinational corporation outsourcing. His research includes articles published in *Technology Analysis and Strategic Management*, *World Economy*, and *Nankai Economy Studies* and recent books include *Super-Ownership Advantages and Risk Governance of Firms International Investment* (2019) and *Super-Ownership Advantage and Study of OBOR Investment Strategy* (2017).

Roxanne Zolin is Adjunct Professor at the Noble International Business School in Ghana. Roxanne completed her doctorate at Stanford University and holds a Masters in Sociology, Master of Business Marketing, and Bachelor of Business. She published 50 papers on topics such as the entrepreneurial success of women, migrants, and seniors. Roxanne teaches entrepreneurship in developing nations such as the Congo, Mozambique, Papua New Guinea, and Kenya. She helped to establish a business center in the Congo and presents at entrepreneurship conferences in Kenya.

1. Introduction: The Asian entrepreneurial family enterprise

Hung-bin Ding and Phillip H. Phan

The definition of a family enterprise, that which is owned, controlled, and managed by a family, is rigidly defined in the practice or the literature. Many family enterprises consist of owners from unrelated families. The population of this type of enterprise is also heterogenous, with very different levels of family control, ownership, and management styles. Yet, the topic of family enterprises has been a popular source of inspiration for writers and researchers across cultures and mediums. The commercial success of Downton Abbey[1] and, for the more vintage among us, Dallas,[2] are just two fun examples.

Scholars have observed that in the business landscape, family enterprises are among the most noteworthy. First, as a class they are the longest lived continually operating organizations, as long as 600 years old. These enterprises are still controlled and/or managed by the founding family or other family.[3] Some have familiar names – Beretta (firearms), Zildjian (cymbals), Ford (automobiles) – while others, Kongo Gumi (construction), Barovier & Toso (glass), Richard de Bas (paper), are less familiar. Their long lives contrast with the 30 percent 10-year survival rate of United States private enterprises.[4]

Second, family enterprises are entrepreneurial in nature and values. They have to be so, to survive as long as they have. They vary in size from large multinational corporations (Ford, Samsung, Walmart, and Volkswagen) to small boutique ones (Barovier & Toso, Richard de Bas, and Ed Meier) that few people know of. The ones that grow large often come to dominate the economies in which they operate. They represent brands that have transformed such industries as information technology (Tata), retail (Walmart, Aldi), construction (Toll Brothers), and transportation (Swire) (Bain, 2020).

Third, they are ubiquitous. With the exception of centrally planned economies in which private ownership of capital is prohibited, these enterprises and the social institutions (hospitals, schools, culture, community assistance) they support comprise 50–90 percent of the gross domestic product of economies around the world (Neubauer & Lank, 1998: 10; Colli, Perez, & Rose, 2000; Donckels & Frohlich, 1991).

The family enterprise has been studied from a multitude of disciplinary lenses. Business ownership represents a family's choice in how it will make a living. Such choices are intertwined with the historical, sociological, cultural, psychological, economic, and political tensions impinging on the family unit over long periods of time. For example, understanding the environmental factors driving the motivations to launch a business enterprise was a focus of early sociological studies. The American laundry industry used to be dominated by Chinese immigrant families from the late nineteenth century through to most of the twentieth century. Such dominance was not the result of coordinated action among early Chinese immigrants but the consequence of institutional changes in nineteenth-century America that pushed them toward this industry (Jung, 2007; Siu & Tchen, 1987). In the mid-nineteenth century Chinese laborers were imported to the United States in great numbers to build the Transcontinental Railroad (Chang, 2019). The Chinese eventually came to comprise 90 percent of the labor force for the western part of the railroad and this led to an increase in social tensions that resulted in anti-Chinese movements from as early as the 1850s (Boswell, 1986; Siu & Tchen, 1987). The regional movements coalesced into a series of national campaigns in the 1860s and 1870s that culminated in the 1882 Chinese Exclusion Act (Boswell, 1986; Office of the Historian, n.d.). As a consequence, Chinese laborers and their families were forced to leave their jobs in farms, construction sites, and mines to move into industries, such as laundry, that were considered undesirable by the Americans (Jung, 2007; Siu & Tchen, 1987).

This example illustrates the importance of a multidisciplinary perspective in researching family enterprises. Only a historical sociocultural perspective can explain the origins, heterogeneity, and consequence of immigrant family enterprises. The history of the Chinese-American experience is intertwined with the formation of the American laundry industry. Therefore, scholars looking for theories or general descriptions of the phenomenon should not ignore its distinctive aspects because these will be determined by region, culture, and history. Isolating these distinctive aspects of the experience provide greater explanatory power for the status quo. From a methodological perspective, such historical observations provide unique insights into the dynamics of the family enterprise and their interactions with the immigration experience, host institutions, and other immigrant family networks.

The co-evolution of societies and the families in them suggest that the study of family enterprises needs to include an understanding of the social dynamics in an economy (Martinez & Aldrich, 2014). The wide variation in the success and failure of family enterprises around the world has inspired business scholars to explore the reasons for these outcomes (Donnelley, 1964; Yasuoka, 1984; Ward, 1986). These early scholarly pathfinders led to the inception of the *Family Business Review* in 1988, in which the creation of this academic forum and other similar venues effectively facilitated the growth of family enterprise research in business schools. The resulting scholarly inquiry into the distinctiveness of family business organizations and their strategic choices related to survival and growth greatly increased in the last three decades (Martinez & Aldrich, 2014; De Massis, Frattini, & Lichtenthaler, 2013; Perez & Lluch, 2016; Calabrò et al., 2019).[5]

This volume is a collection of intellectual contributions from eight interdisciplinary research teams. They represent recent attempts to expand the frontier of family enterprise research, often by locating the research in less well-researched contexts (countries, industries, and strategic situations). Deliberately, these chapters represent a diversity of contexts and issues in family enterprises while still being rooted in the scholarly traditions typifying research of the family–business interface. Furthermore, the growing research on family enterprises from other social science disciplines has provided us with new lenses for examining the phenomenon and these perspectives have been introduced, where appropriate, in the chapters.

The purpose of this chapter is to offer a framework for viewing the most recent discussions on family influence in business enterprises, and of the chapters in this book. Although the family of an entrepreneur can be viewed as separate from the business, a family enterprise is defined by the sometimes indistinguishable overlap between the family and the enterprise. These overlaps represent potential sources of theoretical insight and innovation from a research standpoint, and potential sources of competitive advantage for the family enterprise from a practical standpoint.

This subject of family–business interconnectivity or coupling is perhaps a defining area of research in family enterprises. It is one of the earliest topics of inquiry in the field (Ward, 1986). Research in this area falls into the intersection of family and business as shown in our illustration of Davis and Tagiuri's (1989) three-circle model of the family enterprise (Figure 1.1). Here, we discuss what this intersection means, the implications, and highlight the research in succession and governance as the two structural issues most commonly investigated. Our objective is not to review the extensive literature on family and business dynamics, of which many have been conducted, but to highlight the unique issues emerging from the interface of the family unit and an economic organization. For example, in any firm the problems associated with top management team (TMT) processes and performance and firm governance are critical issues, but in the family enterprise these topics take on additional layers of complexity because of the inheritance and succession questions (Ward, 1986; Schulze, Lubatkin, Dino, & Buchholtz, 2001; Young, Peng, Ahlstrom, Bruton, & Jiang, 2008). If done right, effective governance and succession can rejuvenate the entrepreneurial spirit of an established

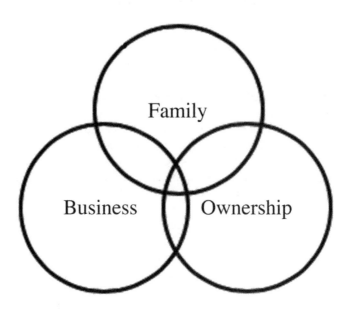

Figure 1.1   *Davis and Tagiuri's (1989) three-circle model of the family enterprise*

family enterprise (Anderson & Reeb; 2003; Au, Chiang, Birtch, & Ding, 2013). If done wrong, these can lead to ossification, decline, and failure.

We then discuss family-related matters that are independent of the business enterprise but are no less important to the understanding of these enterprises. We discuss the fact that a family is a social system in its own right. Some family factors have significant implications for the enterprise. For example, women tend to assume traditional gender roles in paternalistic societies. These often spill over into the roles assumed by female members of the business enterprise (Lyman, 1988; Overbeke, Bilimoria, & Perelli, 2013). When these roles evolve because of changing social norms, enterprise leadership is also affected. Over time, women's roles have expanded from primary caregiver in the home to primary provider; so that in more paternalistic societies, we are witnessing more family enterprises being led by women, where before such events were relatively rare (Jimenez, 2009). Finally, the family is a dynamic social system, which means that system-specific factors, such as the relationship between the family and its social environment, matter (Combs, Shanine, Burrows, Allen,

& Pounds, 2020). Traditionally, these questions have fallen squarely in the family-only domain of the three-circle model (Figure 1.1) but we are seeing more research to link the family social system to the broader societal system, so that a more expansive model now includes a "societal" circle. Societal systems do not always interact directly with the business system, except in the regulations that impact the business or changing consumer demands for its products and service. Societal systems do interact directly with the family system since an aspect of family continuity is its legitimacy in the society in which it is embedded. Hence, in the case of the family enterprise, societal dynamics are more closely connected to the business, because of the family, compared to non-family enterprises.

All the chapters in this book explore the family factors that impact business decisions. While some of them build from the management literature, others have extensive references to studies from sociology, anthropology, and economics. Next, we briefly introduce each chapter and discuss them in relation to the framework in this chapter.

WHEN FAMILY AND BUSINESS OVERLAP

Individuals pursuing business ownership do so with a wide variety of motivations (DeMers, 2015). The successful outcome of this economic choice requires significant commitment from the entrepreneur. Many business owners work longer hours than employees. A recent survey to the subscribers of the New York Enterprise Report found that 33 percent of small business owners work more than 50 hours a week. The same survey also reports that about a quarter of the responding business owners work more than 60 hours a week (Sutter, 2019). While many business owners feel that the extra work is overwhelming (Callahan, 2006), another survey reported that they considered the work justified by the independence they enjoy (Di Gangi, 2016).

Becoming an entrepreneur involves a series of decisions to manage personal and economic trade-offs. While entrepreneurs can sometimes choose to earn less money in order to improve family life, the sources of these tensions exist throughout the business life cycle (Jahanmir, 2016). For example, starting a home business can be an economic solution for young parents to manage child caregiving but can translate to longer working hours because the natural barrier between home and workplace disappears. The family enterprise is a special case of this phenomenon, especially if more than one family member is involved or has ownership shares. In this circumstance, the family enterprise embeds the trade-offs between home, work, and extended family. Additionally, although families are traditionally considered a common source of startup funds, not all family-invested startups become family enterprises. It depends on the interest of family members to participate, whether a succession to the second generation from founding occurs, and the continued interest of family investors to support the growth of the firm. Hence, a family enterprise becomes one when the *family*, not just the founder, eventually controls and manages the business.

Since family resources and labors were contributing factors of a new business venture's survival or success, the family becomes an influential stakeholder of the family enterprise. Therefore, although the venturing process of a family enterprise and a non-family one are conceptually similar (opportunity identification, resource orchestration, risk mitigation, investment for growth), the organizations created through these two processes can be very different (Hoy & Verser, 1994).

The degree of interconnectivity or overlap between the family and the business enterprise varies. In some instances, the family enterprise *is* the family because it provides the economic means for the family to be sustained. In the United States, for example, Asian Indian immigrant families are commonly found in the motel industry. Motels are multi-employee businesses and therefore natural job creation "machines" for family members. More importantly, in these businesses the workplace and living place greatly overlap. Historical accounts of the immigrant businesses in the United States provide detailed descriptions of immigrant families living in the retail store such as Chinese laundries (Jung, 2007; Siu & Tchen, 1987) and Korean groceries (Min, 2011). These home-based family enterprises are not related to immigrant families only. Recent observations from Mexico (Ramirez-Solis, Baños-Monroy, & Rodríguez-Aceves, 2016), Taiwan (Shieh, 1993), and Australia (Holmes, Smith, & Cane, 1997) offer a few other examples.

Family enterprise researchers often use the three-circle model (Tagiuri & Davis, 1982) to capture the relationship between the family and business ties and the business owner. One way to visualize this model is that the circles can overlap to different degrees. If we consider the degree of family–business interconnectivity on a spectrum, the home-based family enterprise represents a situation in which the family and the business completely overlap. On the opposite end of the spectrum, there is no overlap between the family and the business. The family enterprise may still own majority shares or control the board through alliances, but no family member remains on the payroll.

Family inclusion is sometimes crucial to the survival of many family enterprises. In part, this is because of human capital costs but more importantly, immediate family members are more trustworthy in cash-dominant businesses. Many Chinese immigrants' laundry and Korean immigrants' grocery businesses in America probably would not have survived if the founders' spouses and children were not actively involved in operations (Jung, 2007; Siu & Tchen, 1987; Min, 2011). In addition, family members provide important social capital. The business networks created by generations of Chinese migrants in South East Asia are closely associated with the family networks of their business owners. Ethnic Chinese business families dispersed their business interests, sometimes intentionally, to locations around the world to manage the risks of unfamiliar environments (Redding, 1995). The uncertain environments they face require managers to be given high degrees of autonomy in personnel and financial decision making. Hence, the branch managers in these "bamboo network" locations are usually family members (Weidenbaum & Hughes, 1996). While the family network and business connected through family ties maximize the survivability and long-term success of large, multigenerational family enterprises in South East Asia, the network stemmed from collaborative relationships among different families in a single region creates highly flexible and agile hubs of small manufacturers in suburban and rural Taiwan (Shieh, 1993) and played a significant role in the emergence of Chinese family enterprises (Bian, Breiger, Galaskiewicz, & Davis, 2005).

Both the family system and business system have specific requirements for effectiveness. These can be aligned through appropriate structural designs, which is the overarching theme of Chapters 3 and 7 in this volume. Here, the two most frequently studied topics are succession and governance. In the general management literature, succession in the TMT is an important issue. Extant TMT research has identified the environmental, organizational, and personnel factors driving successful and unsuccessful executive team turnover (Barron, Chulkov, & Waddell, 2011) and chief executive officer succession (Berns & Klarner, 2017). While the findings from the TMT literature are instructive for researchers on family enterprise succession, they do not consider the importance of the *family* in these decisions. Seldom are family enterprise successions solely the decision of the founder when family members are involved in the operations of the firm or when ownership is shared by family members or branches of the family tree.

Family enterprise succession is a business founder's plan for exiting the business but unlike typical successions in a non-family enterprise, family enterprise founders have the option to leave the ownership, control, and management of the business to other family members to ensure that their departure does not decouple the family from the business. More importantly, succession is often accompanied by a transfer of control and wealth from one generation to another or from one branch of the family tree to another. Therefore, the decision is deeply fraught with political and social considerations, and also historical implications for the family and its relationship to the community in which it is embedded. In a way, the prolonged coupling of family and business is one reason for the long-lived nature of these enterprises, since families tend to have more enduring legacies than economic organizations.

Managing family succession is challenging in practice. Early studies on succession have identified such issues as training and the selection of successors (Seymour, 1993; Scranton, 1992) and the planning (Schaefer & Frishkoff, 1992; Lansberg & Astrachan, 1994) and implementation (Welsch, 1993; Schwartz, 1954) of succession processes. Several writers have suggested that a family enterprise may need to plan 15–20 years ahead of the succession (Ward, 1990; Stalk & Foley, 2012). Given the complexity and attention needed to keep the family enterprise in the hands of the family, successful execution of succession across the generations is a key factor in family enterprise longevity (Stalk & Foley, 2012).

Underlying the succession event is the corporate governance of an enterprise. The general literature has shown that good corporate governance practices minimize the opportunistic behaviors of managers while safeguarding the interests of shareholders (Neubauer & Lank, 1998). Good corporate governance also ensures or improves organizational performance (Neubauer & Lank, 1998; Mirela-Oana & Melinda-Timea, 2015). Although many corporate governance studies do not examine the specific challenges of family enterprises, their findings are still applicable to family enterprises in which the family and business operations do not overlap, i.e., they no longer employ family members. These organizations are still considered family enterprises because their boards of directors are controlled by family members through the ownership structure. However, family members may not hold executive positions in these organizations anymore. For example, Anderson and Reeb (2003) studied the relationship between family ownership and performance of Standard & Poor's (S&P) 500 list of the largest United States public corporations. They canvassed the S&P 500 between 1992 and 1999 and identified 141 family enterprises. While the founding families still owned fractions of shares, few have family members that are employed in them. Although the founding families may exercise strong influence on the board, the family–business overlap is much weaker than an enterprise that is fully controlled, owned, and staffed by family members.

When a family is still closely connected to the business it founded, the family enterprise may encounter two unique governance issues. The first is the agency problem between majority and minority shareholders (Schulze et al., 2001; Young et al., 2008). This principal–principal agency problem refers to the subversion of minority holders' interest by the majority shareholders. In other words, when a family is a majority shareholder, but not sole owner of a business, the family can exercise control over corporate decisions that benefit the family but harm other shareholders. Additionally, when such business is part of a portfolio of companies controlled by the family, the latter can take steps to shift earnings and valuable assets to other wholly owned entities of the family. This minority shareholder exploitation tactic is known as tunneling (Johnson, La Porta, Lopez-de-Silanes, & Shleifer, 2000), which can have a negative impact on the performance of the enterprise (Johnson et. al., 2000).

The second governance issue is known as the bifurcation bias (Verbeke & Kano, 2010; 2012). This refers to the differential treatment of family and non-family employees in a family enterprise. When a family enterprise gives family employees preferable treatment over non-family employees such as higher compensation or faster promotion, non-family members can be demotivated or seek to pursue opportunities outside of the business. Therefore, reducing or even eliminating bifurcation bias helps reduce employee opportunism and turnover in a family enterprise (Verbeke & Kano, 2010; 2012).

NON-BUSINESS FAMILY FACTORS THAT AFFECT THE BUSINESS

Although business researchers tend to focus on the impact of family inclusion in the business–ownership dyad, the family social system is also affected by being involved in the business. As illustrated in Figure 1.2, the family and its business enterprise are recursively connected to each other. The influence of family is not limited to safeguarding family interests in the business or wealth creation for future generations. Other family factors independent of the family's business interests can also impact business decisions. Family enterprise succession is a good example. Although the responsibilities of being head of the family and leader of the family enterprise are distinct and separate, many family enterprises combine these roles, especially if the founder and patriarch are still alive (Hamilton & Kao, 1990; Mehrotra, Morck, Shim, & Wiwattanakantang, 2013). These types of role configurations can lead business decisions to be suboptimal for the business but optimal for the family. For example, businesses are driven by efficiency considerations in decisions on asset sales and dispositions. Families, on the other hand, have longer time horizons and are more willing to take investment risks to grow family wealth for future generations.

These family factors fall into three categories. The first category is the family structure, which refers to the expected roles of family members and the relational boundary of the family. Some families define themselves by blood and marriage whereas others may define themselves more expansively. Within the definition of "blood," the ties may vary according to the relational distance between a family member and the patriarch and founder. Spouses have special definitions that vary by family. If a spouse is employed by the family enterprise or is a co-founder of the enterprise, their status and influence in the family, because of the business, is likely to be more significant than a spouse who is simply connected by marriage. The degree of separation between a spouse's partner to the patriarch and founder will similarly affect the degree of influence that person wields in the family, and by extension, the family enterprise.

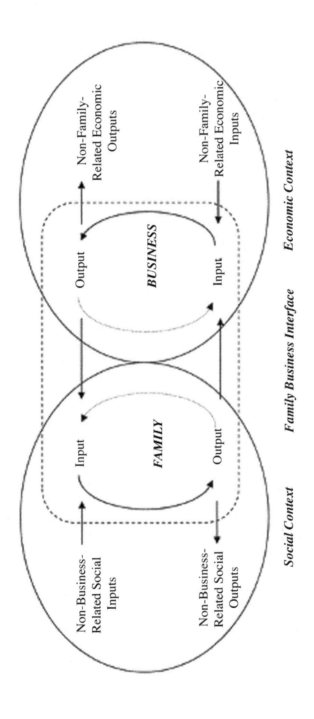

Source: Litz, 2008: 225.

Figure 1.2   *The family–business and business–family as a Möbius strip*

Early studies on this topic looked at spouses' interactions at home and how they balance the competing demands of family and business by role sharing and role specialization (Marshack, 1993; Pratt, 2009). More recently, there has been a growing interest on the topic of women in family enterprises, concomitant with the rise in general interest in women in the workplace and women as corporate leaders. In addition to co-founding businesses with their spouses, women become entrepreneurs to create supplemental income for the family (Oppenheimer, 1977). Many cultures encourage women entrepreneurship (Overbeke et al., 2013) rather than becoming engaged in the core business. These choices are often made because caregiving and other social roles demand more personal resources than full involvement in the core family enterprise can afford. Such limits to women entrepreneurs are particularly prevalent in developing economies (World Bank, 2018). Research has found that women entrepreneurs that are strongly supported by their families are more likely to succeed (Wu, Chang, & Zhuang, 2010) since such support allows them to ease the tension between caregiving and employment. That said, the research as shown that women's social role as primary caregiver continues to influence their choices when navigating the tension between family and business aspirations (Lyman, 1988).

While caregiving can represent a limitation to the economic potential of women as business leaders, the role confers non-active women participants in the family enterprise a higher degree of influence compared to their male counterparts. As primary caregiver, women tend to focus on the durability of future generations and are the conduit by which family values are propagated forward in time. Hence, their willingness to participate in such matters as business succession, wealth transfer, and wealth accumulation is more likely to be taken more seriously. In the same way, spouses of family enterprise owners may perform work that is unpaid (Rowe & Hong, 2000), and hence create social and political capital that can be deployed in the future.

The contribution from spouses, especially wives, extends beyond free labor. Their role as caregiver confers the ability to mediate conflicts and foster cohesion among family members, which are important during times of crises. This cohesion-building function is particularly relevant when there are serious disagreements within the family over a course of action for the business (Campopiano, De Massis, Rinaldi, & Sciascia, 2017; Jimenez, 2009). Strong cohesion in a family creates the foundation for a strong family enterprise (Fernández-Aráoz, Iqbal, Ritter, & Sadowski, 2019). Finally, female family members are increasingly active family enterprise participants (Jimenez, 2009; Campopiano et al., 2017). They may join the board of the family enterprise or join the company as full-time employees. Increasingly, in traditionally paternalistic societies daughters and daughters-in-law are being seen as potential successors in their family enterprises (Overbeke et al., 2013).

Families grow over time. The growth of the family expands the number of family stakeholders, either through employment or ownership. The expansion of the family increases the complexity of stakeholder interests (Ding, 2008). The solution to such a complexity can be family-centric or business-centric. The two approaches are not mutually exclusive, but their foci are different. A family-centric approach generally focuses on ways to consolidate interests within family around ensuring the durability of the family. Common examples of the family-centric approach include family councils (Ward, 1986), family constitutions (Arteaga & Menéndez-Requejo, 2017), and family offices (Rosplock, 2014). The business-centric approach to resolving stakeholder conflict involves approaches to consolidating interests within family around ensuring the durability of the business. Common practices of this approach are to place family members in the family enterprise or to allow representatives of family branches into the board of directors (Ding, 2008).

A second category of family factors has to do with the family system. *Family system* refers to two different concepts in the family enterprise literature. The more common is the reference to the family sub-system defined in the three-circle model (Davis & Tagiuri, 1989; Hoy & Verser, 1994). According to this definition, a family system is a self-sustaining social actor whose members are connected by blood, marriage, or adoption. Hence, the family system has a well-defined boundary, often typified by a last name. The other definition of a family system comes from systems theory (Hall & Fagen, 1956), in which members of a family are connected by exchange relationships. Because these relationships can be semi-permanent, the definition allows for more porous conceptualizations of the family system. Of interest is the behavior of the system as a unit, for example, in how it adapts to environment shocks. A system has the property of being homeostatic, meaning that adjustments to the system's responses to environmental change are always aimed at maintaining equilibrium between inputs and outputs. Family systems theorists study such factors as quality of communication among family members (Cabrera-Suárez, Déniz-Déniz, & Martín-Santana, 2014), family cohesion (Arteaga & Menéndez-Requejo, 2017), conflict (Claßen & Schulte, 2017), and family transitions including life events such as births, deaths, marriages, and divorce (Combs et al., 2020). The concept of the family system in this view allows for the system and its environment to co-evolve, so that the family can affect its environment (White & Klein, 2002). Hence, the degree to which a family system is embedded in the societal meta-system tells us the degree to which the family influences its environment.

The third category of family factors is related to the growth and development of future generations. The upbringing of family members is the caregiving and instruction that they receive during childhood. The sources of the caregiving and instruction may include parents and family (Avloniti, Iatridou,

Kaloupsis, & Vozikis, 2014), neighborhoods and educational institutions (Venkataramani, Cheng, Solomon, & Pollack, 2017), and the institutions of society such as media, schools, and social organizations (Sarche & Spicer, 2008). The outcome of a child's upbringing includes life skills (Martin, Côté, & Woodruff, 2016), personal well-being including personal safety, emotional competence, and social competence (National Academies of Sciences, Engineering, and Medicine, 2016), attitudes toward change (Lupu, Spence, & Empson, 2017), gender ideology (Dekas & Baker, 2014), and personal values (Pratap & Saha, 2018). The shaping of the upbringing outcomes can be intentional and formal, or unintentional and informal. For example, children develop a religious identity by following their parents' religious guidance and participation in religious services (Bengtson, 2013). In the context of family enterprises, children develop attitudes toward work–life balance by observing their parents' struggles to maintain the balance between work and family (Lupu et al., 2017).

Empirical studies have confirmed that children growing up in families with family enterprises are more likely to pursue entrepreneurial careers (Tarling, Jones, & Murphy, 2016). The training and education of the younger generation is a major topic of discussion in the succession planning literature (Walsh, Bruehl, & Di Loreto, 2020). Children growing up in a family that is constantly in conflict with each other are more likely to experience difficulty in maintaining a cohesive family system with their own siblings later in life (Avloniti et al., 2014). When these unresolved conflicts are transferred to the business, failure is not far behind. A recent study on the impact of material conditions on the development of leadership reports that children from families with high parental income are more likely to develop narcissism, which can negatively affect their future leadership effectiveness (Martin et al., 2016). At this time, the business literature is scant on the topic of upbringing in the family enterprise. We hope that this volume moves us away from this condition (Combs et al., 2020). That said, although none of the chapters in this book specifically examines the effect of upbringing, the research on conflict behaviors in family enterprises makes important contributions to this end.

CHAPTERS IN THIS BOOK

The chapter authors in this book report, from their various perspectives, on how family factors influence the family business enterprise. The following is a brief introduction.

Chapter 2 investigates the effect of long-term orientation in family enterprise innovation. Innovation in family enterprise is a quickly growing field of study. Family factors may affect the outcome and process of innovation activities in the family enterprise (Calabrò et al., 2019). Family may also play a role in setting the priorities and objectives of innovation investments in the business (Huang, Ding, & Kao, 2009). In this chapter, Taylor, Aslani, and Zheng review the family involvement literature and propose that long-term orientation, a trait of family enterprises, can moderate the relationship between family involvement and innovation output. This chapter provides new insights to the family enterprise *and* innovation literature by introducing a new influential factor to the ongoing debate.

Chapter 3 connects internationalization strategy and business succession to shed light on how these two business decisions interact with each other. Shi argues that family enterprise owners make decisions regarding successor selection and development, management transfer, and ownership transfer to support the strategic goals of internationalization. Based on data collected from 11 Chinese family enterprises, the author identifies three distinctive approaches to succession. By connecting two important and popular subjects of research in the field, this chapter brings new ideas to succession decisions.

Chapter 4 focuses on a different context and perspective of internationalization. Human families are governed by an institutional logic, which include a set of socially acceptable rules and guidelines for the family. The family institutional logic is relatively stable as long as the macro environment such as religion, community, law remain unchanged (Friedland and Alford, 1991). However, a major change of the macro environment will force the family to reconcile the differences of institutional logics between the home country and the new destination. The context of this theoretical study is the migrant family businesses. Two culturally similar societies can have very different institutional logics. The authors posit that the migrant entrepreneurs need to make sense of the different institutional logics of the host country when they formulate strategic responses to the new environment. Specifically, the immigrant entrepreneurs' business decisions are moderated by the entrepreneurs' identity commitment, institutional logic adherence, and efforts to obtain legitimacy in the host country.

Conflicts occur in families and can spill over into the businesses they run. Growing empirical evidence on the impact of family on family enterprises has grown with the interest in family conflict (Claßen & Schulte, 2017). Using the critical incident technique, the authors in Chapter 5 interviewed 22 Indonesian family enterprise members who have experienced recent conflict to identify contributing factors of conflict behaviors between family members in an enterprise. The authors identified six patterns of conflict behaviors dependent on an individual's emotional regulation and conflict-resolution style. The authors also found that conflicts between individuals with certain conflict-behavior patterns can easily escalate the conflict while other combinations may not.

While Chapter 5 opens the discussion of family dynamics by zeroing in on conflict, Chapter 6 aims to explore the relationship between business strategies on family dynamics, with conflict embedded in the strategy-making process. The authors conducted qualitative data collection from three Chinese family enterprises after the Great Recession that ended in 2010. Their research reports that e-commerce adoption in these organizations was a reaction to the need to reach more markets by moving sales activities online. Such extensive strategy changes required managers to change business processes. Concomitant with these changes, family members found themselves having to change work–life patterns to adapt. Although the research design did not allow observations of the long-term effects, their findings open new ways to understand the interconnectivity between a family and its business.

Managerial coaching is an important talent-development practice in modern organizations. Although there have been many studies on coaching, this is a relatively new practice in Chinese family enterprises. The authors of Chapter 7 surveyed more than 900 part-time MBA students from 11 Chinese cities to analyze the differences between family and non-family enterprises. The results of the survey confirm the difference in the approaches to managerial coaching adopted in family and non-family enterprises. The authors also report a generational difference in coaching approaches when they compare their survey results from students in their 20s and 30s.

Chapter 8 employs an anthropological methodology to report on a feminist observation of a Taiwanese family enterprise. This case features a matriarch who is the sister of the co-founders. She becomes a paternal aunt when her brothers marry and have families, eventually assuming the dual roles of head of the family and the business. As the extant research on women's participation in family enterprises focuses on the matriarch's career decisions, this chapter redirects readers toward the role and influence of grown-up daughters in the family enterprise. As more family enterprises are transitioning through the succession process, daughters are playing more important roles (Campopiano et al., 2017), so this chapter offers a way to conceptualize this phenomenon.

Finally, Chapter 9 reports on a longitudinal case study of a Chinese agricultural business group. Based on multiple interviews and corporate documents, the authors report on the family decisions and related business choices of the Dawu Group from its founding in the 1980s to the present day. This case illustrates bifurcation bias theory (Verbeke & Kano, 2012), which we discussed earlier in this introduction. During a major crisis, the employees of Dawu demonstrated strong loyalty and commitment to the family enterprise. In order to maintain such loyalty, Dawu adopted an innovative organizational design, which also addressed potential feelings of inequity arising from the succession and governance challenges of the enterprise. While the Dawu approach may not be for every company, it is a unique example that might foster theory development in the organization theory domain.

In conclusion, it was our intention for this volume to be a resource for scholars in family enterprise research. The ideas presented in this book draw from extant knowledge of the field to support a framework that suggests less travelled contexts and new avenues of theory development. Entrepreneurial families continue to encounter new challenges and opportunities in their pursuit of business success. As a social institution, modern families are also evolving with new social mores surrounding gender roles, definitions of the family, and definitions of economic sustainability of business enterprises. This book is a snapshot of what we believe are the important dynamics of evolving family and business systems as they interact in the third decade of the twenty-first century.

NOTES

1. www.imdb.com/title/tt1606375/?ref_=nv_sr_srsg_0 (accessed July 4, 2020).
2. www.imdb.com/title/tt0077000/?ref_=fn_al_tt_1 (accessed July 4, 2020).
3. www.worldatlas.com/articles/the-oldest-companies-still-operating-today.html (accessed February 1, 2020).
4. www.fundera.com/blog/small-business-survival (accessed February 1, 2020).
5. The authors ran an article search using "family enterprise" and "family business" as the key words on the EBSCO database. There were 175 peer-reviewed academic papers published before 1988. The earliest publication year was 1945. Using the same key words, EBSCO located 4,521 peer-reviewed papers published between 1989 and 2019.

REFERENCES

Anderson, R., & Reeb, D. (2003). Founding-family ownership and firm performance: Evidence from the S&P 500. *Journal of Finance*, 58(3), 1301–28.

Arteaga, R., & Menéndez-Requejo, S. (2017). Family constitution and business performance: Moderating factors. *Family Enterprise Review*, 30, 320–38.

Au, K., Chiang, F., Birtch, T., & Ding, Z. (2013). Incubating the next generation to venture: The case of a family enterprise in Hong Kong. *Asia Pacific Journal of Management*, 30(3), 749–67.

Avloniti, A., Iatridou, A., Kaloupsis, I., & Vozikis, G.S. (2014). Sibling rivalry: Implications for the family enterprise succession process. *International Entrepreneurship and Management Journal*, 10, 661–78.

Bain, D. (2020). The world's top 750 family businesses ranking. *Family Capital*, March 1.

Barron, J.M., Chulkov, D.V., & Waddell, G.R. (2011). Top management team turnover, CEO succession type, and strategic change. *Journal of Business Research*, 64(8), 904–10.

Bengtson, V.L. (2013). *Families and Faith: How Religion Is Passed Down across Generations*. New York: Oxford University Press.

Berns, K., & Klarner, P. (2017). A review of the CEO succession literature and a future research program. *Academy of Management Perspectives*, 31(2), 83–108.

Bian, Y.J., Breiger, R., Galaskiewicz, J., & Davis, D. (2005). Occupation, class, and social networks in urban China. *Social Forces*, 83(4), 1443–68.

Boswell, T.E. (1986). A split labor market analysis of discrimination against Chinese immigrants, 1850–1882. *American Sociological Review*, 51(3), 352–71.

Cabrera-Suárez, M.K., Déniz-Déniz, M.D.L.C., & Martín-Santana, J.D. (2014). The setting of non-financial goals in the family firm: The influence of family climate and identification. *Journal of Family enterprise Strategy*, 5, 289–99.

Calabrò, A., Vecchiarini, M., Gast, J., Campopiano, G., De Massis, A., & Kraus, S. (2019). Innovation in family firms: A systematic literature review and guidance for future research. *International Journal of Management Reviews*, 21, 317–55.

Callahan, T. (2006). Business owners work twice as much as employees, survey finds. *Inc*, April 13.

Campopiano, G., De Massis, A., Rinaldi, F., & Sciascia, S. (2017). Women's involvement in family firms: Progress and challenges for future research. *Journal of Family Enterprise Strategy*, 8, 200–12.

Chang, G.H. (2019). *Ghosts of Gold Mountain: The Epic Story of the Chinese Who Built the Transcontinental Railroad*. New York: Houghton Mifflin Harcourt.

Claßen, C.A.E., & Schulte, R. (2017). How do conflicts impact change in family enterprise? The family system and familiness as a catalytic converter of change. *Journal of Organizational Change Management*, 30, 1198–212.

Colli, A., Perez, P., & Rose, M. (2003). National determinants of family firm development? Family firms in Britain, Spain, and Italy in the nineteenth and twentieth centuries. *Enterprise and Society*, 4(1), 28–64.

Combs, J.G., Shanine, K.K., Burrows, S., Allen, J.S., & Pounds, T.W. (2020). What do we know about business families? Setting the stage for leveraging family science theories. *Family Enterprise Review*, 33(1), 38–63.

Davis, J., & Tagiuri, R. (1989). The influence of life stage on father–son work relationships in family companies. *Family Enterprise Review*, 2(1), 47–74.

De Massis, A., Frattini, F., & Lichtenthaler, U. (2013). Research on technological innovation in family firms: Present debates and future directions. *Family Business Review*, 26, 10–31.

Dekas, K.H., & Baker, W.E. (2014). *Adolescent Socialization and the Development of Adult Work Orientations: Research in the Sociology of Work*. Bingley: Emerald Group Publishing.

DeMers, J. (2015). 50 reasons to start your own business. *Entrepreneur*, February 23, www.entrepreneur.com/article/243145.

Di Gangi, M. (2016). Attitude check: Small business owners say it's all worth It. Blog, changematters.bankofthewest.com/2016/07/26/attitude-check-small-business -owners-say-worth/.

Ding, H.B. (2008). Family involvement in family firms: Antecedents and moderators, in J. Butler (ed.), *Theoretical Developments and Future Research in Family Enterprise* (pp. 177–94). Charlotte, NC: Information Age Publishing.

Donckels, R., & Fröhlich, E. (1991). Are family enterprise really different? European experiences from STRATOS. *Family Enterprise Review*, 4(2), 149–60.

Donnelley, R.G. (1964). The family enterprise. *Harvard Business Review*, 42(4), 93–105.

Fernández-Aráoz, C., Iqbal, S., Ritter, J., & Sadowski, R. (2019). 6 traits of strong family enterprise. *Harvard Business Review*, June 18.

Friedland, R. and Alford, R.R. (1991). Bringing society back in: Symbols, practices, and institutional contradictions, in W. W. Powell and P. J. DiMaggio (eds), *The New*

Institutionalism in Organizational Analysis (pp. 232–66). Chicago: University of Chicago Press.

Hall, A.D., & Fagen, R.E. (1956). Definition of a system. *General Systems*, 1, 18–28.

Hamilton, G., & Kao, C.-S. (1990). The institutional foundations of Chinese business: The family firm in Taiwan. *Comparative Social Research*, 12, 95–112.

Holmes, S., Smith, S., & Cane, G. (1997). Gender issues in home-based business operation and training: An Australian overview. *Women in Management Review*, 12(2), 68–73.

Hoy, F., & Verser, T.G. (1994). Emerging business, emerging field: Entrepreneurship and the family firm. *Entrepreneurship Theory and Practice*, 19(1), 9–23.

Huang, Y.C., Ding, H.B., & Kao, M.R. (2009). Salient stakeholder voices: Family enterprise and green innovation adoption. *Journal of Management and Organization*, 15(3), 309–26.

Jahanmir, S.F. (2016). Paradoxes or trade-offs of entrepreneurship: Exploratory insights from the Cambridge eco-system. *Journal of Business Research*, 69(11), 5101–5.

Jimenez, R.M. (2009). Research on women in family firms: Current status and future directions. *Family Business Review*, 22(1), 53–64.

Johnson, S., La Porta, S., Lopez-de-Silanes, F., & Shleifer A. (2000). Tunneling. *American Economic Review*, 90, 22–7.

Jung, J. (2007). *Chinese Laundries: Tickets to Survival on Gold Mountain*. n.l.: Yin and Yang Press.

Lansberg, I., & Astrachan, J.H. (1994). Influence of family relationships on succession planning and training: The importance of mediating factors. *Family Enterprise Review*, 7(1), 39–59.

Litz, R.A. (2008). Two sides of a one-sided phenomenon: Conceptualizing the family enterprise and business family as a Möbius strip. *Family Enterprise Review*, 21(3), 217–36.

Lupu, I., Spence, C., & Empson, L. (2017). When the past comes back to haunt you: The enduring influence of upbringing on the work–family decisions of professional parents. *Human Relations*, 71(2), 155–81.

Lyman, A.R. (1988). Life in the family circle. *Family Enterprise Review*, 1(4), 383–98.

Marshack, K.J. (1993). Co-entrepreneurial couples: A literature review on boundaries and transitions among copreneurs. *Family Enterprise Review*, 6(4), 355–69.

Martin, S.R., Côté, S., & Woodruff, T. (2016). Echoes of our upbringing: How growing up wealthy or poor relates to narcissism, leader behavior, and leader effectiveness. *Academy of Management Journal*, 59(6), 2157–77.

Martinez, M.A., & Aldrich, H. (2014). Sociological theories applied to family enterprise, in L. Melin, M. Nordquist, & P. Sharma (eds), *Sage Handbook of Family Business* (pp. 83–98). Los Angeles: Sage.

Min, P.-G. (2011). *Ethnic Solidarity for Economic Survival: Korean Greengrocers in New York City*. New York: Russell Sage.

Mirela-Oana, P., & Melinda-Timea, F. (2015). Literature review on corporate governance: Firm performance relationship. *Annals of Faculty of Economics*, 1(1), 98–854.

Mehrotra, V., Morck, R., Shim, J., & Wiwattanakantang, Y. (2013). Adoptive expectations: Rising sons in Japanese family firms. *Journal of Financial Economics*, 108(3), 840–54.

National Academies of Sciences, Engineering, and Medicine (2016). *Parenting Matters: Supporting Parents of Children Ages 0–8*. Washington, DC: National Academies Press.

Neubauer, F., & Lank, A. (1998). *The Family Enterprise: Its Governance for Sustainability*. Houndmills: Macmillan.

Office of the Historian (n.d.). Chinese immigration and the Chinese Exclusion Acts. https://history.state.gov/milestones/1866-1898/chinese-immigration.

Oppenheimer, V. (1977). The sociology of women's economic role in the family. *American Sociological Review*, 42(3), 387–406.

Overbeke, K., Bilimoria, D., & Perelli, S. (2013). The dearth of daughter successors in family enterprise: Gendered norms, blindness to possibility and invisibility. *Journal of Family enterprise Strategy*, 4, 201–12.

Perez, P.F., & Lluch, A. (2016). Introduction, in P. Fernández Pérez & A. Lluch (eds), *Evolution of Family enterprise Continuity and Change in Latin America and Spain* (pp. 1–22). Cheltenham, UK and Northampton, MA, USA: Edward Elgar Publishing.

Pratap, S., & Saha, B. (2018). Evolving efficacy of managerial capital, contesting managerial practices, and the process of strategic renewal. *Strategic Management Journal*, 39(3), 759–93.

Pratt, J.H. (2009). Who operates the business? A comparison of husband and wife copreneurs from the Survey of Business Owners. *USASBE 2009 Proceedings*, 568–89.

Ramirez-Solis, E., Baños-Monroy, V., & Rodríguez-Aceves, L. (2016). Family enterprise in Latin America: The case of Mexico. In F. Kellermans & F. Hoy (eds), *The Routledge Companion to Family Enterprise*. New York: Routledge.

Redding, G. (1995). Overseas Chinese networks: Understanding the enigma. *Long Range Planning*, 28(1), 61–9.

Rosplock, K. (2014). *The Complete Family Office Handbook: A Guide for Affluent Families and the Advisors Who Serve Them*. New York: Bloomberg Press.

Rowe, B.R., & Hong, G.S. (2000). The role of wives in family enterprises: The paid and unpaid work of women. *Family Enterprise Review*, 13, 1–13.

Sarche, M., & Spicer, P. (2008). Poverty and health disparities for American Indian and Alaska Native children. *Annals of the New York Academy of Sciences*, 1136(1), 126–36.

Schaefer, M.A., & Frishkoff, P.A. (1992). Evaluation of auditors' going-concern risk in family enterprise. *Family Enterprise Review*, 5, 63–76.

Schulze, W., Lubatkin, M., Dino, R., & Buchholtz, A. (2001). Agency relationships in family firms: Theory and evidence. *Organization Science*, 12, 99–116.

Schwartz, E.L. (1954). Will your busines die with you? *Harvard Business Review*, 32(5), 110–22.

Scranton, P. (1992). Learning manufacture: Education and shop floor schooling in the family firm. *Family Enterprise Review*, 5, 323–42.

Seymour, K.C. (1993). Intergenerational relationships in the family firm: The effect on leadership succession. *Family Enterprise Review*, 6, 263–81.

Shieh, G.S. (1993). *Boss Island: The Subcontracting Network and Micro-Entrepreneurship in Taiwan's Development*. New York: Peter Lang Publishing.

Siu, P.C.P., & Tchen, J.K.W. (1987). *The Chinese Laundryman: A Study of Social Isolation*. New York: New York University Press.

Stalk, G., Jr., & Foley, H. (2012). Avoid the traps that can destroy family enterprise. *Harvard Business Review*, January–February.

Sutter, B. (2019). How hard small business owners work. *SCORE*, August 7, www.score.org/blog/how-hard-small-business-owners-work.

Tagiuri, R., & Davis, J.A. (1982). Bivalent attributes of the family firm. Working Paper, Harvard Business School. Reprinted 1996, *Family Enterprise Review*, 9(2), 199–208.

Tarling, C., Jones, P., & Murphy, L. (2016). Influence of early exposure to family enterprise experience on developing entrepreneurs. *Education and Training*, 58(7/8), 733–50.

Venkataramani, M., Cheng, T.L., Solomon, B.S., & Pollack, C.E. (2017). Addressing parental health in pediatrics: Physician perceptions of relevance and responsibility. *Clinical Pediatrics*, 56(10), 953–8.

Verbeke, A., & Kano, L. (2010). Transaction cost economics (TCE) and the family firm. *Entrepreneurship Theory and Practice*, 34(6), 1173–82.

Verbeke, A., & Kano, L. (2012). The transaction cost economics theory of the family firm: Family-based human asset specificity and the bifurcation bias. *Entrepreneurship Theory and Practice*, 36(6), 1183–205.

Walsh, J.L., Bruehl, S., & Di Loreto, N. (2020). Is the next generation of your family enterprise entrepreneurial enough? *Harvard Business Review*, May 8.

Ward, J.L. (1986). *Keeping the Family Enterprise Healthy: How to Plan for Continuing Growth, Profitability, and Family Leadership*. New York: Jossey Bass.

Weidenbaum, M.L., & Hughes, S. (1996). *The Bamboo Network: How Expatriate Chinese Entrepreneurs are Creating a New Economic Superpower in Asia*. New York, Free Press.

Welsch, J. (1993). Family enterprises in the UK, the Federal republic of Germany, and Spain: A transnational comparison. *Family Business Review*, 4(2), 231–61.

White, J.M., & Klein, D.M. (2002). The systems framework, in J.M. White, T.F. Martin, & K. Adamsons (eds), *Family Theories: An Introduction* (pp. 117–42). New York: Sage.

World Bank (2018). Female entrepreneurs: The future of the African continent, www.worldbank.org/en/news/opinion/2018/11/29/women-entrepreneurs-the-future-of-africa.

Wu, M., Chang, C.-C., & Zhuang, W.-L. (2010). Relationships of work–family conflict with business and marriage outcomes in Taiwanese copreneurial women. *International Journal of Human Resource Management*, 21, 742–53.

Yasuoka, S. (1984). Capital ownership in family companies: Japanese firms compared with those in other countries, in A. Okochi (ed.), *Family Enterprise in the Era of Industrial Growth: Its Ownership and Management* (pp. 1–32). Tokyo: University of Tokyo Press.

Young, M.N., Peng, M., Ahlstrom, D., Bruton, G., & Jiang, Y. (2008). Corporate governance in emerging economies: A review of the principal–principal perspective. *Journal of Management Studies*, 45(1), 196–220.

2. When and how high family involvement helps a family business: The role of long-term orientation and innovativeness

Dina L. Taylor, Soroush Aslani and Dexi Zheng

INTRODUCTION

Family business success is essential to the health of the economy given that 80 percent of businesses in the United States are family owned (Gomez-Mejia, Larraza-Kintana, & Makri, 2003). The impact of family businesses on the economy has increased the interest in family business studies since research shows that family businesses have important differences from non-family businesses (Anderson & Reeb, 2003). The most important differences are: (a) the involvement of family members in the business through ownership and in management and (b) the fact that the firm's performance is connected to the concentration of wealth of the family (Zahra, 2005; Gomez-Mejia, Haynes, Nunez-Nickel, Jacobson, & Moyano-Fuentes, 2007).

Some of the past research has argued that family firms may be less likely to invest in long-term projects and therefore limit opportunities to increase firm performance (Munari, Oriani, & Sobrero, 2010), especially through innovation. Such firms are concerned about jeopardizing the family fortune and consider it a priority to be risk-averse (Gomez-Mejia et al., 2007). Consequently, one may assume that family businesses, especially those with higher involvement of family members in ownership and management of the firm, may show such risk-averse tendencies.

However, family businesses are not a homogeneous group of firms (Chua, Chrisman, Steier, & Rau, 2012) and the evidence from the real world shows several cases where family firms, with high involvement of family members, could in fact experience boosts in their innovation and ultimately their performance. For example, Meijer, which is a privately held family business and national grocery store chain, has four generations of family ownership and management of the company. Meijer has remained a privately held family business with involvement of the founder's grandsons and other family members who serve as key company executives and board members. They believe that there is a link between growing the business for family generations and remaining innovative. Meijer claims to be committed to "keeping our competitive spirit strong and staying nimble and flexible to win in the market-place" (Meijer, 2019a). For example, Meijer is savvy in its online shopping, which has kept them competitive against large businesses such as Walmart (Buss, 2016). Apparently, a high level of family involvement did not interrupt their investment in innovation.

Another family business, Perdue Farms, prominently features its family business heritage. It showcases its family ownership since 1920 by the presence of family members in leadership roles throughout different decades, and by the involvement of the next generation of family members at high levels of management (Perdue Farms, 2019b). They are also innovative and lead the market as the only major poultry producers studying alternative breeds (Perdue Farms, 2019a).

Overall past research and practice have provided some different, and at times contradicting, findings about important processes and outcomes in family firms, especially the innovation process. Despite some reasons for less risky decisions in general, and lower innovation investments in particular, among family firms, we know that growth is also important to family firms and particularly to owners who are motivated to increase and transfer the family business down to future generations (Chua, Chrisman, & Sharma, 1999; Anderson & Reeb, 2003). Thus, they need to take some calculated risks and make investments to boost firm performance through innovation. Due to this anomaly in research regarding the tendency of family firms to make innovation investments, it is important to examine why, and under what circumstances, family firms are more likely to invest in innovation that helps their firm performance. We look at a specific factor in the composition of a family business, namely family involvement.

Drawing on the familiness perspective (Habbershon & Williams, 1999; Habbershon, Williams, & MacMillan, 2003), in this chapter we focus on family involvement and how it influences firm performance, especially as it relates to innovation. Family involvement is defined as the extent to which family members are present in ownership and management of the business (Songini & Gnan, 2015). The goal to transfer the family business down to future generations makes family involvement in the business an important factor in shaping firm performance (Chua et al., 1999; Anderson & Reeb, 2003). In this research we consider family involvement as a resource in a firm and examine under what conditions family involvement can contribute to higher innovation and ultimately the performance of family firms.

Some past research found that family involvement may limit firm performance, because firms with high family involvement may avoid making risky yet calculated investment decisions, fearing that those decisions may threaten the future wealth of the family (Gomez-Mejia et al., 2007). However, other research found that family involvement in leadership can increase investments in value-enhancing projects like innovation because their leadership persists on pursuing strategies that preserve the business for the future (Chua et al., 1999; Anderson & Reeb, 2003; Hoffmann, Wulf, & Stubner, 2016). Thus, family involvement in ownership and management may be helpful to family businesses.

These contrasting findings are our motivation to further investigate the role of family involvement in family businesses, and especially to understand how it affects firms' performance when making business decisions. Therefore, our research question is under what conditions, and how, family involvement can help firm performance.

In this chapter, we argue that a family firm's long-term orientation (LTO) can play a key role in determining whether family involvement can help or hurt a family business. LTO is defined as the "tendency to prioritize the long-range implications and the impact of decisions and actions that come to fruition after an extended time period" (Lumpkin, Brigham, & Moss, 2010, p. 241). Although LTO may play a crucial role in all firms, we argue that in family firms, family involvement with an LTO mindset is particularly important to business decisions that support the firm's success. This in turn leads to the accumulation of wealth for the family.

Therefore, a central thesis of this chapter is that in family firms with a high level of family involvement, the presence of LTO can increase the chance of success for the firm. We argue that such an effect becomes possible through an important change in the mindset of the firm, namely innovativeness, which in turn leads to more entrepreneurial activities in the firm and consequently its higher firm performance. Innovativeness is a firm's willingness to adopt the development of technology, create new products and services, and improve operations to be more competitive (Lumpkin & Dess, 1996; Slevin & Covin, 1995). Past studies showed that innovativeness is tied to increased firm performance (Sirmon, Gove, & Hitt, 2008; Duran, Kammerlander, Van Essen, & Zellweger, 2016). However, there are gaps in this research, such as understanding the conditions under which family businesses can experience higher innovativeness and firm performance. In this chapter we argue that family businesses with higher levels of family member involvement can develop high levels of innovativeness when they also have high LTO. This will lead to higher firm performance. In other words, innovativeness is the mediator between family involvement and firm performance, and LTO moderates the family involvement–innovativeness relationship.

This chapter contributes to the family business scholarship in two ways. First, it helps scholars obtain a better understanding of family businesses, particularly about the relationship between family involvement and firm performance, by proposing LTO as a moderator in this relationship. Empirical studies on the impact of LTO on family firms are emerging (Brigham, Lumpkin, Payne, & Zachary, 2014) and, thus, theorizing through familiness may spur more discussion and facilitate future research. Second, this chapter argues that firms with higher LTO can benefit more from their family involvement through higher innovativeness, which subsequently influences other important processes and outcomes in family firms. This opens opportunities for further studies on other constructs (related to firm resources and capabilities) that mediate the relationship between a firm's involvement and its performance. The chapter also has implications for practitioners in that it will help them to understand how and why family involvement and LTO can affect outcomes of family businesses.

In the following sections we will first introduce our theoretical framework, review the literature, and clarify the constructs in our model. Next we will develop three propositions through the familiness paradigm. Finally, we will discuss future research, implications, and will wrap up with a conclusion. Figure 2.1 shows our theoretical model.

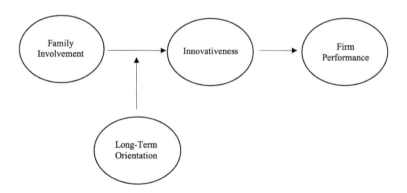

Figure 2.1   Theoretical model

THEORETICAL DEVELOPMENT

Familiness and Firm Performance

The familiness paradigm was introduced by Habbershon and Williams (1999) and Habbershon et al. (2003) as an extension to the resource-based view (Barney, 1991). Familiness refers to "the unique bundle of resources a particular firm has because of the systems interactions between the family, its individual members, and the business" (Habbershon & Williams, 1999, p. 11). Family businesses are unique in that they comprise of both a family system and organizational system. Despite considerable heterogeneity across family firms, much of the past literature has made broad generalizations on family businesses without recognizing this heterogeneity. By addressing heterogeneity, the familiness paradigm looks closely into family-specific firm resources and matches them to the firm's capabilities and key outcomes, such as its performance.

Firm performance is often regarded as one of the ultimate outcome variables of study (if not "the" ultimate outcome variable of study) in the research on family businesses; however, other variables such as succession, commitment, and survival have also been studied in this line of research. Yu, Lumpkin, Sorenson, and Brigham (2012) conducted a review of 257 empirical studies on family business in the years 1998–2009 and reported a comprehensive list of outcome variables studied in past research. While these outcomes are all important, outcomes such as survival and succession are often predicated on successful firm performance as there would be no need to plan for succession if a firm does not have sufficient performance to survive for the long term. Therefore, in this chapter we focus on firm performance (as the ultimate outcome) because it is an important measure to gauge a firm's financial health and its ability to sustain itself, and it is also an indicator of the way the firm uses resources to produce earnings (Kimmel, Weygandt, & Kieso, 2010). The familiness paradigm specifies that family and firm resources are critical to firm performance (Habbershon & Williams, 1999). We extend this line of reasoning to suggest that familiness resources are matched to achieve firm performance.

The family system and the firm system are comprised of familiness resources such as physical capital, human capital, organizational capital, and process capital (Habbershon & Williams, 1999). These resources are unique to each family firm and can have a positive impact on performance (Habbershon et al., 2003). For example, resources such as leadership, trust within the organization, human or political capital, etc. may provide a competitive advantage. However, by applying the familiness concept to family businesses, researchers may determine how the resources lead to firm performance.

In this chapter, we particularly look at the level of family involvement as one such family-specific resource (Chrisman, Chua, & Litz, 2003), and examine how it can be more effective in generating a competitive advantage for the firm. Furthermore, in our application of the familiness framework, we examine how the impact of family involvement on performance may be moderated by LTO and mediated by innovativeness.

Family Involvement

Family involvement is defined as the extent to which family members are present in ownership and management of the business (Songini & Gnan, 2015). Chua et al. (1999, p. 24) refer to the decision makers who shape the vision of the family firm as the dominant coalition; they are the powerful actors in a firm who control the overall organization's agenda and make business decisions that implement the strategy. Their connections to family members and their high degree of power and legitimacy raise their desire to focus on decisions that favor firm outcomes and the wealth generation of the family business (Chua et al., 1999).

When family involvement increases in the dominant coalition, the dominant coalition may struggle with tension between two conflicting concerns: maximizing wealth generation through long-run high-return investments (e.g. effective research and development) versus minimizing the risk of failure and focusing on short-term returns. On the one hand, past studies have shown that involvement of family firm owners and managers in the dominant coalition can increase their willingness to invest in innovation projects and explore possible opportunities for earning strategic advantages (Lumpkin & Brigham, 2011; Miller & Le Breton-Miller, 2005; Zahra, Hayton, & Salvato, 2004). On the other hand, some studies have shown that family businesses may be more risk-averse and thus neglect investments in domains such as long-run research and development to avoid business failure or losing control (Gomez-Mejia et al., 2007). As firms go through generational transitions, gradual, yet considerable, changes in the composition and nature of resources (e.g. changes in experience, management style, stakeholder relationships, and cultural values) can transform the firm's once distinctive familiness (i.e. positive sources of uniqueness that give them competitive advantage; see Habbershon & Williams, 1999) to constrictive familiness (i.e. burden and inaction caused by unnecessary repetition of past practices; Habbershon & Williams, 1999) and create inertia toward healthy risk taking and innovation.

We argue that whereas a high level of family involvement in the dominant coalition may provide the owners with a sense of security and commitment toward boosting the firm performance and ultimately accumulating transgenerational wealth, this relationship between family involvement and firm performance is not universal and depends on a key moderator, namely LTO. This approach is consistent with what Habbershon and Williams (1999) argue in their familiness framework: instead of making overly broad and generalized propositions on family businesses, scholars should identify a firm's familiness, and assess its impact on the firm's strategic capabilities. To reach this goal, one should examine under what conditions a specific resource or characteristic of a family firm can create value.

Long-Term Orientation

In strategic management, LTO refers to a firm's tendency to prioritize the outcomes of decisions and actions that are realized in the long run (Le Breton-Miller & Miller, 2006; Lumpkin et al., 2010, p. 241). LTO is a disposition held within the dominant coalition of leaders in the family firm. Long term is typically considered greater than five years (Le Breton-Miller & Miller, 2006), but researchers suggest that LTO is a disposition, or mindset, that changes over time (Lumpkin & Brigham, 2011), rather than a specific time period. LTO has received attention as an important concept in recent years (Lumpkin & Brigham, 2011; Lumpkin et al., 2010; Gentry, Dibrell, & Kim, 2016), and it can help us explain some anomalies in family business research.

Choosing between long-term versus short-term courses of action can be complicated. Short-term courses of action, such as responding to customer demands, leadership changes, and new technology changes, may impact performance and survival. However, family firms are sometimes hesitant to make quick short-term decisions because they tend to favor long-range planning and, thus, need more time to evaluate the impact of such decisions on both the firm and family (Lumpkin & Brigham, 2011). To further understand family firms' behaviors and the logic behind their decisions, research on LTO can be further developed.

Lumpkin and Brigham (2011) and Lumpkin et al. (2010) introduced a multidimensional LTO construct that could prompt further examination of LTO. This construct can help explain the dominant logic for the decisions in family firms that support the firm's sustainability. LTO was later validated in three dimensions: futurity, perseverance, and continuity (Brigham et al., 2014).

The first dimension, futurity, is a firm's belief that "forecasting, planning, and evaluating long-range consequences of current actions have utility." It is an indicator of a firm's top management's "shared beliefs about the strategic direction" (Lumpkin & Brigham, 2011, p. 1152). Firms that value futurity are more salient in the long run.

The second dimension, perseverance, is noticed in firms which do not compromise the core beliefs or venture from long-term goals (Le Breton-Miller & Miller, 2006). Strong commitment levels and the desire to pass the firm on to future generations manifest in perseverance (Brockhaus, 2004). Additionally, patient capital investments and a strong long-term horizon for investment opportunities are characteristics of firms that persevere (Sirmon & Hitt, 2003; Zellweger, 2007).

Finally, the third dimension, continuity, represents a desire to uphold trans-generational ownership thereby keeping important, long-lasting traditions that consider prior and future generations (Lumpkin & Brigham, 2011). Succession planning is a significant signal that continuity is a goal of the firm. Each LTO dimension can contribute to an understanding of family key processes.

Since LTO is ultimately rooted in individual experiences that are transferred to and embedded in the firm, here we briefly refer to social cognitive theory (SCT) to understand how LTO manifests in family firms (Bandura, 1986). According to SCT, individuals draw from experiences or knowledge before a certain behavior begins (Bandura, 1986). As we consider the nature of individuals and assumptions of SCT, individuals draw on past experiences before making decisions. SCT can help us explain how individuals are drawing on their available knowledge, using forethought to consider the ramifications of their behavior, and learning directly from their own experiences or indirectly from others' experiences to determine the standards that help them regulate their behavior. For example, the nature of a family firm's LTO disposition is that the dominant coalition draws from the past experiences and traditions, considers the potential outcome on the family firm longevity, reflects on the outcomes of their past decisions, and exercises self-control against risky business decisions.

Under high levels of LTO, high levels of family involvement can lead to using various forms of family-related process intervention (family meetings, management team meetings, consultant facilitation), which in turn contribute to continual reevaluation and replenishment of the familiness resources. However, when LTO is low a high level of family involvement is more likely to result in conservative inertia for the firm. It does not properly invest in replenishing, augmenting, and upgrading its familiness as a valuable resource; it can quickly become a familial encumbrance.

Innovativeness

Innovativeness is a firm's willingness to adopt the development of technology, create new products and services, and improve operations to be more competitive (Lumpkin & Dess, 1996; Slevin & Covin, 1995). Innovativeness was reintroduced by Lumpkin and Dess (1996) as one of the five dimensions of entrepreneurial orientation (EO). It is recognized as the leading force of EO, having gained most attention amongst the five EO dimensions (Baker & Sinkula, 2009; Wales, Gupta, & Mousa, 2013). This chapter extends other research that firm performance is increased through innovativeness (Hult & Ketchen, 2001; Dibrell, Craig, & Neubaum, 2014).

Innovation has been considered a key factor, contributing to entrepreneurship for decades (Schumpeter, 1934; 1942). It is a component of the entrepreneurial process of combining existing resources. Schumpeter (1934) described five types of innovation: (a) new good creation, (b) new production method creation, (c) creation of new markets, (d) obtaining new sources of supply, and (e) creation or destruction of a monopoly. Schumpeter (1942) described the economics of entrepreneurship as creative destruction in which firms have an opportunity to create wealth in the current market by shifting resources away from competitors or by creating a new market. A firm that does not continuously dedicate effort to innovation may not possess high levels of innovativeness, as the notion of innovativeness implies that the firm holds a mindset that encourages it to "continuously introduce new products and services that are more attuned to current and emerging market needs, and are able to quickly enter into new markets that might represent a better strategic fit for their innovation-based capabilities" (Kreiser, Marino, Kuratko, & Weaver, 2013, p. 276). Regardless of the innovation approach, innovativeness as a mindset is one of the most important forces of EO.

In the next section we propose that a healthy interaction between family involvement and LTO encourages innovativeness because the familiness in family firms will create a synergy that supports the needs and desires of the family and firm. We will introduce our propositions through the familiness framework and suggest a series of relationships between family involvement, LTO, innovativeness, and firm performance.

PROPOSITIONS

Family Involvement and Innovativeness

Many family firms desire to pass the business down for generations, and thus they may be willing to adopt an innovativeness mindset (Gomez-Mejia et al., 2007; Kellermanns, Eddleston, Barnett, & Pearson, 2008; Le Breton-Miller & Miller, 2006). Furthermore, they realize that if they do not innovate, or fail to introduce new products or business models (Covin & Wales, 2019), they risk becoming obsolete. With the desire to pass the business to future generations, family firms would want to develop an innovativeness mindset to protect the family from hazards against losing wealth because the family and business systems are intertwined in family firms (Gomez Mejia et al., 2007; Zahra, 2005). The level of family involvement in a firm can be an important factor affecting the innovativeness of that firm.

One may argue that firms with high levels of family involvement are less likely to adopt an innovativeness mindset due to two main reasons. First, a high level of family involvement (especially in ownership) often means a strong tendency or concern in the firm to maintain control in key decisions. High investment in innovation typically requires them to surrender some of that control by accepting external capital from the stock market or by increasing debt levels.

Second, high family involvement encourages investment in less risky projects because investment in risky projects can seriously threaten family wealth concentration. A high level of family involvement may thus imply that the firm faces a limited availability of financial resources for investment into innovation and instead prefers investments characterized by low levels of uncertainty. This is consistent with past research that family firms prefer investing in less risky assets such as buildings and machinery (Anderson, Duru, & Reeb, 2012; Duran et al., 2016). A related (though not fully parallel) line of research on the different types of family ownership also showed that firms with lone owners had higher levels of research and development intensity, spending, and productivity than those with multiple owners (Block, 2012) and research and development investment was reduced as the levels of family ownership increased (Munari et al., 2010).

Consistent with these arguments, Gomez et al. (2007) studied Spanish olive oil mill family firms who were given an opportunity to invest in a co-op that brought all businesses together under one legal co-op entity. Investing in the co-op meant that family businesses relinquished some of their control over their family business, whereas in return the co-op could provide higher financial rewards for the firm. This article implies that in family firms where family involvement in ownership and management was higher, firms tended not to join the co-op, and consequently they avoided risk and reduced investments in innovation that could have yielded a positive outcome. Instead they kept the family involved in control of the business to preserve the socioemotional wealth of the family business (Berrone, Cruz, & Gómez-Mejía, 2012).

Therefore, we propose:

Proposition 1a: Family involvement is negatively associated with innovativeness.

However, family businesses are not a homogeneous group of firms (Chua et al., 2012) and a characteristic like family involvement can have positive impacts on innovativeness in other contexts. For example, when family involvement is high, family members can maintain activities that support the long-run interest and focus on strategic advantages to secure the family firm's financial well-being (Miller & Le Breton-Miller, 2005; Lumpkin & Brigham, 2011; Zahra et al., 2004).

The two companies introduced earlier, Meijer and Perdue Farms, have high family involvement, and at the same time they believe that investments in innovative initiatives are necessary for business growth and the family. For example, Perdue Farms showcases its high family involvement by stating that it has multiple generations of Perdue family members involved in its operations. It believes that its "path forward is about getting better, not just bigger, using our scale to drive positive change" (Perdue Farms, 2019c). While it leaves no doubt that it is a firm with high family involvement, it is also embracing and leading innovative efforts to meet the changing expectations. It specifically indicates that "ongoing investments keep our operations on the forefront of food safety and production technology" (Perdue Farms, 2019c).

According to the familiness paradigm, family business resources come through family involvement (Habbershon & Williams, 1999). In our reference to the above two companies, in the context of innovation, high family involvement helps the firm to closely and efficiently monitor the innovation process (Fama & Jensen, 1983) and minimize the associated agency costs (Songini & Gnan, 2015). This is also consistent with past research that found personalized family-member involvement can foster more creativity in family firms (Pervin, 1997) and encourage them to pay closer attention to research and development (Ward, 1997), especially considering that the family business is the ultimate long-term investor (Dreux, 1990).

The involvement of family members in the business may reflect their desire to focus on the goal of passing the business to future generations rather than immediate profit, and thus increase investments in innovative endeavors (Le Breton-Miller & Miller, 2006). Additionally, drawing on SCT, we argue that high levels of family involvement help the accumulation and retention of tacit knowledge in the family business, which in turn can encourage an innovativeness mindset by learning from the past.

Therefore, we propose as a rival hypothesis to Proposition 1a:

Proposition 1b: Family involvement is positively associated with innovativeness.

Considering the above two rival hypotheses, in the next section we will argue that the LTO mindset may serve as a moderator in this relationship between family involvement and innovativeness.

The Moderating Role of Long-Term Orientation

Family firms generally care about passing the business to future generations, but that is assuming that the family members make a present business decision with the future of the family and firm in mind. In this context, LTO may function as a valuable, rare, and inimitable resource that a family firm uses to guide its decision-making process. Family beliefs and goals are among the shared resources eminent in LTO when we examine the familiness of a firm (Habbershon & Williams, 1999). In a related line of research, Zahra et al. (2004) argued that the presence of LTO can boost entrepreneurial activities ensuring the future success of a family business.

Our central argument is that a combination of high family involvement and LTO can create a major competitive advantage for family firms through empowering them to adopt an innovativeness mindset. High family involvement can facilitate such an innovativeness mindset when the family business heavily relies on collaboration networks (Spriggs, Yu, Deed, & Sorenson, 2012) and takes advantage of knowledge and resources that are not typically accessible through transactional market exchanges (Rothaermel & Hess, 2007). We argue that trust is crucial in making this possible and is appreciated and maintained best when the family business has high LTO. Under high LTO high family involvement leads to building and maintaining long-term and trust-based connections with suppliers, customers, and other external stakeholders (Duran et al., 2016), some of whom may be family businesses themselves. Such long-term and trust-based connections can help them receive valuable support from these partners, which leads them to manage the innovation process much more efficiently (e.g. by quick marketing of newly developed products; Schreier & Prugl, 2008) and effectively (e.g. through early and frequent interaction in the development and testing of prototypes; Thomke, 2003). All these potentials, unlocked by a combination of high family involvement and LTO, encourage family firms to adopt an innovativeness mindset.

Furthermore, we argue that under high levels of LTO, high levels of family involvement can lead to using various forms of family-related process interventions such as family meetings, management team meetings, and consultant facilitation. Such family-related process interventions in turn contribute to continual reevaluation and replenishment of the familiness resources (Habbershon & Williams, 1999). They can also help the family business create a "family language" (Tagiuri & Davis, 1996) that allows the family business to communicate better and exchange more information with privacy through efficient information channels while enhancing trust and loyalty in the firm (Habbershon & Williams, 1999). The presence of such elements in a firm's familiness can facilitate its innovativeness. Whereas there are inherent uncertainties of the outcome associated with innovation, the presence of high LTO, along with high family involvement, can help family firms manage this risk and continually introduce new products and services.

As an example, in Perdue Farms one may notice LTO in different parts of the corporate statement such as "our company has remained family-owned and operating since 1920. Two generations currently work in the company and the family is committed to keeping Perdue Farms a family-owned business" (Perdue Farms, 2019b). Under the values and vision established decades ago by their founders, one of Perdue Farm's aspirations is "to our customers, we want to be their most trusted partner, providing innovative products and service solutions" (Perdue Farms, 2019c).

The innovativeness of Perdue Farms is shown in being the only major poultry company actively studying alternative breeds and also in bringing together experts, advocates, customers, farmers, and the company's leadership in an Animal Care Summit (Perdue Farms, 2019a). For Perdue Farms the concept of familiness is evident in its presentation of family, family members, and business as an integral unit. For example, when introducing the next generation of Perdue family members, it states that "four members of the next generation of Perdues are currently working in the family" (Perdue Farms, 2019b). There is not a distinction of family and firm, but rather an integral unit that continues to pursue the vision of their family and firm – "To be the most trusted name in food and agricultural products" (Perdue Farms, 2019c). Perdue Farms is an example consistent with the argument that family firms with high LTO can leverage their high family involvement toward being more innovative.

Meijer has four generations in family ownership and management of the company including the founder's grandsons and other family members who serve as key company executives and board members. It also believes that there is a link between growing the business for family generations and remaining innovative. It justifies some of its innovative initiatives such as launching the "one stop shopping" concept, providing online shopping opportunities and home delivery, as a way to provide busy customers with a more convenient shopping experience (Meijer, 2019b). Through a long-term mindset, it argues that in pursuing such initiatives the company should "take care of … customers, team members, and community. [If it does so,] all of them will take care of you, just like a family" (Meijer, 2019a).

Conversely, when LTO is low a high level of family involvement is more likely to result in conservative inertia for the firm. The firm will tend to not properly invest in replenishing, augmenting, and upgrading its familiness as a valuable resource; it does not invest in long-term and trust-based ties that are crucial for innovative mindsets, and it can quickly become a familial encumbrance and even make complacent decisions. Consequently, high family involvement without a high level of LTO may result in decisions that do not emphasize the innovativeness mindset.

Although family firms typically do not experience the classic owner–manager agency conflict common in non-family firms, they face other types of agency conflicts, such as the conflicts of interest between family members in different roles and the conflicts of interest between family members and non-family members (Songini & Gnan, 2015). We argue that in the absence of LTO, higher family involvement exacerbates some agency conflicts and requires the family firm to more heavily rely on agency cost-control mechanisms. This weakens collaborative trust-based ties in the firm and ultimately hurts its innovativeness mindset. However, when there is a strong LTO in the firm, many of those interests are relatively aligned or the conflicts among them are minimized.

Finally, as we argued above, a high level of family involvement (especially in ownership) often means a strong tendency, or concern, in the firm to maintain control in key decisions. High investment in innovation typically requires them to surrender some of that control by actions such as accepting external capital from the equity market or by increasing debt levels. For example, in the olive oil mills case these family firms elected not to join the co-op and refused to reduce their control over the business. Consequently, a high level of family involvement may discourage firms from innovation investments. However, under high LTO, family owners will be less concerned about raising such debt levels because they know that innovation will in the long run add to the firm profits and accumulation of wealth in the family. They may even take advantage of high family involvement as an opportunity to manage significantly lower costs of debt financing than non-family firms (Anderson, Mansi, & Reeb, 2003).

Therefore, we propose:

Proposition 2: Long-term orientation moderates the relationship between family involvement and innovativeness:

Proposition 2a: Under high long-term orientation, family involvement will be positively associated with innovativeness.

Proposition 2b: Under low long-term orientation, family involvement will be negatively associated with innovativeness.

Innovativeness and Firm Performance

According to the familiness paradigm (Habbershon & Williams, 1999), each family firm can use its unique bundle of resources to create a competitive advantage and achieve higher firm performance. Resources include physical, human, organizational, and process capitals. Within an effective system of familiness, the family business can mobilize valuable, rare, and inimitable resources for a competitive advantage through family involvement.

Past research suggests that investment in firm resources for innovation is important to higher firm performance (De Massis, Frattini, Kotlar, Petruzzelli, & Wright, 2016). An innovativeness mindset in firms helps them mobilize resources toward strategies that help firms adapt to changing customer demands, markets, technology, and competition. Innovativeness requires a willingness to gain information, knowledge of internal process capabilities, and networks (De Massis et al., 2016). The decision to identify and evaluate resources that should be mobilized is a critical management decision; thus, mobilizing resources toward innovation is important to attain a competitive advantage and achieve higher firm performance (Barney, 1991).

Therefore, we propose:

Proposition 3a: Innovativeness is positively associated with family firm performance.

Family firms have a special family language that can make communications more efficient and allows for greater privacy and trust to make informal decision-making channels more efficient as well (Tagiuri & Davis, 1996). According to the familiness paradigm, the unique combination of the family system and the firm system for a family business can achieve a competitive advantage for the family firm. In competitive markets, firms that operate without innovativeness in mind often risk becoming obsolete. As we discussed in the two examples, Meijer and Perdue Farms show that through innovativeness they can achieve higher firm performance, and a healthy interaction between high family involvement and high LTO facilitates that for them. In family firms, a dominant coalition with a high LTO disposition can successfully identify and evaluate the right mix of resource investments to mobilize toward innovation as the firm moves to achieve long-range economic and non-economic goals. Hence, those firms can better adapt to changes and protect family members' wealth which is connected to the firm performance. In this sense, innovativeness will result in expending financial resources toward new product development or process improvements. We thus argue that family firms can rely on innovativeness as a mediator or mechanism in the relationship among the family involvement, LTO, and performance.

Therefore, we propose:

Proposition 3b: Through a moderated-mediation effect, innovativeness mediates the relationship between "family involvement long-term orientation" interaction and firm performance.

IMPLICATIONS FOR FUTURE RESEARCH AND PRACTICE

In this chapter, we argued that a healthy interaction between family involvement and LTO can encourage innovativeness as the familiness within family firms can create synergy that supports the needs and desires of the family and firm. Such synergy between the family and the firm – which tends to happen under high family involvement and high LTO – can promote innovativeness and willingness to explore new opportunities or improve processes. Conversely, when LTO is low and family involvement is high, the firm may avoid allocating resources toward innovativeness to conserve resources for the family. For example, LTO may be lower in situations of conflict among family members and in situations where firms face higher agency costs. Thus, the family firm will tend to stay conservative and less willing to adopt innovativeness, which will limit its outcomes.

This chapter has implications for future research. Based on the familiness paradigm, we suggest that family involvement is a resource contributing to the innovation efforts of family firms. Here we proposed that LTO moderates the family involvement–innovativeness relationship. In doing so, we illustrated that these two independent factors (family involvement and LTO) can work together as a unique bundle of resources for the family and the business to achieve organizational goals as prescribed by the familiness paradigm.

Future research could also examine and distinguish this effect on different financial performance measures, such as market value and firm growth. Similarly, future research can look at the impact of different types of family involvement, such as family involvement in the board of directors versus in the top management positions, in this moderated mediation model. This may add to governance literature in family business and help further understand the family involvement role in evaluating the adoption of innovativeness. Finally, it is important to note that LTO is a multidimensional construct. Future research may examine the influences of each dimension on the family involvement to firm performance relationship.

Although it is intuitive to assume a positive direct relationship between LTO and innovativeness, we did not discuss that relationship because the focus of this chapter was the relationship between family involvement and innovativeness and the boundary conditions of that relationship. In that regard, LTO was just a moderator in our model. In other words, family involvement is the main independent variable that affects a firm's innovativeness, while LTO is the moderating factor that can determine the direction and/or strength of that relationship. Future research may empirically test this moderated mediation relationship we propose here, as well as a possible direct relationship between LTO and innovativeness, or LTO and performance.

This research also has implications for practitioners. Family firms should consider family involvement and LTO as resources working together to promote innovativeness and to boost firm performance. Like Meijer and Perdue Farms, family firms can develop the right combination of family involvement in the dominant coalition in the board of directors, and within the management ranks, and promote LTO in a way that supports the adoption of innovativeness. Depending on the situational and temporal context that a family firm is experiencing, some or all of the three dimensions of LTO (futurity, perseverance, and continuity) can be encouraged to inspire stronger LTO. For instance, in the case of Spanish olive oil mills, encouraging futurity (i.e. evaluating the long-range consequences of their current actions) can help them adopt a stronger LTO. A high level of LTO can then translate their high family involvement into high innovativeness.

Hence, by connecting the links between family involvement, LTO, innovativeness, and firm performance, family firms can remain competitive in the market and achieve their goals for transgenerational wealth. This suggestion is in line with a broader implication that family firms should evaluate whether the family system and business system are aligned to achieve the best long-term outcome for the firm's specific familiness.

CONCLUSION

In this chapter we presented a set of propositions on the relationship between family involvement and firm performance. In particular we examined when and how family involvement can positively affect firm performance. We argued that the presence of LTO in a family firm can facilitate a positive relationship between family involvement and firm performance because it promotes an innovativeness mindset in the family firm. In this regard, LTO can serve as an important moderator, and innovativeness can serve as an important mediator in the relationship between family involvement and firm performance.

REFERENCES

Anderson, R. C., & Reeb, D. M. (2003), "Founding-family ownership and firm performance: Evidence from the S&P 500," *Journal of Finance*, **58** (3), 1301–28.
Anderson, R. C., Mansi, S. A., & Reeb, D. M. (2003), "Founding family ownership and the agency cost of debt," *Journal of Financial Economics*, **68** (2), 263–85.
Anderson, R. C., Duru, A., & Reeb, D. M. (2012), "Investment policy in family controlled firms," *Journal of Banking and Finance*, **36** (6), 1744–58.

Baker, W. E., & Sinkula, J. M. (2009), "The complementary effects of market orientation and entrepreneurial orientation on profitability in small businesses," *Journal of
Small Business Management*, **47** (4), 443–64.

Bandura, A. (1986), *Social foundations of thought and action: A social cognitive
theory*. Englewood Cliffs, NJ: Prentice-Hall.

Barney, J. (1991), "Firm resources and sustained competitive advantage," *Journal of
Management*, **17** (1), 99–120.

Berrone, P., Cruz, C., & Gómez-Mejía, L. R. (2012), "Socioemotional wealth in
family firms: Theoretical dimensions, assessment approaches, and agenda for future
research," *Family Business Review*, **25** (3), 258–79.

Block, J. H. (2012), "R&D investments in family and founder firms: An agency perspective," *Journal of Business Venturing*, **27** (2), 248–65.

Brigham, K. H., Lumpkin, G. T., Payne, G. T., & Zachary, M. A. (2014), "Researching
long-term orientation: A validation study and recommendations for future research,"
Family Business Review, **27** (1), 72–88.

Brockhaus, R. H. (2004), "Family business succession: Suggestions for future research,"
Family Business Review, **17** (2), 165–77.

Buss, D. (2016), Forbes, August 30, www.forbes.com/sites/dalebuss/2016/08/30/
meijer-expands-curbside-pick-up-to-compete-with-other-giants-in-its-midwest
-battleground/#38448fbf2266.

Chrisman, J. J., Chua, J. H., & Litz, R. (2003), "A unified systems perspective of family
firm performance: An extension and integration," *Journal of Business Venturing*, **18**
(4), 467–72.

Chua, J. H., Chrisman, J. J., & Sharma, P. (1999), "Defining the family business by
Behavior," *Entrepreneurship Theory and Practice*, **23** (4), 19–39.

Chua, J. H., Chrisman, J. J., Steier, L. P., & Rau, S. B. (2012), "Sources of heterogeneity in family firms: An introduction," *Entrepreneurship Theory and Practice*, **36**
(6), 1103–13.

Covin, J. G., & Wales, W. J. (2019), "Crafting high-impact entrepreneurial orientation
research: Some suggested guidelines," *Entrepreneurship Theory and Practice*, **43**
(1), 3–18.

De Massis, A., Frattini, F., Kotlar, J., Petruzzelli, A. M., & Wright, M. (2016),
"Innovation through tradition: Lessons from innovative family businesses and directions for future research," *Academy of Management Perspectives*, **30** (1), 93–116.

Dibrell, C., Craig, J. B., & Neubaum, D. O. (2014), "Linking the formal strategic planning process, planning flexibility, and innovativeness to firm performance," *Journal
of Business Research*, **67** (9), 2000–7.

Dreux, D. R. (1990), "Financing family business: Alternatives to selling out or going
public," *Family Business Review*, **3** (3), 225–43.

Duran, P., Kammerlander, N., Van Essen, M., & Zellweger, T. (2016), "Doing more
with less: Innovation input and output in family firms," *Academy of Management
Journal*, **59** (4), 1224–64.

Fama, E. F., & Jensen, M. C. (1983), Separation of ownership and control, *Journal of
Law and Economics*, **26** (2), 301–25.

Gentry, R., Dibrell, C., & Kim, J. (2016), "Long-term orientation in publicly traded
family businesses: Evidence of a dominant logic," *Entrepreneurship Theory and
Practice*, **40** (4), 733–57.

Gomez-Mejia, L. R., Larraza-Kintana, M., & Makri, M. (2003), "The determinants
of executive compensation in family-controlled public corporations," *Academy of
Management Journal*, **46** (2), 226–37.

Gomez-Mejia, L. R., Haynes, K., Nunez-Nickel, M., Jacobson, K., & Moyano-Fuentes, J. (2007), "Socioemotional wealth and business risks in family-controlled firms: Evidence from Spanish olive oil mills," *Administrative Science Quarterly*, **52** (1), 106–37.

Habbershon, T. G., & Williams, M. L. (1999), "A resource-based framework for assessing the strategic advantages of family firms," *Family Business Review*, **12** (1), 1–25.

Habbershon, T. G., Williams, M. L., & MacMillan, I. C. (2003), "A unified systems perspective of family firm performance," *Journal of Business Venturing*, **18** (4), 451–65.

Hoffmann, C., Wulf, T., & Stubner, S. (2016), "Understanding the performance consequences of family involvement in the top management team: The role of long-term orientation," *International Small Business Journal*, **34** (3), 345–68.

Hult, G. T. M., & Ketchen, D. J., Jr. (2001), "Does market orientation matter? A test of the relationship between positional advantage and performance," *Strategic Management Journal*, **22** (9), 899–906.

Kellermanns, F. W., Eddleston, K. A., Barnett, T., & Pearson, A. (2008), "An exploratory study of family member characteristics and involvement: Effects on entrepreneurial behavior in the family firm," *Family Business Review*, **21** (1), 1–14.

Kimmel, P. D., Weygandt, J. J., & Kieso, D. E. (2010), *Accounting: Tools for business decision makers*. New York: John Wiley & Sons.

Kreiser, P. M., Marino, L. D., Kuratko, D. F., & Weaver, K. M. (2013), "Disaggregating entrepreneurial orientation: The non-linear impact of innovativeness, proactiveness and risk-taking on SME performance," *Small Business Economics*, **40** (2), 273–91.

Le Breton-Miller, I., & Miller, D. (2006), "Why do some family businesses out-compete? Governance, long-term orientations, and sustainable capability," *Entrepreneurship Theory and Practice*, **30** (6), 731–46.

Lumpkin, G. T., & Brigham, K. H. (2011), "Long-term orientation and intertemporal choice in family firms," *Entrepreneurship Theory and Practice*, **35** (6), 1149–69.

Lumpkin, G. T., & Dess, G. G. (1996), "Clarifying the entrepreneurial orientation construct and linking it to performance," *Academy of Management Review*, **21** (1), 135–72.

Lumpkin, G. T., Brigham, K. H., & Moss, T. W. (2010), "Long-term orientation: Implications for the entrepreneurial orientation and performance of family businesses," *Entrepreneurship and Regional Development*, **22** (3–4), 241–64.

Meijer (2019a), About Meijer, http://newsroom.meijer.com/about.

Meijer (2019b), News room, http://newsroom.meijer.com/2019-05-21-From-Our-Store -to-Your-Door-Meijer-Launches-Home-Delivery-Service-in-Suburban-Cleveland.

Miller, D., & Le Breton-Miller, I. (2005), *Managing for the long run*. Boston, MA: Harvard Business School Press.

Munari, F., Oriani, R., & Sobrero, M. (2010), "The effects of owner identity and external governance systems on R&D investments: A study of Western European firms," *Research Policy*, **39** (8), 1093–104.

Perdue Farms (2019a), *2018 Highlights Report*, www.perduefarms.com/responsibility/ animal-care/2018-highlights-report/.

Perdue Farms (2019b), *Our Legacy*, www.perduefarms.com/company/legacy/.

Perdue Farms (2019c), *Vision and Values*, www.perduecareers.com/content/culture -and-values/.

Pervin, A. (1997), "A conversation with Henry Mintzberg," *Family Business Review*, **10** (2), 185–98.

Rothaermel, F. T., & Hess, A. M. (2007), "Building dynamic capabilities: Innovation driven by individual-, firm-, and network-level effects," *Organization Science*, **18**, 898–921.

Schreier, M., & Prugl, R. (2008), "Extending lead-user theory: Antecedents and consequences of consumers' lead userness," *Journal of Product Innovation Management*, **25**, 331–46.

Schumpeter, J. A. (1934), *The theory of economic development*. Cambridge, MA: Harvard University Press.

Schumpeter, J. A. (1942), *Capitalism, socialism and democracy*. New York: Harper and Row.

Sirmon, D. G., & Hitt, M. A. (2003), "Managing resources: Linking unique resources, management and wealth creation in family firms," *Entrepreneurship Theory and Practice*, **27** (4), 339–58.

Sirmon, D. G., Gove, S., & Hitt, M. A. (2008), "Resource management in dyadic competitive rivalry: The effects of resource bundling and deployment," *Academy of Management Journal*, **51** (5), 919–35.

Slevin, D. P., & Covin, J. G. (1995), "Entrepreneurship as firm behavior: A research model," *Advances in Entrepreneurship, Firm Emergence, and Growth*, **2**, 175–224.

Songini, L., & Gnan, L. (2015), "Family involvement and agency cost control mechanisms in family small and medium-sized enterprises," *Journal of Small Business Management*, **53** (3), 748–79.

Spriggs, M., Yu, A., Deeds, D., & Sorenson, R. L. (2012), "Too many cooks in the kitchen: Innovative capacity, collaborative network orientation, and performance in small family businesses," *Family Business Review*, **26** (1), 32–50.

Tagiuri, R, & Davis, J. A. (1996), "Bivalent attributes of the family firm," *Family Business Review*, **9** (2), 199–208.

Thomke, S. H. (2003), *Experimentation matters: Unlocking the potential of new technologies for innovation*. Boston, MA: Harvard Business Press.

Wales, W. J., Gupta, V. K., & Mousa, F.-T. (2013), "Empirical research on entrepreneurial orientation: An assessment and suggestions for future research," *International Small Business Journal*, **31** (4), 357–83.

Ward, J. L. (1997), "Growing the family business: Special challenges and best practices," *Family Business Review*, **10** (4), 323–37.

Yu, A., Lumpkin, G. T., Sorenson, R. L., & Brigham, K. H. (2012), "The landscape of family business outcomes: A summary and numerical taxonomy of dependent variables," *Family Business Review*, **25** (1), 33–57.

Zahra, S. A. (2005), "Entrepreneurial risk taking in family firms," *Family Business Review*, **18** (1), 23–40.

Zahra, S. A., Hayton, J. C., & Salvato, C. (2004), "Entrepreneurship in family vs. non-family firms: A resource-based analysis of the effect of organizational culture," *Entrepreneurship Theory and Practice*, **28** (4), 363–81.

Zellweger, T. (2007), "Time horizon, costs of equity capital, and generic investment strategies of firms," *Family Business Review*, **20** (1), 1–15.

3. Making sense of succession in family business internationalisation: An exploratory approach

Henry Shi

INTRODUCTION

The internationalisation of family businesses has become a topic of interest following the global and regional economic integrations (e.g., Arregle et al., 2012; Pukall & Calabrò, 2014). It is recognised that family businesses make important contributions to socio-economic well-being, locally and globally (Kontinen & Ojala, 2010). Existing studies, in general, contend that internationalisation is a strategic process that results in business growth and a strengthened market position of the firm. Along this process, a wide range of issues have been examined, including management involvement and commitment (Graves & Thomas, 2006), networking and relationship building (Yeung, 2000), decision-making (George et al., 2005), market and entry mode selection (Child et al., 2002; Claver et al., 2007), resource and capability creation (Davis & Harveston, 2000; Tsang, 2002), and generational impact on internationalisation (Fernández & Nieto, 2005; Menéndez-Requejo, 2005).

Interestingly, despite the long tradition of defining family business as a combination of family ownership and family management (Gersick et al., 1997), as well as generational transfer of not only the ownership and management (Handler, 1989) but also family values and legacy (Shi et al., 2015) through intergenerational succession, most prior studies on family business internationalisation concentrate on the ownership and management aspects. Empirical work on the effect of succession emerges only recently (e.g., Claver et al., 2009; Menéndez-Requejo, 2005; Meneses et al., 2014) with fragmented and inconclusive findings. Some report that the longevity of the family business across generations is positively related to an internationalisation strategy and performance (Fernández & Nieto, 2005; Graves & Thomas, 2004). Others argue that multi-generational family businesses attempt to maintain a family paradigm in the business over time, which leads to resistance to changes that depart from this paradigm (Davis, 1983), hence a lack of motives for internationalisation (Crick & Chaudhury, 2013; Okoroafo, 1999). These conflicting conclusions suggest that succession varies considerably in its effects on the internationalisation of family businesses.

Given that family business is at the intersection of the family system and the business system, succession in family businesses involves not only the transfer of business leadership[1] but also deep changes in the family (Seymour, 1993; Shi et al., 2015). The interaction between both systems makes succession a dynamic process that can have significant, and often nuanced, effects on the firm's strategic choices (Cadieux, 2007). Therefore, to understand the impact of succession on family business internationalisation, we first need to investigate how succession proceeds in the family and the business, before evaluating its influences on internationalisation. Thus, this study endeavours to explore how family businesses differ in their succession processes and how succession influences the internationalisation of family businesses.

This study attempts to extend our understanding of the nuances between the succession process and internationalisation strategy in small to medium-sized family businesses. It also contributes to the international entrepreneurship literature, which has recently begun to include a family business perspective (e.g., Piva et al., 2013; Swoboda & Olejnik, 2013).

LITERATURE REVIEW

This section first focuses on the succession process, that is, how succession begins and proceeds in small and medium-sized family businesses, and its impact on firm strategy and performance. It then concentrates on family business internationalisation and its relevance to intergenerational succession. By drawing on the assumption that internationalisation is a firm's entrepreneurial activity beyond its home market, this section builds conceptual links between succession, internationalisation, and entrepreneurship within the family business contexts.

Family Business Succession

Intergenerational succession is arguably a defining feature of family businesses, distinguishing them from other forms of business organisations where the transfer is mostly a business consideration (Handler & Kram, 1988) and barely affects relationships external to the business paradigm. In family businesses, especially those of a small to medium size, business leadership is typically undifferentiated from leadership in the owning family (Gersick et al., 1997; Gómez-Mejía et al., 2011; Le Breton-Miller et al., 2004). Therefore, succession in family businesses is a complex process that occurs over time across the business system and the family system (Handler, 1994; Ibrahim et al., 2001), which often restructures the business model and shakes up family relationships (Shi et al., 2015).

Research on intergenerational succession prevailed in the early family business literature (e.g., Ambrose, 1983; Barnes & Hershon, 1976; Birley, 1986), which revealed the challenges in the process and attempted to provide solutions to achieve a "smooth succession" (Handler & Kram, 1988, p. 361) or "successful succession" (Barach & Ganitsky, 1995, p. 131; Le Breton-Miller et al., 2004, p. 306). Both notions pointed to the view that intergenerational succession in family businesses is a "multi-phased evolutionary process that needs to take place over many years" (Le Breton-Miller et al., 2004, p. 312). In line with this view, the literature highlights the importance of effective succession planning that emphasises not just business performance but also the interest of multiple stakeholders within and external to the family business (Cabrera-Suárez et al., 2001; Morris et al., 1997).

Indeed, succession in small and medium-sized family businesses is far more complicated, and often more time-consuming, than that in other forms of organisations, partly because of the owner-manager's dual leadership role across the business and the family (Seymour, 1993). The power in family businesses is not solely derived from the business side (Brockhaus, 2004; Molly et al., 2010); rather, it is at times the family side that plays a crucial role in the firm's decision-making (Davis & Harveston, 2000; Shepherd & Zacharakis, 2000). Therefore, succession planning often begins with the family values and attitude (Birley, 1986), family relationships (Seymour, 1993), family socialisation (Shi & Dana, 2013), and family involvement and governance (Nordqvist et al., 2013), which are in effect antecedents to the actual succession process prior to the occurrence of key succession events (Davis & Harveston, 2000).

Existing literature establishes that intergenerational succession in family businesses is a dynamic process that involves various participants and stakeholders and evolves among multiple contexts (Morris et al., 1997; Sharma et al., 2012). For example, Brockhaus (2004) contends that central to family business succession are two major processes – successor selection and development, and both are nuanced by relationship issues (Davis & Harveston, 2000). Echoing Handler and Kram (1988), Barach and Ganitsky (1995) suggest that although numerous stakeholders are involved in family business succession, it is the relationship between the incumbent and the successor that exerts the most decisive influence on succession processes and outcomes. Le Breton-Miller et al. (2004) further contextualise the inquiry and submit that the incumbent–successor dynamics do not only develop within the family business context, but also interplay with the family, industry, and wider social contexts.

Despite the general agreement on the participants, stakeholders, and contexts of the succession process, most prior work has been devoted to the effect of succession on next-generation performance (e.g., Molly et al., 2010; Shepherd & Zacharakis, 2000), with the nature of the process underexamined. Among the very few attempts, Miller et al. (2003) investigate relationships between the past and the present within the family business and document three types of intergenerational succession, namely conservative, wavering, and rebellious. Inappropriate relationships are identified in each pattern, primarily because of the successor's reaction to the incumbent's intention to *perpetuate* the firm's existing heritage and vision. This negatively influences the firm's strategy, governance, organisation, and culture, and consequently gives rise to "poor performance that ended either in successor dismissal or bankruptcy" (Miller et al., 2003, p. 516).

Miller et al. (2003) provide valuable insights for the current study. On the one hand, the authors operationalise the process of family business succession by comparing the traits of succession events and classifying pattern types. Therefore, a ground is paved on which succession processes and their conse-quences can be comparatively studied among family businesses, which departs from the dichotomous tradition of comparing family and non-family busi-nesses (Nordqvist et al., 2013). Overall, Miller et al. (2003) suggest that there is no one "best practice" succession pattern and that each pattern has certain traits that hinder the business from achieving its best possible performance.

In a similar vein, this study does not intend to make judgments on the "quality" of succession. Rather, it is committed to making sense of the relation-ships between succession and internationalisation in small and medium-sized family businesses and advocating the inclusion of succession in family busi-ness internationalisation studies. The study borrows Miller et al.'s (2003) idea of clustering succession processes into common patterns. However, unlike Miller et al. (2003), whose investigation concentrates on succession failures, this study considers a wider range of intergenerational relationships and dynamics that occur in various contexts (cf., Le Breton-Miller et al., 2004).

Family Business Internationalisation

Existing literature takes a variety of perspectives and mixed approaches to examine the internationalisation of family businesses. Much has been done to understand the impact of family ownership and management on internationali-sation (e.g., Carr & Bateman, 2009; Fernández & Nieto, 2005, 2006; Graves & Thomas, 2004; Sciascia et al., 2012; Zahra 2003), family business strategy and its effect on internationalisation (e.g., Banalieva & Eddleston, 2011; Basly, 2007; Claver et al., 2009; Graves & Thomas, 2006; Thomas & Graves, 2005), and the internationalisation processes of family businesses (e.g., Claver et al., 2007; Graves & Thomas, 2008; Menéndez-Requejo, 2005; Piva et al., 2013; Tsang, 2002).

The findings and conclusions, however, are notably inconsistent and somehow contrasting. For example, Sciascia et al. (2012), among others (e.g., Fernández & Nieto, 2006; Graves & Thomas, 2006), hold that family businesses are less motivated to internationalise. This is primarily because the family emphasises continued control and stability of the business, hence high risk-aversion (Gallo et al., 2004) and a home-market orientation (Banalieva & Eddleston, 2011), as opposed to a growth and diversification strategy (Gómez-Mejía et al., 2010). However, others (e.g., Carr & Bateman, 2009; Zahra, 2003) have provided evidence that family-related attributes can drive small and medium-sized family businesses, in comparison with their non-family counterparts, to be more active in pursuing entrepreneurial opportunities internationally (Cruz & Nordqvist, 2012). For example, Huang (2009) finds that key family members' attitudes play a significant role in the firm's decision to internationalise. Similarly, Demir et al. (2017) argue that the owner-manager's expertise and experience is an important contributor to the family firm's growth strategy. Once the family is determined to expand into the international market, the firm is committed to an internationalisation strategy and prepared to take the risks associated with the international entrepreneurial processes.

The development of international entrepreneurship as a field of research provides useful insights to understanding family business internationalisation through both international business and entrepreneurship lenses. Arguably, internationalisation develops with "the discovery, enactment, evaluation and exploitation of opportunities – across borders – to create future goods and services" (Oviatt & McDougall, 2005, p. 540). Internationalisation is especially relevant to small and medium-sized businesses whose competitiveness often relies on their responsiveness to market opportunities, in addition to their ability to access and organise resources (Partanen et al., 2014). Pukall and Calabrò (2014) submit that the family's network relationships play a significant role in the firm's opportunity exploration and exploitation (Partanen et al., 2014), as well as resource acquisition and organisation in international markets (Semrau & Werner, 2014; Sullivan & Ford, 2014). Likewise, prior studies have also revealed that networking is an important source of social capital for small and medium-sized family businesses (Shi et al., 2015), which underpins their entrepreneurial performance both within and beyond the home market (Graves & Thomas, 2004; Kontinen & Ojala, 2010).

The international entrepreneurship literature yields two important insights for this study. First, evidence suggests that entrepreneurial family businesses, by capitalising on their social capital through networking and socialisation (Shi & Dana, 2013), are able to achieve advantages in levering not only liability of foreignness (Anderson et al., 2005; Child et al., 2002), which is primarily a result of psychic distance (Johanson & Vahlne, 1977), but also the liability of outsidership (Casillas et al., 2007), which stems from uncertainty in the unfamiliar international market (Johanson & Vahlne, 2009). Second, the literature has documented the next-generation involvement in family business internationalisation and argued that next-generation owner-managers tend to be more actively seeking entrepreneurial opportunities in home and foreign markets to outgrow the incumbents' heritage (Fernández & Nieto, 2005; Menéndez-Requejo, 2005). Prior studies suggest that the incoming generation is usually equipped with international awareness and readiness (cf., Graves & Thomas, 2008) and more likely to adopt a growth orientation, which under-pins the internationalisation of the previously home-market-oriented family business.

Family Business Succession and Internationalisation

There has been a tradition of featuring family business with family ownership and management (Gersick et al., 1997), as well as intergenerational transfer of the ownership and management (Handler, 1989). The impact of family own-ership and family management on the firm's internationalisation has attracted enormous interest and produced rich results, although such results are notably disjointed and disagreeable. In contrast, research on the role of intergenera-tional transfer, namely succession, tends to be surprisingly scarce and still (cf., Kontinen & Ojala, 2010; Pukall & Calabrò, 2014), which inhibits our under-standing of the essence of family business in general, and entrepreneurship in family business in particular, especially on the international arena.

The notion of born-again-global has provided insights (e.g., Fernández & Nieto, 2005; Graves & Thomas, 2004; Menéndez-Requejo, 2005). However, its limitations are also explicit. Arguably, most internationalised family businesses are of a small to medium size and typically follow an incremental approach to internationalising. Besides their entrepreneurial orientation and performance in the international markets, small and medium-sized family businesses emphasise control and heritage (Gallo et al., 2004; Okoroafo, 1999) and tend to consider international engagement as an extension or reinforcement of the existing domestic operations (Claver et al., 2009). This practice presents a different strategy from the born-again-global firms, which often overwrite their domestic market orientation with a rapid and radical internationalisa-tion approach (Meneses et al., 2014) and result in business rebirth globally. Although intergenerational succession can be a critical incident that triggers a born-again-global strategy (Graves & Thomas, 2008), the born-again-global framework can barely capture the "mainstream" family businesses that inter-nationalise through intergenerational succession.

Meneses et al. (2014) elaborate on the impact of succession on family busi-ness internationalisation from the successor's perspective. The examination focuses on the successors' demographical and experiential characteristics, and social networks, which are related to the firm's internationalisation. Findings confirm that intergenerational succession constitutes a disruptive incident, which is likely to redirect the domestically established family businesses to foreign markets (Graves & Thomas, 2004; Kontinen & Ojala, 2012). Meneses et al. (2014) argue that some successor characteristics – such as technical knowledge, prior international experience, and innovative spirit – are closely related to the firm's internationalisation (cf., Thomas & Graves, 2005; Tsang, 2002; Westhead et al., 2001).

Despite the conceptual and managerial implications provided by Meneses et al. (2014), it is argued in this study that besides the successor's personal characteristics, the succession processes – namely, how intergenerational succession occurs – exerts crucial influence on the next generation's business motivation, objectives, and capabilities (Shi et al., 2015). Neither succession nor internationalisation is a static phenomenon, but are dynamic and evolving over time. Therefore, research efforts should be directed to the succession process to yield authentic insights to understanding the relationships and nuances that are critical for the internationalisation of entrepreneurial family businesses.

METHODOLOGY AND METHODS

This study seeks to investigate a range of cognitive and behavioural activities by exploring the role of intergenerational succession in the internationalisation of family businesses. These activities are generally under-researched and inadequately understood in the context of family businesses, partly because "the bulk of research conducted within business schools has ignored the family dimension of enterprises" (Heck et al., 2008, p. 318). Neither a grounding theory nor promising evidence is available at the point of intersection between family business succession and internationalisation. Most prior studies take a quantitative approach, which lacks "sophistication concerning measures of family involvement, thus making it difficult to deduct strong statements related to the influence of the family on the businesses internationalization" (Pukall & Calabrò, 2014, p. 109). This study adopts a qualitative approach that provides methods to generate "quality, depth and richness in the findings" (Marshal & Rossman, 1999, p. 16) and to support systematic understanding of what is likely to be found in the shortage of existing information (Eisenhardt & Graebner, 2007), with which conceptualisation and theorisation on social relations become possible (Edmondson & McManus, 2007).

In line with this thinking, case studies were conducted in Jiangsu, one of China's first industrialised regions that is characterised by rapid develop-ment of family businesses, private entrepreneurship, and an export-oriented

Table 3.1   *Case profiles*

Case ID	Founded	Main business	Workforce	SOM's siblings	Founder left for
C1	1998	Chemical manufacturing	150	1 younger sister	Other business
C2	1995	Chemical manufacturing	120	1 younger brother	Health
E3	2002	Electronics manufacturing	250	1 elder brother	Retirement
F4	1991	Footwear manufacturing	80	1 younger sister	Retirement
F5	1995	Footwear manufacturing	60		Retirement
M6	1983	Machinery manufacturing	90	2 elder sisters	Retirement
M7	1994	Machinery manufacturing	120		Other business
M8	1990	Machinery manufacturing	70	1 younger brother	Retirement
M9	1995	Machinery manufacturing	160	2 elder siblings	Retirement
T10	1992	Textile manufacturing	180	1 younger brother	Health
T11	1990	Textile manufacturing	110		Other business

economy. Although a universally agreed definition of family business has yet to emerge, there is a general consensus that a family business is normally at the nexus of family ownership and management (Chua et al., 1999). Therefore, this study defines a family business as one that is majority-owned by a family and has at least one family member on the management team. On the other hand, a fundamental selection criterion was that the second-generation owner-managers (SOMs) are key decision-makers, even if the "retired" founders are still involved at times. Also, to understand how succession processes influence the firm's strategic choices across generations, cases were chosen from those that internationalised through, or immediately after, the succession processes. In other words, each case firm performed business activities in at least one market other than China.

As interviews and observations continued, information was increasingly repeated, signalling that subsequent emergence of new themes would be less likely (Creswell, 1994). This saturation enabled an understanding of the succession processes and their effects on the internationalisation of entrepreneurial family businesses, which in turn led to the development of a conceptual model and theory building (Eisenhardt & Graebner, 2007). Eventually, this study included 11 small to medium-sized family businesses (see Table 3.1).

To collect data, this study employed semi-structured interviews, personal observations, and document inspections to reduce reliance on a single method and increase sources of information that are potentially triangulated (Eisenhardt & Graebner, 2007). Three to four interviews were conducted in each case firm, with the SOMs, managers, employees, owning family members and relatives, as well as external stakeholders like business partners and government officials, which added up to 37 interviews in total. Each semi-structured interview lasted around an hour, at which pre-designed questions were used as guidelines for the interviewees to respond with relevant information. As information of interest emerged, in-depth discussions followed up, which allowed further and more specific information to be captured. Such information was recorded for subsequent data processing. At times, personal observations in the case firms provided contextual insights to interpreting the interview data. Documents, including the firms' categories, publicly accessible news reports, and government registers in some cases, were inspected as a supplementary source of information.

Data analysis began while fieldwork continued, which informed the judgement on information saturation. Interview recordings were first transcribed in Chinese, verbatim, and then translated into English. Overarching themes were identified from repeated readings, word repetitions, and keyword searching. A cluster analysis was used to group similar meanings to yield common themes. To check the accuracy and credibility of the data translation, the back translation technique (Harkness 2003) was used by a third-party professional who did not participate in this study.

FINDINGS AND DISCUSSION

This section compares the succession processes and examines their relevance to the internationalisation of the case firms. The discussion focuses on the patterns of succession process and their effects on the firms' entrepreneurial processes and outcomes in the international markets.

Succession Patterns

All 11 case firms completed their succession. In both legal and operational terms, all are in their second generation. Both systematic similarities and differences were identified in their succession processes. Based on these similarities and differences, their succession processes can be clustered into three pattern types – evolutionary, co-evolutionary, and revolutionary (cf., Miller et al., 2003), highlighting the intergenerational dynamics and relationships. Table 3.2 provides the main features of each pattern.

Table 3.2   *Succession patterns*

Succession pattern	Successor selection	Successor development	Management transfer	Ownership transfer
Evolutionary	Founder initiated Primogeniture as a guiding principle Decisions made at founder's discretion	Founder driven Events designed purposefully for successor's capabilities related to existing business	Progressively transferred as on-the-job training and rotation proceeded Under founder's close supervision	Occurred after management transfer Concluded succession process
Co-evolutionary	Self-nominated candidature open to all children of founder Selection based on candidates' motivation and merit Intergenerational reconciliations	Guided and facilitated by founder Often involved both external and internal experiences Built up a wide range of successor capabilities	Progressively transferred through on-the-job rotation Jointly decided by founder and successor Successor initiative and autonomy allowed and encouraged	Occurred before management transfer completed Subject to judgement on successor's readiness
Revolutionary	Successor's self-given exclusive candidature Often with intergenerational disputes or conflicts	Successor generated and implemented Successor capabilities distant from existing business	Wrested by successor rather than transferred from founder Rapid and complete	Forced ownership transfer once successor's sole candidature established

First, the evolutionary succession pattern consists of C1, C2, F4, M9, and T11. These businesses have strong and powerful founders, who initiated the succession planning long before the actual succession process began, and dominated the entire succession process, including successor selection and development (Brockhaus, 2004). In successor selection, four of the five founders followed the primogeniture tradition and considered exclusively the first-born (C1, C2, F4) or the only son (T11) as a successor candidate. As C2's founder reflected, "Successor candidature has never been an issue, and no one [in the family and the business] has ever thought it is an issue," which indicates that there was a tacit agreement among the family and business that his first son be the successor. M9 is the only one where the primogeniture principle was discounted. The founder chose his second son because the first son was "neither interested nor talented to be at the helm." The first son, now M9's marketing manager, admitted that his younger brother was better gifted with business leadership and competence.

Successor development in all five businesses was driven by the founders. As an essential part of succession planning and successor development, all SOMs worked in the businesses before succession. Most rotated their positions to accumulate substantial knowledge of the products and production, as well as relations with internal and external stakeholders (cf., Cabrera-Suárez et al., 2001). The SOMs of F4 and T11 started as frontline workers in their businesses and were subsequently promoted to management positions. M9's SOM was the only successor who did not rotate his roles. Instead, he remained deputy to his father until the handover. Still, this role allowed him enough experience to maintain existing business and to explore new opportunities. Management transfer occurred gradually in all five firms. C2's SOM described his pre-succession roles as an "advanced placement programme," in which he was appointed to serial positions and gained authority in these positions one by one. "It was like passing prerequisite courses and moving up to the next level until I satisfied all conditions did my father pass me the baton," recalled the SOM. Arguably, the ownership transfer in these businesses was largely the result of management transfer, which followed a gradual process step by step. Like C2, all the other four businesses changed their ownership at the end of the succession process, when the founders eventually stepped down as leaders.

Second, the co-evolutionary succession pattern includes E3, F5, and T10. Compared to their evolutionary counterparts, successors of these businesses present a stronger role in the succession process. F5's SOM is the founder's only child, hence the sole successor candidate. The other two businesses had an open process of successor selection, based on the candidates' self-nomination and the founders' approval. This process entitled all children of the founder successor candidature, making no distinction between sons and daughters or birth order. "My father certainly wanted us to work in the business, but he did not force my brother or me; instead, he let us develop individually and choose our own career paths," revealed the SOM of E3, who is the founder's second son and became successor as he chose to remain when his brother moved overseas. Likewise, T10's SOM was not assigned to be successor by the founder but stepped forward by himself and acquired the successor's status through a series of discussions and reconciliations within the family and the business.

Likewise, successor development in these businesses was a joint effort between the founder and successor. All SOMs started their business careers with external work experience by choice. Such experiences were highly regarded by the SOMs because they provided diverse insights to business management and complemented experiences that they acquired later in their own business. The founders took a facilitator's role in successor development, rather than dictating the process. Particularly, they assisted the successors with building up business confidence and capabilities. Ownership was transferred before the completion of management transfer. The founders remained active in some management roles after they officially transferred ownership to the SOMs and until they were fully assured of the SOMs' capability. The metaphor made by F5's founder can be insightful and representational, "The ageing monarch had better abdicate as soon as the crown prince is ready, and assist him to be a wise king – this, and only this, is in the best and long-term interest of the royal family."

Third, the revolutionary succession pattern was performed by M6, M7, and M8. This is a radical pattern. None of the three SOMs were selected as a successor. Their candidature was self-given rather than self-initiated, and the process was filled with disputes and conflicts, particularly with the founder. At M6, for example, it was the SOM's eldest sister who was originally selected as successor. This decision was not acceptable to the SOM, who thought she was not offered a chance to compete with her sister. The resentfulness between the SOM and her father led to intense conflicts in the family for a few years, which negatively affected the firm's performance. The SOM eventually won the succession war and expelled her father and sister. M8 presents a similar case, where the SOM's younger brother was the founder's preference and the SOM seized power through a painful revolution. As a result, his younger brother left the business, and the founder was strictly kept away from decision-making, which was dominated by the SOM and his team. M7's revolution illustrates a different scenario. The SOM is the founder's only child and should "by default" become the successor. However, the SOM disagreed with the way his father managed the business. "I was not impatient, but very concerned, and thought everything must be changed immediately," said the SOM, who then managed to shut his father out of the business.

Because of the radical nature of the succession process, successor development was essentially self-generated and self-implemented by the SOMs. On the one hand, they had considerable autonomy in developing expertise and capabilities, with little to no founder involvement. On the other hand, management transfer and ownership transfer happened almost concurrently once the SOMs' succession revolution succeeded, with the founders being kept away from the core management team or the business completely.

Overall, these findings align with existing literature on the complexity of intergenerational succession in family businesses (Handler, 1994; Ibrahim et al., 2001). They also supplement prior studies on succession characteristics and types, particularly that of Miller et al. (2003), who propose three patterns of succession in their exploration of succession failure. On the other hand, this study has travelled a different route from that of Miller et al. (2003) by devoting more to the intergenerational dynamics that contribute to the making of next-generation entrepreneurship in the pursuit of business growth and market diversification. To depict a contrast, the focus here is on the success stories, acknowledging while differentiating from Miller et al.'s (2003) insights yielded from failures.

Effects of Succession on Internationalisation

Arguably, the internationalisation of family businesses is an entrepreneurial undertaking. Unlike born-global firms that engage with international markets from their inception, small to medium-sized family businesses typically establish a home-market orientation (Banalieva & Eddleston, 2011) before they consider international opportunities and proceed to exploit them (Fernández & Nieto, 2005; Graves & Thomas, 2004; Menéndez-Requejo, 2005). Also, differing from the born-again-global firms that shift to a foreign-market orientation with domestic operations marginalised or terminated (Meneses et al., 2014), the internationalisation of established family businesses is an extension or supplement of existing business (Claver et al., 2009). Reflecting these realities, this study chooses to examine established family businesses that internationalise for growth and reinforcement of the existing business, instead of born-global or born-again-global firms. Therefore, rather than adopting a new venture creation framework (cf., Carter et al., 1996), this study embraces a Schumpeterian approach and emphasises the innovative nature of the entrepreneurial behaviours in established businesses (Shane & Venkataraman, 2000). Investigations focus on the relationships between succession processes and the source of international opportunity, resource acquisition and deployment, and international market outcomes.

Regarding their firms' internationalisation, all SOMs reported that it was the succession processes that "triggered" or "facilitated" their growth motivation, opportunity identification, and resource organisation. This is a view in line with existing literature (e.g., Graves & Thomas, 2004; Kontinen & Ojala, 2012), which posits that intergenerational succession provides an opportunity for the home-market-oriented family business to review and update its strategy, and is likely to result in an operation expansion into international markets. However, the way that such impacts exert on the international entrepreneurial process varies across the 11 family businesses, shedding light on the three succession patterns. Table 3.3 summarises the internationalisation processes and outcomes of the 11 case firms.

First, the evolutionary succession process created a structured and progressive approach to the transfer of family business leadership, in which the founder played a dominant role. Such dominance resulted in the successor receiving systematic training and developing a strategic vision aligned with that of the founder. These supported the continuity of existing business strategy and operations across generations. As a result, the SOMs were well

Table 3.3   *The internationalisation process and outcomes*

Succession pattern	Case ID	Initiator	Exporting type	Market scope	Product scope
Evolutionary	C1	Founder	Indirect	2 in EU	Single, standardised
	C2	Founder	Indirect	1 in US	Single, standardised
	F4	Founder	Indirect	1 in EU	Single, standardised
	M9	Founder	Indirect	1 in US	Single, standardised
	T11	Founder	Indirect	1 in US	Multiple, customised
Co-evolutionary	E3	SOM and founder	Direct and indirect	5 in Asia, EU, US	Multiple, standardised and customised
	F5	SOM and founder	Direct and indirect	4 in Asia, EU, US	Multiple, standardised and customised
	T10	SOM and founder	Indirect	3 in EU	Multiple, customised
Revolutionary	M6	SOM	Indirect	1 in Asia	Single, standardised
	M7	SOM	Direct	1 in Asia	Single, standardised
	M8	SOM	Indirect	1 in US	Single, standardised

equipped with knowledge and skills to enhance the firms' existing operations. Not surprisingly, the founders played a crucial role in the internationalisation of these businesses, through their activities pertaining to the discovery and evaluation of international opportunities. The SOMs, on the other hand, faithfully implemented the founders' internationalisation initiative and involved mainly in opportunity exploitation, under the founders' supervision. The internationalisation of these businesses happened through their succession processes, and arguably formed part of their successor development. By the time succession had completed, the firms' exports had regularised and international engagement was established, resulting in business continuity and stability in both domestic and international markets. In effect, these businesses tended to prefer exporting a narrow range of existing products, with little to no modification, to a foreign market through a trade agent with whom a business relationship was established and sustained. Their intention to grow internationally remained low because ambitious growth in remote markets would consume the limited resources that could have been concentrated on home-market operations where the businesses can easily control and monitor with more confidence and certainty.

Overall, an evolutionary succession enhances existing business, high-lights the firm's past entrepreneurial achievements (Miller et al., 2003), and prepares the successor to embrace existing strategy and operations. Here, internationalisation of the business is part of the founder's legacy, which aims at strengthening existing business and improving firm performance without major changes to the firm's existing strategy and structure while minimising costs and risks. Most opportunities are created from the founder's established networks and exploited by deploying existing resources without having to acquire new resources from unfamiliar environments or invest in new capabil-ity development (Shi et al., 2015). Therefore, these businesses are more likely to employ a prudent approach to internationalisation and remain content with small-scaled engagement and limited foreign markets.

Second, businesses in the co-evolutionary pattern went through a succession process that was loosely structured and mostly driven by the SOMs. Overall, the founder–SOM relationship was engaged and agreeable so that different views could be openly discussed and reconciled through family socialisation (cf., Shi & Dana, 2013). Throughout the entire succession process, the SOMs were given considerable autonomy to evaluate the firms' strategic and oper-ational performance and participated in the firms' decision-making and man-agement. With the autonomy and founders' support, the SOMs were able to develop a wide range of business skills and expertise, network resources, and managerial capabilities. They were more actively engaged in the opportunity creation and exploitation internationally. In fact, all three businesses in this pattern captured the initial international market information from the SOMs' networks, including the spouse's family and relatives (T10), alumni (E3), and friends in business (F5), who in turn had access to the information which was later jointly developed by the founders and successors, and their teams, into exporting opportunities. To exploit the opportunities, these businesses were not only able to deploy existing resources but also acquire new resources from sources accessible to the founders and/or the SOMs. As a result, these businesses could exploit a wide range of international market opportunities by exporting both existing and modified products to multiple foreign markets.

In general, a co-evolutionary succession emphasises the successor's ini-tiative, the incumbent's guidance and facilitation, and the intergenerational engagement and collaboration. In effect, entrepreneurial behaviours are nur-tured across generations through the succession process (Nordqvist et al., 2013). When the incumbent and successor jointly reconstruct the firm's strat-egy and resources through succession, an entrepreneurial legacy is created and embraced across generations (Jaskiewicz et al., 2015). Internationalisation is a vehicle of the entrepreneurial reconstruction, which results in the acquisition of new resources and capabilities and business growth into multiple interna-tional markets with both existing and modified products. The businesses are more likely to have a stronger entrepreneurial position as well as an ongoing entrepreneurial orientation (Cruz & Nordqvist, 2012; Thomas & Graves, 2005) that facilitates future entrepreneurial behaviour and performance in both domestic and international markets.

Third, the revolutionary SOMs took a radical approach to succession. Rather than being granted leadership by the founders, they "pushed" the founders and "seized" leadership rapidly. Consequently, the founder–SOM relationship appeared to be unengaged, mutually distrustful, or even inimical. On the business side, most existing operations started by the founders were terminated or significantly altered, because they were not consistent with the SOMs' vision, and more importantly, they represented the past heritage which the new generation deemed as a threat to their own business agenda and rejected to incorporate (Seymour, 1993). The SOMs were active in seeking new opportunities from their own networks and foreign markets. Instead of inheriting existing resources, the SOMs managed to acquire new resources to explore international opportunities. As a result, these SOMs quickly developed new business relationships, through which international market opportunities arose. Unlike their counterparts in the other patterns, these businesses barely relied on existing resources and capabilities in their opportunity evaluation and exploitation. Rather, they mainly used resources accessed and possessed by the SOMs. However, because of the shortage of resources and capabilities, as well as a lack of knowledge and confidence in international markets, these businesses chose to adopt a focus strategy in terms of product range and market scope (cf., Yeung, 2000). All three businesses export a single standardised product to one foreign market only. Although the SOMs were motivated to grow their international engagement, such ambition was notably constrained by their lack of resources and capabilities, market intelligence, and export-related expertise.

In summary, a revolutionary succession is dominantly driven by the successor to radically restructure or replace the existing business and strategy with new developments. Therefore, the primary focus is on present and future entrepreneurial opportunities, as opposed to the past practices (Miller et al., 2003). Besides others, internationalisation is one option that the successor can choose to undermine the past, undertake the present, and underpin the future. Having this in mind, the successors tend to be more proactive in information search, both at home and abroad, as well as opportunity creation. Despite entrepreneurial proactiveness, the successor's entrepreneurial capability is notably restricted by the absence of the incumbent's support, which leads to barriers to resource access, organisation, and deployment (Shi et al., 2015). Also, the successor's "revolutionary" – in other words, rebellious – mindset and behaviours contribute to an unengaged intergenerational relationship. Consciously or subconsciously, the successor chooses to overlook, or reject, the incumbent's advice or offer to help. On the one hand, the conditions for a transgenerational entrepreneurial legacy are nowhere in sight (cf., Jaskiewicz et al., 2015). On the other hand, the performance outcome is less radical than the succession process, with a single or narrow range of product in a limited scope of international markets.

CONCLUSION

Both family business and entrepreneurship literatures have found succession an important construct for understanding family business strategy in general, and internationalisation in particular. However, studies are nascent on the role of succession in the international entrepreneurial behaviour of small to medium-sized family businesses. The main purpose of this study is to contribute to conceptualising and theorising the interplay between family business succession and internationalisation. In particular, the study explores how family businesses differ in their succession processes and how such difference influences their internationalisation. To do this, the study adopts an inductive exploratory approach by focusing on Chinese family businesses. The findings confirm that family business succession takes various patterns, which have a mutual effect with the intergenerational dynamics (Miller et al., 2003) and the firm's pursuit of entrepreneurial opportunities in foreign markets (Meneses et al., 2014).

Contributions of this study are three-fold. First, it contributes to the theorisation of intergenerational succession as an interactive factor with the internationalisation of family businesses. Three patterns of succession are identified by probing into the processes of succession selection, successor development, management transfer, and ownership transfer. After investigating the varying effects of these patterns on the firms' international entrepreneurial processes and outcomes, it is arguable that intergenerational succession is a dynamic construct that develops in different patterns for different purposes, and results in different market outcomes. Second, insights have been provided to understanding intergenerational succession and internationalisation in the Chinese family business context. Although Chinese culture traditionally emphasises longevity and continuity of family values and loyalty, which often result in conservative and past-oriented succession processes (Tsang, 2002; Yeung, 2000), this study has found intergenerational family dynamics that depart from the belief in patriarchy and develop into more present- or future-oriented succession processes. This has implications for many Chinese family businesses, who are in the process of intergenerational succession and considering a strategic stretch into diversified markets domestically and internationally. Third, this study contributes to the international entrepreneurship literature by documenting the systematically different effects of succession patterns and intergenerational dynamics on family business internationalisation (Gómez-Mejía et al., 2010; Sciascia et al., 2012) that are distinct from the born-global and born-again-global paradigms. As such, this study brings the family business dimension back into the international entrepreneurship research.

In addition to the theoretical and empirical contributions, this study provides practical implications for family business owner-managers and policymakers. On the one hand, owner-managers need a balanced view of the firm's past, present, and future to nurture an entrepreneurial legacy that can help the firm thrive by performing entrepreneurship in wider markets across generations (Jaskiewicz et al., 2015). On the other hand, while the Chinese government has advocated for a "modern enterprise system," where private firms are encouraged to be more market-oriented, policymakers need to recognise the family dynamics within the family businesses, especially between generations. This can benefit the firm's strategic and entrepreneurial construction and reconstruction and lead the firm to succeed in new business and markets at home and abroad.

This study extends our understanding of the interrelationship between succession and internationalisation by focusing on Chinese family businesses that experienced intergenerational succession and ventured beyond their domestic market. However, this specific focus can limit the generalisability of the findings as well. Therefore, future exploration is needed into the succession patterns and their effects on internationalisation in other economic and institutional contexts. As the study focuses on newly internationalised family businesses, it is unlikely to ascertain whether family businesses that have yet to internationalise and those with a greater international involvement present additional or alternative succession patterns. The study solely examines succession to the second generation, thus, future investigations can be conducted on how succession beyond the second generation, as well as intra-generational transfers, can influence the internationalisation of Chinese family businesses.

Both family business succession and internationalisation are dynamic and heterogeneous concepts. Therefore, more work is needed to specify the processes as how succession begins and proceeds, and how international opportunities are recognised and exploited, by paying attention to the past–present relationships in the family and the business. Moreover, the impact of institutional environment on the internationalisation of small to medium-sized family businesses requires additional research efforts. To further extend this line of inquiry, large-scale empirical studies are necessary by using mixed methods. Drawing on investigations in the context of China's transitional economy and institutional structure, how succession evolves and how it impacts the internationalisation of family businesses in other economies can also be an interesting and promising area for future research.

NOTE

1. For the purpose of this study, the term 'leadership' is used to describe the key decision-making role or position, rather than the leader's management capability.

REFERENCES

Ambrose, D. M. (1983), "Transfer of the family-owned business," *Journal of Small Business Management*, **21** (1), 49–56.

Anderson, A. R., Jack, S. L., & Dodd, S. D. (2005), "The role of family members in entrepreneurial networks: Beyond the boundaries of the family firm," *Family Business Review*, **18** (2), 135–54.

Arregle, J. L., Naldi, L., Nordqvist, M., & Hitt, M. A. (2012), "Internationalization of family-controlled firms: A study of the effects of external involvement in governance," *Entrepreneurship Theory and Practice*, **36** (6), 1115–43.

Banalieva, E. R., & Eddleston, K. A. (2011), "Home-region focus and performance of family firms: The role of family vs non-family leaders," *Journal of International Business Studies*, **42** (8), 1060–72.

Barach, J. A., & Ganitsky, J. B. (1995), "Successful succession in family business," *Family Business Review*, **8** (2), 131–55.

Barnes, L. B., & Hershon, S. A. (1976), "Transferring power in the family business," *Harvard Business Review*, **54** (5), 105–14.

Basly, S. (2007), "The internationalization of family SME: An organizational learning and knowledge development perspective," *Baltic Journal of Management*, **2** (2), 154–80.

Birley, S. (1986), "Succession in the family firm: The inheritor's view," *Journal of Small Business Management*, **24** (3), 36–43.

Brockhaus, R. H. (2004), "Family business succession: Suggestions for future research," *Family Business Review*, **17** (2), 165–77.

Cabrera-Suárez, K., De Saá-Pérez, P., & García-Almeida, D. (2001), "The succession process from a resource- and knowledge-based view of the family firm," *Family Business Review*, **14** (1), 37–47.

Cadieux, L. (2007), "Succession in small and medium-sized family businesses: Toward a typology of predecessor roles during and after instatement of the successor," *Family Business Review*, **20** (2), 95–109.

Carr, C., & Bateman, S. (2009), "International strategy configurations of the world's top family firms," *Management International Review*, **49** (6), 733–58.

Carter, N., Gartner, W. B., & Reynolds, P. (1996), "Exploring start-up sequence events," *Journal of Business Venturing*, **11** (3), 151–66.

Casillas, J. C., Acedo, F. J., & Moreno, A. M. (2007), *International Entrepreneurship in Family Businesses*. Cheltenham, UK and Northampton, MA, USA: Edward Elgar Publishing.

Child, J., Ng, S. H., & Wong, C. (2002), "Psychic distance and internationalization: Evidence from Hong Kong firms," *International Studies of Management and Organization*, **32** (1), 36–56.

Chua, J. H., Chrisman, J. J., & Sharma, P. (1999), "Defining the family business by behavior," *Entrepreneurship Theory and Practice*, **23** (4), 19–39.

Claver, E., Rienda, L. P., & Quer, D. (2007), "The internationalisation process in family firms: Choice of market entry strategy," *Journal of General Management*, **33** (1), 1–14.

Claver, E., Rienda, L. P., & Quer, D. (2009), "Family firms' international commitment: The influence of family-related factors," *Family Business Review*, **22** (2), 125–35.

Creswell, J. W. (1994), *Research Design: Qualitative and Quantitative Approaches*. Thousand Oaks, CA: Sage.

Crick, D., & Chaudhury, S. (2013), "An exploratory study of UK based, family-owned, Asian firms' motives for internationalising," *Journal of Small Business and Enterprise Development*, **20** (3), 526–47.

Cruz, C., & Nordqvist, M. (2012), "Entrepreneurial orientation in family firms: A generational perspective," *Small Business Economics*, **38** (1), 33–49.

Davis, P. S. (1983), "Realizing the potential of the family business," *Organizational Dynamics*, **12** (1), 47–56.

Davis, P. S., & Harveston, P. D. (2000), "Internationalization and organizational growth: The impact of internet usage and technology involvement among entrepreneur led family business," *Family Business Review*, **13** (2), 107–20.

Demir, R., Wennberg, K., & McKelvie, A. (2017), "The strategic management of high-growth firms: A review and theoretical conceptualization," *Long Range Planning*, **50** (4), 431–56.

Edmondson, A. C., & McManus, S. E. (2007), "Methodological fit in management field research," *Academy of Management Review*, **32** (4), 1155–79.

Eisenhardt, K. M., & Graebner, M. E. (2007), "Theory building from cases: Opportunities and challenges," *Academy of Management Journal*, **50** (1), 25–32.

Fernández, Z., & Nieto, M. J. (2005), "Internationalization strategy of small and medium-sized family businesses: Some influential factors," *Family Business Review*, **18** (1), 77–89.

Fernández, Z., & Nieto, M. J. (2006), "Impact of ownership on the international involvement of SMEs," *Journal of International Business Studies*, **37** (3), 340–51.

Gallo, M. A., Tapies, J., & Cappuyns, K. (2004), "Comparison of family and nonfamily business: Financial logic and personal preferences," *Family Business Review*, **17** (4), 303–18.

George, G., Wilklund, J., & Zahra, S. A. (2005), "Ownership and the internationalization of small firms," *Journal of Management*, **31** (2), 210–33.

Gersick, K. E., Davis, J. A., McCollom-Hampton, M., & Lansberg, I. (1997), *Generation to Generation: Life Cycles of the Family Business*. Boston, MA: Harvard Business School Press.

Gómez-Mejía, L. R., Makri, M., & Larraza Kintana, M. (2010), "Diversification decisions in family-controlled firms," *Journal of Management Studies*, **47** (2), 223–52.

Gómez-Mejía, L. R., Cruz, C., Berrone, P., & De Castro, J. (2011), "The bind that ties: Socioemotional wealth preservation in family firms," *Academy of Management Annals*, **5** (1), 653–707.

Graves, C. R., & Thomas, J. (2004), "Internationalisation of the family business: A longitudinal perspective," *International Journal of Globalisation and Small Business*, **1** (1), 7–27.

Graves, C. R., & Thomas, J. (2006), "Internationalization of Australian family businesses: A managerial capabilities perspective," *Family Business Review*, **19** (3), 207–24.

Graves, C. R., & Thomas, J. (2008), "Determinants of the internationalization pathways of family firms: An examination of family influence," *Family Business Review*, **21** (2), 151–67.

Handler, W. C. (1989), "Methodological issues and considerations in studying family businesses," *Family Business Review*, **2** (3), 257–76.

Handler, W. C. (1994), "Succession in family business: A review of the research," *Family Business Review*, **7** (2), 133–57.

Handler, W. C., & Kram, K. E. (1988), "Succession in family firms: The problem of resistance," *Family Business Review*, **1** (4), 361–81.

Harkness, J. A. (2003), Questionnaire translation. In J. A. Harkness, F. J. R. van de Vijver, & P. P. Mohler (Eds), *Cross-Cultural Survey Methods*. New York: John Wiley & Sons.

Heck, R. K. Z., Hoy, F., Poutziouris, P. Z., & Steier, L. P. (2008), "Emerging paths of family entrepreneurship research," *Journal of Small Business Management*, **46** (3), 317–30.

Huang, X. (2009), "Strategic decision-making in Chinese SMEs," *Chinese Management Studies*, **3** (2), 87–101.

Ibrahim, A., Soufani, K., & Lam, J. (2001), "A study of succession in a family firm," *Family Business Review*, **14** (3), 245–58.

Jaskiewicz, P., Combs, J. G., & Rau, S. B. (2015), "Entrepreneurial legacy: Toward a theory of how some family firms nurture transgenerational entrepreneurship," *Journal of Business Venturing*, **30** (1), 29–49.

Johanson, J., & Vahlne, J. E. (1977), "The internationalization process of the firm: A model of knowledge development and increasing foreign market commitments," *Journal of International Business Studies*, **8** (1), 23–32.

Johanson, J., & Vahlne, J. E. (2009), "The Uppsala internationalization process model revisited: From liability of foreignness to liability of outsidership," *Journal of International Business Studies*, **40** (9), 1411–31.

Kontinen, T., & Ojala, A. (2010), "The internationalization of family businesses: A review of extant research," *Journal of Family Business Strategy*, **1** (2), 97–107.

Kontinen, T., & Ojala, A. (2012), "Internationalization pathways among family-owned SMEs," *International Marketing Review*, **29** (5), 496–518.

Le Breton-Miller, I., Miller, D., & Steier, L. P. (2004), "Toward an integrative model of effective FOB succession," *Entrepreneurship Theory and Practice*, **28** (4), 305–28.

Marshal, C., & Rossman, G. (1999), *Designing Qualitative Research* (3rd ed.). London: Sage

Menéndez-Requejo, S. (2005), "Growth and internationalization of family businesses," *International Journal of Globalisation and Small Business*, **1** (2), 122–33.

Meneses, R., Coutinho, R., & Pinho, J. C. (2014), "The impact of succession on family business internationalisation: The successors' perspective," *Journal of Family Business Management*, **4** (1), 24–45.

Miller, D., Steier, L., & Le Breton-Miller, I. (2003), "Lost in time: Intergenerational succession, change, and failure in family business," *Journal of Business Venturing*, **18** (4), 513–31.

Molly, V., Laveren, E., & Deloof, M. (2010), "Family business succession and its impact on financial structure and performance," *Family Business Review*, **23** (2), 131–47.

Morris, M. H., Williams, R. O., Allen, J. A., & Avila, R. A. (1997), "Correlates of success in family business transitions," *Journal of Business Venturing*, **12** (5), 385–401.

Nordqvist, M., Wennberg, K. J., Bau, M., & Hellerstedt, K. (2013), "An entrepreneurial process perspective on succession in family firms," *Small Business Economics*, **40** (4), 1087–122.

Okoroafo, S. C. (1999), "Internationalization of family businesses: Evidence from north-west Ohio, USA," *Family Business Review*, **12** (2), 147–58.

Oviatt, B. M., & McDougall, P. P. (2005), "Defining international entrepreneurship and modelling the speed of internationalization," *Entrepreneurship Theory and Practice*, **29** (5), 537–53.

Partanen, J., Chetty, S. K., & Rajala, A. (2014), "Innovation types and network relationships," *Entrepreneurship Theory and Practice*, **38** (5), 1027–55.

Piva, E., Rossi-Lamastra, C., & De Massis, A. (2013), "Family firms and internationalization: An exploratory study on high-tech entrepreneurial ventures," *Journal of International Entrepreneurship*, **11** (2), 108–29.

Pukall, T. J., & Calabrò, A. (2014), "The internationalization of family firms: A critical review and integrative model," *Family Business Review*, **27** (2), 103–25.

Sciascia, S., Mazzola, P., Astrachan, J. H., & Pieper, T. M. (2012), "The role of family ownership in international entrepreneurship: Exploring nonlinear effects," *Small Business Economics*, **38** (1), 15–31.

Semrau, T., & Werner, A. (2014), "How exactly do network relationships pay off? The effects of network size and relationship quality on access to start-up resources," *Entrepreneurship Theory and Practice*, **38** (3), 501–25.

Seymour, K. C. (1993), "Inter-generational relationships in the family firm: The effect on leadership succession," *Family Business Review*, **6** (3), 263–81.

Shane, S., & Venkataraman, S. (2000), "The promise of entrepreneurship as a field of research," *Academy of Management Review*, **25** (1), 217–26.

Sharma, P., Chrisman, J., & Gersick, K. (2012), "25 years of family business review: Reflections on the past and perspectives for the future," *Family Business Review*, **25** (1), 5–15.

Shepherd, D. A., & Zacharakis, A. (2000), "Structuring family business succession: An analysis of the future leader's decision-making," *Entrepreneurship Theory and Practice*, **24** (4), 25–39.

Shi, H. X., & Dana, L.-P. (2013), "Market orientation and entrepreneurship in Chinese family business: A socialisation view," *International Journal of Entrepreneurship and Small Business*, **20** (1), 1–16.

Shi, H. X., Shepherd, D. M., & Schmidts, T. (2015), "Social capital in entrepreneurial family businesses: The role of trust," *International Journal of Entrepreneurial Behavior and Research*, **21** (6), 814–41.

Sullivan, D. M., & Ford, C. M. (2014), "How entrepreneurs use networks to address changing resource requirements during early venture development," *Entrepreneurship Theory and Practice*, **38** (3), 551–74.

Swoboda, B., & Olejnik, E. (2013), "A taxonomy of small- and medium-sized international family firms," *Journal of International Entrepreneurship*, **11** (2), 130–57.

Thomas, J., & Graves, C. R. (2005), "Internationalization of the family firm: The contribution of an entrepreneurial orientation," *Journal of Business and Entrepreneurship*, **17** (2), 91–113.

Tsang, E. W. K. (2002), "Learning from overseas venturing experience: The case of Chinese family businesses," *Journal of Business Venturing*, **17** (1), 21–40.

Westhead, P., Wright, M., & Ucbasan, D. (2001), "The internationalization of new and small firms: A resource-based view," *Journal of Business Venturing*, **16** (4), 333–58.

Yeung, H. W. (2000), "Limits to the growth of family-owned business? The case of Chinese transnational corporations from Hong Kong," *Family Business Review*, **13** (1), 55–70.

Zahra, S. A. (2003), "International expansion of US manufacturing family businesses: The effect of ownership and involvement," *Journal of Business Venturing*, **18** (4), 495–512.

4. The impact of logics-based immigrant context on migrant family enterprises

Stone Han, Artemis Chang and Hsi-Mei Chung

INTRODUCTION

Family business scholars in recent years increasingly recognize that institutions have significance for family firm operation, because, as context, they impinge on the behaviors and decisions of important stakeholders within the firm (Soleimanof, Rutherford, & Webb, 2018; Wright, Chrisman, Chua, & Steier, 2014). While numerous advances have been made in understanding the role that institutions may play for family business, there is still much to learn. For example, a great many family firms are established by individuals who have left their country of origin (home country) to find life in a new country (host country). Certainly, as immigrants, they and their family members are likely to face foreign institutional elements that affect their thoughts and behaviors, which in turn influence business orientations. Presently, we know little about how such immigrant context may impact those who operate migrant family enterprises.

In the past, scholars have touched upon this topic, but in a fragmented way. For example, the immigrant entrepreneurship literature examines in detail various aspects of the host country's socio-economic and politico-institutional environment and its impact on migrant enterprises (Kloosterman & Rath, 2001). It also mentions family resources and personnel as often crucial to migrant business start-ups (Sanders & Nee, 1996; Verver & Koning, 2018). However, researchers in this literature do not examine migrant enterprises as family firms per se, and hence, do not deal with many of the issues that are central to business families (Chrisman, Kellermanns, Chan, & Liano, 2010), leaving us with a partial understanding of the repercussions of the immigrant context for migrant family businesses.

Other studies, such as those involving diaspora business (e.g., Chinese overseas business; Wong, McReynolds, & Wong, 1992) and ethnicity in entrepreneurship (Danes, Lee, Stafford, & Heck, 2008), do examine migrant enterprises as family-controlled ventures, but focus more on entrepreneurs' ethnic traditions and network relations as determinants of what happens inside these ventures, and less on the influence of societal-level institutional factors. In this chapter, we aim to reduce fragmentation in this area of study by integrating analysis of foreign institutional environment and immigrant business families to build toward a systematic assessment of the role that immigrant context may play for migrant family businesses.

While the immigrant context can consist of various institutional elements that affect immigrant family entrepreneurs, we are mainly concerned with understanding the theoretical and practical implications of institutional logics. Institutional logics are "systems of cultural elements (values, beliefs, and normative expectations) by which people, groups, and organizations" make sense, evaluate, and organize their everyday activities (Haveman & Gualtieri, 2017). They originate from institutional spheres of life, such as the family, the market, and the state, just to name a few, that pervade societies and manifest as material practices, symbolic constructions, motives of action, and sense of self and identity (Friedland & Alford, 1991; Thornton, Ocasio, & Lounsbury, 2012). As such, these institutional logics can act as behavior guidelines and organizing principles for individuals in working environments, having consequences for organizational outcomes. For example, Almandoz (2012) finds that whether founders of United States community banks draw upon financial logic (priority is profit) or community logic (priority is good of the community) can influence the extent to which their banks achieve entrepreneurial success.

While an institutional sphere of life may be found to exist in all societies, practices based on its central logic may not be the same across societies. Given a specific institutional logic, individuals in different societies can "elaborate" on its instantiation (Friedland & Alford, 1991). Such "elaborations" rely heavily upon behaviors and rules that are particular to the cultural traditions of each society (Redding, 2008). Hence, practices associated with any institutional logic may be subject to cross-country variations. When individuals immigrate, they carry within them logics from their home country and a taken-for-granted understanding of how these logics may be "elaborated." Upon arriving in the host country and attempting to establish business ventures, they face unfamiliar logics, i.e., logics they've never encountered before, as well as novel "elaborations" of familiar logics. Under these circumstances, which logics or "elaborations" would they align with? What factors facilitate such decisions? How would this affect their economic actions and the enterprises that they own/manage? These are the questions that we address in this chapter.

We organize this chapter in two parts. In the first part, we develop a framework that delineates the nature of the logics-based immigrant context and implications for its inhabitants, the immigrants. Our framework covers three aspects. First, we offer a typology of logics differences that immigrants may encounter between home and host country. Second, we examine the types of response strategies they may adopt with regard to such conflicting logics. And third, we highlight three key factors that may impact immigrants' responses: adherence to logics, legitimacy concerns, and identity commitment. In the second part of the chapter, we link logics-based immigrant context specifically to how migrant business families operate, focusing in particular on their transgenerational intent (Williams, Zorn, Crook, & Combs, 2013). For parents, transgenerational intent refers to their desire to pass their business to their children (De Massis, Sieger, Chua, & Vismara, 2016). For children, it refers to their willingness to succeed their parents (Stavrou & Swiercz, 1998).

Our motivation for looking at business family members' transgenerational intent in immigrant context stems from research which shows that forces within the immigrant context often compel immigrant entrepreneurs to rely on their families for their ventures (Zhou, 2004). If immigrant context is known to facilitate initial family involvement in migrants' entrepreneurial efforts, a logical follow-up question, which surprisingly has received little attention so far, is, does immigrant context also influence migrants' desire to sustain such involvement over generations? We hope to shed some light on this issue in the second part of this chapter.

Since our topic of interest is not covered by any one single literature, but is spread out over diverse areas of study, we mainly draw from literatures on institutional logics perspective and family business, but also utilize studies on institutional theory, identity theory, immigrant experience, and family science. From these literatures, we aim to identify elements and factors that may be important for an initial understanding of how immigrant business families handle home and host country logics, and thereby influence how they go about operating their business. The ultimate purpose of this chapter is not to be definitive or comprehensive, but rather to be generative in such a way that promotes further research on this topic.

THE ROLE OF INSTITUTIONS FOR MIGRANT ENTERPRISES

Scholars have found that immigrants who attempt to establish businesses in a host country can be influenced by the structural impact of different institutional spheres (Zhou, 2004). The state can provide immigrants advantages or disadvantages to establish enterprises through its regulations and policies (Collins, 2003; Kontos, 2003). The market can marginalize immigrants in labor hiring and compel them into self-employment (Blume, Ejrnaes, Nielsen, & Wurtz, 2009). The ethnic community can enable immigrants to do business catering only to its members, without relying on the mainstream population (Ndofor & Priem, 2011; Zhou, 2004). The family can offer immigrants the resources they need to initiate start-ups (Sanders & Nee, 1996). Thus, the state, the market, the community, and the family make up four significant institutional spheres for migrant businesses.

Past research, however, can only tell us half of the story about the impact of these institutions on immigrants' entrepreneurial activities. Researchers agree that institutional spheres exert influence on individual actions, not only through formal structures, such as rules, regulations, policies, and laws (North, 1990), but also informally through taken-for-granted assumptions and beliefs about how individuals should act and organize activities (Meyer & Rowan, 1977; Zucker, 1977). Presently, we know much about how formal institutions affect immigrants' efforts to establish ventures, but less about the role that informal, "cognitive" elements of institutions may play. This chapter provides a greater understanding of how one particular form of informal institution, institutional logics, impacts immigrants' entrepreneurial activities. We do so by conceiving immigrant context as exposure to foreign logics, with an interest in how this exposure would impact migrant family enterprises. In the next section, we start by explicating the nature of this logics-based immigrant context.

EXPOSURE TO FOREIGN LOGICS

Society consists of interinstitutional systems (Friedland & Alford, 1991). Given each country's interinstitutional systems evolve from distinctive historical and cultural development (Mutch, 2018), immigrants will likely experience institutional logics differences between home and host country. There are two types of logics differences that they will encounter.

Interinstitutional Difference

First, immigrants may encounter brand new logics that they've not experienced before in their home country. This kind of difference is interinstitutional in nature. An example of such logic is mainstream versus ethnic logic (Brubaker, Loveman, & Stamatov, 2004). Mainstream versus ethnic logic identifies social groups, within larger social groups, in a society for the purpose of differential and unequal treatment (Meyers, 1984). It is salient in many countries with diverse populations. Immigrant business family members who come from a home country that has a homogeneous population may not have been exposed to this type of logic beforehand. They experience this logic when they migrate to a host country and find themselves, for example, as targets of ethnic discriminatory policies and practices.

Intra-Institutional Difference

The second type of logics difference that immigrants may encounter is novel "elaboration" of logics for institutional spheres that are common to both countries. This is called intra-institutional difference (Meyer & Hollerer, 2016). In reading the literatures, we find that such intra-institutional differences can manifest in three ways: content of practice, meaning of practice, and power. First, scholars for many years have examined cross-national variations in practice content of institutional logics. For instance, research on varieties of capitalism and national business systems focus on how market logic practices differ across countries (Witt et al., 2018). Similarly, studies on the sociology of religion show how religion logic practices differ from one nation to another (e.g., Ruiter & van Tubergen, 2009).

Second, besides differences in practice content, countries can also differ in institutional logics in terms of practice meaning. Such differences have been studied for family logic, for example. Research shows that the meaning of having children for parents varies in many countries (Kagitcibasi, 1982). For some, the worth of raising children lies more in their utility for old-age security. In others, meaning of childbearing leans toward the psychological values it provides, in terms of ties, affection, and love. Another example is the meaning of child independence for parents. Chao (1995) finds that by independence for children, European American mothers tend to mean self-expression, individuality, and separateness from parents. For Taiwanese American mothers, independence for their children represents the ability to take care of themselves at home, allowing parents to do other duties.

Lastly, cross-country differences in institutional logics may also involve differences in power. Societies place different values on institutional spheres (Abrutyn & Turner, 2011). Those institutional spheres deemed as having greater value may be conferred greater power. For example, in communist Russia, the institution of state has tremendous power, probably more so than others. In Israel, the institution of religion may be argued to have influence over all other institutions. When an institution has power, it is able to impact how other institutional spheres operate. For instance, in Chinese society, due to Confucianism, the family has great power (Hwang, 2012). In traditional Chinese family logic, parents have the say over the welfare of the entire family, including the education, career, marriage, and living arrangements of their children. In other words, Chinese parents have power over how their children function in other institutional spheres of life. This power is not given to family or parents in non-Confucianist, Western countries (Smetana, 2002).

RESPONSE STRATEGIES

In the face of logics from home and host country that differ and conflict with each other, how can immigrants respond? Extant literature, on the institutional logics perspective, do offer some answers in terms of how individuals handle conflicting logics (e.g., McPherson & Sauder, 2013; Raaijmakers, Vermeulen, Meeus, & Zietsma, 2015). Discussions in this area center around individuals' various response strategies, as well as factors that drive adoption of such strategies (e.g., Pache & Santos, 2013). However, these studies largely deal with what happens for members inside an organization (e.g., social enterprise, law firm, university, and medical school; see Thornton et al., 2012), as opposed to for newcomers in a foreign country. Below, we examine how these response strategies, and relevant determining factors covered in the extant literature, may apply to the immigrant context.

Experiencing new logics or novel "elaborations" of logics can bring forth awareness of differences between home and host country, leading to sensemaking (Raaijmakers et al., 2015). Sensemaking is "the process through which people work to understand issues or events that are novel, ambiguous, confusing, or in some other way violate expectations" (Maitlis & Christianson, 2014: 57). Immigrants' sensemaking likely involves getting to know foreign logics and then making comparisons with home logics. Based on evaluating the personal/social benefits and costs of adopting one logic over another, immigrants may come to a decision about which logic they will comply with.

There can be five types of individual responses to conflicting logics: ignorance, compliance, defiance, combination, or compartmentalization (Pache & Santos, 2013). Ignorance refers to an absence of response to logic. Compliance is full enactment of the practices of a home or host country logic. Defiance is resistance toward a logic to the extent of purposely contradicting it. Compartmentalization is complying with both home and host country logics but picking and choosing when and where to comply with each one, enacting all but keeping them separate. Combination is blending values, norms, and practices of both home and host country logics (Pache & Santos, 2013).

Institutional scholars have conjectured that various factors may drive individuals within organizations to adopt certain strategies in response to conflicting logics. Three factors that they have identified include adherence to logics, legitimacy judgment, and identity commitment. In the next section, we examine each of these factors, highlighting how they influence immigrants' response strategies.

FACTORS THAT MODERATE RESPONSE STRATEGIES

Adherence to Logics

Pache and Santos (2013) suggest that a basic factor to individuals' response strategies to conflicting logics is a degree of adherence to logics. They differentiate three types of adherence to logics. The first type is called novice. This is the case in which individuals have virtually no knowledge of the logic and hence have low adherence to the logic. A second type of relation is that in which individuals are familiar with a logic. In this type, they have knowledge and experience with the logic, but are not committed ideologically or emotionally to it. Adherence to a logic for those who are familiar with the logic is moderate. The third type of relationship to a logic is the case in which individuals identify with a logic. For this type, adherence is high, because the logic forms the basis for their identity (Pache & Santos, 2013).

Pache and Santos (2013) propose that individuals have different responses to conflicting logics within organizations, depending on how they relate to each of the conflicting logics. Individuals, they suggest, will tend to comply with logics they identify with and ignore those that they have moderate or low adherence to. However, if the logics with which they have low or moderate adherence dominates the organizational environment, individuals may be forced to compartmentalize or combine logics (Pache & Santos, 2013).

Applying this notion of logic adherence to the immigrant context, we can suppose that immigrants can be novice with some home country logics, familiar with others, and identify with still other home country logics, but are mostly novice with host country logics. In the case where they are novice to a certain logic in both home and host country, such logic elicits no response on their part, since they are barely aware of its existence. In the case where immigrants are familiar with a particular home country logic but novice with the way it is elaborated in the host country, they are likely to lean toward complying with the home country's version of elaboration. However, one factor may force them to do otherwise: legitimacy concerns. In the next section, we look at the role that legitimacy may play in moderating immigrants' response strategies.

Legitimacy Concerns

Individuals tend to align with logics that appear to them as being legitimate. Legitimacy is "a generalized perception or assumption that the actions of an entity are desirable, proper, or appropriate within some socially constructive system of norms, values, beliefs, and definitions" (Suchman, 1995: 574). Legitimacy judgments can come from two sources: from individuals themselves and from those around them. Below we examine each of these two sources.

Individuals can make a legitimacy judgment along three dimensions: instrumental, relational, and moral (Tost, 2011). Instrumental evaluation considers a logic in terms of how it contributes to their material interests. Relational evaluation frames the logic in terms of how it promotes their social status, dignity, and self-worth. Moral evaluation scrutinizes the logic in terms of whether the logic conforms to their moral convictions (Tost, 2011). Legitimacy judgments can also be based on social context. When making a judgment regarding logics, individuals can not only consider appropriateness in their own eyes, but often must take into account the expectations of the people in groups, organizations, and society at large to which they belong (Suddaby, Bitektine, & Haack, 2017). This is because if they stray from social legitimacy, there can be sanctions and other forms of negative consequences.

Naturally, logics from the home country will tend to appear legitimate in the eyes of immigrants and host-country logics, that conflict with home-country logics, appear to be illegitimate. However, in the host country, host-country logics have a certain degree of legitimacy, whereas home-country logics may have less legitimacy. Hence, immigrants likely feel the pressure, at varying degrees, to adapt and conform to host-country logics.

However, this does not mean that social legitimacy always takes precedence. In certain situations, immigrants may deem personal legitimacy to be more important. To the extent certain home-country logics may be internalized by immigrants, when host-country logic conflicts with those of the home country, although host-country logic may have more social legitimacy, it may not have personal legitimacy with the immigrant. The host-country logic may go against immigrants' moral conviction, for example. In this case, the immigrant will likely resist host-country logic and lean toward home-country logic, despite making a choice that may be unpopular with social sensibility.

Invariably, immigrants' response to strategy decisions, with regard to conflicting logics, involve a certain degree of tradeoff between personal and social legitimacy. However, this tradeoff may be less severe to the extent home-country logics have legitimacy in the host country. Although home-country logics may conflict with those of the host country, they could still be perceived as having legitimacy, such as in the context of multicultural society where people are open to logics embodied in different ethnic groups. The question is, how much legitimacy do home-country logics have in the host country? The legitimacy of home-country logics and practices can range from being illegal in the host country to being totally acceptable. When social norms permit conflicting logics from different countries, immigrants can more freely make logics compliance choices based on their own personal judgments as opposed to being pressured to conform to social expectations.

Even though immigrants may be pressured to succumb to the social legitimacy of the host country, they may find ways to avoid having to do so. A clear example is the existence of ethnic communities. In ethnic communities, where they are surrounded by individuals of similar logics, immigrants may not have to deal with social legitimacy that goes against their sensibility daily, and have the room to enjoy practices and lifestyles that align with their preferred home-country logics.

Identity Commitment

In the case in which immigrants are identified with a certain home-country logic but novice with the way it is elaborated in the host country, immigrants will likely lean toward complying with the home-country version. However, as we mentioned above, social legitimacy may force immigrants to comply with host-country logics. The degree to which immigrants may comply with host-country logics that go against their identity depends on a third factor: identity commitment.

Institutional logics scholars recognize that many individuals' identities can be tied to logics (Meyer & Hammerschmid, 2006; Lok, 2010; Wry & York, 2017). Individuals develop logic-based identities when they are socialized in various institutional spheres of life. For example, parental identity arises from family institutional spheres of life. Executives have managerial identity based on managerial logics. Pastors have religious identity based on the logic from their religion. Even though individuals have multiple identities, they are not equally committed to them (McCall & Simmons, 1978). For example, executives who are married with children and go to church on Sundays have identities as manager, parent, and Christian. These identities, however, may not be equally important to them. Some may be more committed to their managerial identity; others, their identity as Christians; and still others, their identity as a family member.

Individuals commit to certain identities because they are the basis for ties to important others and a source of positive feedback, such as gained rewards and emotional satisfaction (Burke & Reitzes, 1991). Viewed in this way, there is a cost to giving up a committed identity. For immigrants, the more they are committed to an identity associated with a home-country logic, the more they are likely to resist a host-country logic that conflicts with that home-country logic. In the face of social pressure to conform, identities that receive less commitment from immigrants may be let go, facilitating the adoption of host-country logics.

Change over Time

Before we move to the second part of this chapter, it is important to stress that in the immigrant context, adherence to logics, legitimacy concerns, identity commitment, and ultimately response strategies are not stable variables that tend to remain the same, but are likely to shift over time. Socialization in a new country invariably leads individuals to change certain degrees of their "cultural patterns," i.e., practices, values, and identities (Ward & Geeraert, 2016). As this change takes place, immigrants' initial legitimacy judgments may no longer hold, or public opinion about what is appropriate may reverse. Also, their commitment to identities may change, in response to events that take place in the host country. Furthermore, as they learn about host-country culture and logics, their adherence with host-country logics may shift upward, from novice, to familiar, to identified, while adherence to home-country logic may go downward. As a result of all these changes in factors, some logics that are rejected at an earlier time may now be accepted. Others that are adopted in the beginning may later be abandoned. These are the natural ebbs and flows of immigrants adjusting to and living in a foreign land. Hence, individual responses to conflicting logics for immigrants are not a one-time decision, but can change and evolve as part of a continuous process that stretches over a long period of time.

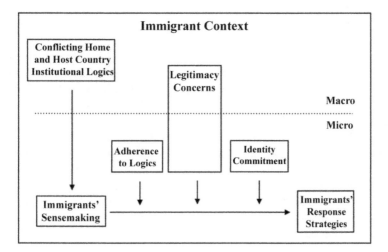

Figure 4.1   *Response strategies to conflicting logics in the immigrant context and factors that moderate such responses*

FRAMEWORK

Here we summarize our framework (Figure 4.1). Immigrants encounter logics differences in a host country. Such differences require them to make sense of practices that appear novel and conflicting. This sensemaking process involves getting to know and comparing logics. Eventually, immigrants will decide which home- and host-country logics they will ignore, defy, comply with (partially or fully), and/or combine. Three factors play a role in the process by which they make such decisions: adherence to logics, legitimacy concerns, and identity commitment.

IMPLICATIONS FOR MIGRANT BUSINESS FAMILIES

In the second part of this chapter, we examine the implications of logics-based immigrant context for migrant business families. The specific question that we aim to tackle is, how do conflicting logics between home and host country impact transgenerational intent of migrant business family members? Our motivation for doing so arises from a desire to address a gap in the literature. Extant literature shows that the immigrant context tends to encourage family involvement in immigrants' enterprises (Zhou, 2004). However, there is little discussion on whether such involvement is likely to extend over generations.

This is an important issue for two reasons. First, when immigrants initiate their enterprises, the family likely becomes involved mainly due to limited resources (Zhou, 2004). If the business family's intention changes from simply being involved in the business to hoping to extend involvement over generations, the firm makes a transition from operating initially as a so-called family-managed firm to one that is a full-fledged family firm (Chua, Chrisman, & Sharma, 1999). Thus, for us to examine how the logics-based immigrant context may influence immigrant business family members' transgenerational intent is to investigate the role that immigrant context may play in either leading the migrant enterprise to become a family business or hindering it from becoming one.

Second, transgenerational intent also implicates the sustainability of family control in firms. The less the intent, the lower the possibility for intra-family succession (Williams et al., 2013). Thus, investigating the relationship between immigrant context and transgenerational intent provides insights on the long-term prospects of the migrant family enterprise. Below we first provide a short summary of the extant research on transgenerational intent and then go into addressing our research question.

Transgenerational Intent in Family Business

Transgenerational intent is central to the concept of family firms. A widely accepted definition of family business is as follows:

> The family business is a business governed and/or managed with the intention to shape and pursue the vision of the business held by a dominant coalition controlled by members of the same family or a small number of families in a manner that is potentially sustainable across generations of the family or families. (Chua et al., 1999: 25)

In this definition, family firms' intention to shape and pursue their vision of the business across generations of the family captures transgenerational intent. Not all business families have this transgenerational intent, however. Very early on, family business researchers find that many business family members do not see their business as a family business, even though there is a high level of family involvement (Carsrud, 1994). In such cases, there is very little or no transgenerational intent.

Family business scholars see transgenerational intent in family firms as involving some key points. First, they recognize that transgenerational intent exists for two types of individuals: incumbents, i.e., those family members "who currently hold the top management position in the firm and who must relinquish that position before another family member can take over" (De Massis et al., 2016: 278), and successors. Second, they find that the intention to transfer business across generations is largely influenced by factors relating to individual (incumbent and successor) attributes, family relations, business characteristics, succession process elements, and environmental conditions (De Massis, Chua, & Chrisman, 2008; Stavrou & Swiercz, 1998; Williams et al., 2013). The majority of these studies focus on individual, family, business, and process-related variables, with very few examining environmental factors. In terms of environmental factors, researchers have mentioned market conditions (Stavrou & Swiercz, 1998), district norm (Zhou, Hu, Yao, & Qin, 2016), relationship with external stakeholders (De Massis et al., 2008), and national culture (Yan & Sorenson, 2006). In this chapter, we further illuminate the effect that a broader environment may have on business family members' transgenerational intent by highlighting cross-national differences in institutional logics. In the next section, we expound how this effect takes place.

LOGICS AND TRANSGENERATIONAL INTENT

The framework that we develop in the first part of the chapter provides guidance for how we go about understanding the impact of conflicting logics in immigrant context on the transgenerational intent of migrant business family members. Based on our framework, we pose three questions to help with our analysis: first, what logics differences between home and host country can be relevant to business family members' transgenerational intent? Second, what response strategies would business family members adopt? And third, how would their responses implicate their transgenerational intent? We suggest that four logics may be particularly salient for migrant business families' transgenerational intent: family logic, business family logic, market logic, and mainstream/ethnic logic. Below is our analysis with regard to each of these logics.

Family Logic

In the immigrant context, differences in family logic between home and host country may influence the transgenerational intent of immigrant business family members. We define family logic as the commonly held values, beliefs, norm expectations, and practices that guide interactions between family members (Hess & Handel, 1959). Immigrant parents may be inclined to run their family based on the family logic of the home country, since they are raised and brought up by parents who operate under such logic. Immigrant children, who receive education in a new country, however, may identify with the family logic of the host country. When there are differences in family logic between parents and children, parents' practices, meaning, and power can appear illegitimate in the eyes of children and vice versa, leading to conflict between them (Park, Kim, Chiang, & Ju, 2010).

Two family logic elements that may be points of conflict between parents and children are family communication patterns (Guan & Li, 2017) and family obligations (Lansford et al., 2016). When children and parents have different ideas about family communication, parents, on the one side, may admonish children for talking to them in a way that is disrespectful; children, on the other side, can accuse parents of not giving them a chance to express themselves. In terms of family obligations, parents may, for example, complain that their children don't spend enough time with their family; children, in turn, may feel that parents seem to want to control their free time. Another element in family logic that provides grounds for contestation is parental power. By their family logic, some parents may interfere with children's career and marriage choices. These practices would not have legitimacy in the eyes of children who identify with host-country family logic that does not confer such power to parents.

When these conflicts between children and parents persist, children's identification with their family may weaken. This affects their goals and identity in relation to their family. They may shy away from goals that involve working with their parents. Also, they may have reduced commitment to their family identity, since conflicts provide negative, rather than positive, feedback in their interactions with parents. When children neither have goals to work with parents, nor commitment to family identity, their transgenerational intent is likely to be low.

While conflicts over different "elaborations" of family logic can debilitate a family, it doesn't always have to be the case. Through these conflicts, children and parents can become aware of logics differences and begin to make sense of such differences. This sensemaking process may involve identifying elements of family logic where they differ and weighing the social/personal benefits and costs of continuing conflicts between them. Through consideration of family legitimacy issues, parents can make a decision about where they are willing to let go some elements of their family logic and modify their logic for the sake of their children. Children, likewise, can make a decision about how much of their parents' family logic they can accept. If some middle ground about family logic can be reached, where parents and children find a way to combine values, beliefs, and/or norm expectations from both home- and host-country family logics, a hybrid logic may be created. This hybrid logic can bring about harmony between parents and children, thereby increasing goal setting toward family and commitment to family identity, which translates into increased transgenerational intent for the children.

Business Family Logic

Immigrant parents can be part of a bigger business family in their home country, or in the host country (the case when the large business family moves to the host country together). The presence of a large business family, either in the home country or host country, can influence the transgenerational intent of immigrant parents and their children, by providing a business family logic (Brundin, Samuelsson, & Melin, 2014). This logic espouses values, beliefs, and norm expectations regarding members' family obligations to the business family. Under this circumstance, the business family acts as a proximal social structure, defined as a "social network close to individuals that provide social relationships based on a specific role identity" (Merolla, Serpe, Stryker, & Schultz, 2012: 150). As such, it serves to legitimize business family goals, such as those involving transfer of business across generations, and increase members' commitment to the business family role as incumbents and successors. Hence, where immigrant parents and children have family relations belonging to a larger business family, they are likely to have higher transgenerational intent.

Market Logic

Differences in market logic between home and host country can influence transgenerational intent of immigrant business family members. Market logic is defined as commonly held values, beliefs, norm expectations, and practices that "guide firm behavior with the aim of improving efficiency, profits, and market status" (Jaskiewicz, Heinrichs, Rau, & Reay, 2016: 793). When facing market logic differences, immigrant business family members will likely have to comply with host-country market logic. It is difficult to do business in the host country using home-country market logic, given there is less legitimacy for home-country market practices (e.g., see Christopherson, 2007). However, compliance with host-country market logic usually puts immigrant business family members at a disadvantage, since they are not familiar with the logic.

Lack of familiarity with host-country market logic can create the condition for necessity entrepreneurship. Necessity entrepreneurs are defined as entrepreneurs whose aspiration is to simply fulfill basic needs (Dencker, Bacq, Gruber, & Haas, forthcoming). Studies show that the business they end up operating tends to have limited growth potential, since they take the best available option (Block & Wagner, 2010). Immigrant business family members may become necessity entrepreneurs for several reasons. First, it takes time to make sense of logics differences and the process may involve trial and error before immigrant business family members learn what to do and what not to do in a host-country market. Second, because they don't know the market well, they may not have control of the opportunities that appear. And third, they may initially fail at establishing enterprises. After they have failed several times, with capital dwindling, they tend to take whatever opportunities that come along. If the business that immigrant business family establishes is more out of necessity than opportunity, both parents and children may not find the migrant family enterprise to be appealing. This likely leads to low transgenerational intent for them both.

Immigrant business families may have the option of adopting home-country market logic instead of host-country market logic, if a vibrant ethnic community is available (Zhou, 2004). Doing business in an ethnic community, to a certain degree, allows them to operate based on home-country market logic. However, a disadvantage for doing business in an ethnic community can be limited market size. Thus, transgenerational intent for both parents and children will be low if the profit and growth of the business is limited by the size of the ethnic community. There will only be a motivation for parents to pass the business to their children if the market has sustainable profit or growth potential.

Mainstream versus Ethnic Logic

Mainstream versus ethnic logic is the last logic that we will examine in relation to immigrant business family members' transgenerational intent. For immigrants, ethnicity is not something that they necessarily recognize as a part of who they are. It only has meaning in relation to mainstream population. When adopting ethnic logic, they take on so-called "enclosed ethnicity," in which they surround themselves with people and things of their ethnic group in a way that they are able to maintain their "sense of peoplehood, their basic, unreflected identity" (Pieterse, 1997: 375). Such logic informs where they prefer to live and/or do business.

For parents who find little legitimacy in a mainstream way of life, they may adopt ethnic logic and choose to do business and live in an ethnic community, virtually isolating themselves in an ethnic cocoon. Although parents comply with ethnic logic, and develop strong ethnic identity, this may not be the case for their children. Through their schooling and friends, children are likely to become socialized in, and identify with, mainstream logic. While parents remain committed to their ethnic identity and set corresponding goals, children may align more and more with their mainstream identity and goals, which takes them farther and farther away from ethnic community, toward the mainstream society.

A key to this growing gap between parents and children concerns their understanding of mainstream society. Immigrant business family parents generally want their children to succeed in the mainstream society. However, the less they understand the mainstream society, the less they will be able to help their children, in terms of giving advice and providing guidance (Qin & Han, 2014). As a result, they and their children end up living more and more in separate worlds (Mann, 2004). Under such circumstances, children are left to their own devices to make it on their own. They become disengaged with their parents' world. Unless children cannot find a job and seek temporary employment with their parents, children do not aim to get involved with their parents' business. Likewise, parents do not expect their children to do so. In this case, transgenerational intent for both parents and children is low.

To summarize, in immigrant context, conflicting logics give rise to sensemaking that takes legitimacy concerns involving mainstream versus ethnic, business family (family of origin), current family, and migrant enterprise issues into account. Compliance with four logics, one from the home country (business family logic), two from the host country (market logic and mainstream versus ethnic logic), one a combination of both (hybrid family logic), may give rise to identities and goals, which in turn influence business family members' transgenerational intent (Figure 4.2).

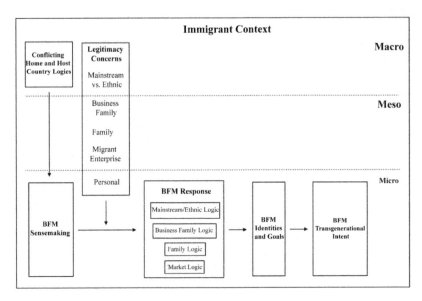

*Figure 4.2   Impact of conflicting logics on transgenerational intent of
                 business family members (BFM) in the immigrant context*

DISCUSSION

The purpose of this chapter has been to establish links between institutional
elements and family business in the immigrant context. We start out by conceiving immigrant context as exposure to foreign institutional logics. Previous
research in immigrant entrepreneurship has largely framed immigrant context
as exposure to foreign culture (Laurence, 2016; Robertson & Grant, 2016).
We think that foreign institutional logics can explain the effect of immigrant
context on migrant family enterprises above and beyond those of culture.
Present conceptions tend to view national culture as mainly homogeneous
(Tung, 2008). It is assumed that people from a similar cultural background
likely would experience host-country culture (also viewed as homogenous)
in similar ways. However, the institutional logics perspective sees society as
constituted by subsystems of heterogeneous institutions, whose logics can
lead to conflicting values, beliefs, norm expectations, and motives for action.
Hence, conceiving immigrant context as exposure to foreign logics allows us
to look at how immigrants may react to different parts of the host country in
different ways.

Take the case of entrepreneurs from Taiwan and China relocating to
Australia, for example. Although Taiwan and China have similar cultural

backgrounds and scholars tend to view immigrant business owners from both countries as belonging to the same ethnic group (i.e., Chinese), these two countries have very different ways of "elaborating" the institutional sphere of the market. Due to this difference, entrepreneurs from Taiwan and China may have different responses to market logic in Australia, even though they come from a similar culture. Hence, by using the institutional logics perspective, we can investigate the nuances of what happens when two cultures clash. Understanding how immigrant business owners react to the institutional spheres that exist in the host country can provide a more refined picture of how migrant enterprises are susceptible to the influence of immigrant context.

In exploring the implications of logics-based immigrant context for family business, we show that indeed foreign institutional environments may not have a uniform effect on transgenerational intent of immigrant business family members. Parents' and children's transgenerational intent may be susceptible to a wide range of logics that lead to conflicting outcomes. Furthermore, we point out in both our framework and our examination of the immigrant business family that due to the varying nature of institutional logics, adoption of home-/host-country logics can be contingent on several factors, such as comparative evaluation of logics, capital that immigrants have on hand, success/failure rate with venture creation, and family dynamics between parents and children. The value of taking the institutional logics approach to immigrant context, for us, is that it can offer insights into the micro-level complexity that immigrant business family members face as they attempt to establish ventures in a foreign land.

This chapter contributes to two literatures. First, we contribute to the literature on institutional logics. Previous research has examined logics differences at the country level, such as those focusing on national business systems (Witt et al., 2018) or cross-national variations in corporate governance (Aguilera, Judge, & Terjesen, 2018). There has been little attention paid to how cross-cultural differences in institutional logics may matter for individuals. We offer insights into individual experiences involving encounters with foreign logics and how such encounters may impact individual outcomes. In doing so, we extend understanding of institutional logics in cross-cultural context as well as in micro-level processes.

Second, we contribute to the literature on family business. Previous studies that look at what happens when family businesses venture into other countries tend to take an internationalization approach (Kontinen & Ojala, 2010; Pukall & Calabro, 2014), focusing on how business families deal with foreign operations from their own home country. This study shifts attention to those business families who call a foreign country home. We show that for immigrant business families, the foreign terrain can be treacherous, with logics tensions, relationship difficulties, and challenging issues related to legitimacy concerns and identities.

This chapter also sheds light on the antecedents of transgenerational intent in migrant family enterprises. Scholars acknowledge that individual, family, and business factors play a central role in transgenerational intent of business family members (Stavrou & Swiercz, 1998; Williams et al., 2013). Through the application of our immigrant context framework to this area of topic, we suggest that "cognitive" elements in the institutional environment, such as logics, can impact the individual, family, and business aspects of the migrant family enterprise in a way that influences the business family's transgenerational intent.

Future Research

By drawing attention to the phenomenon of a logic-based immigrant context, and by laying out some of its implications for migrant family enterprises, we hope that we can generate further research in this area of study. Here we suggest some avenues of research for scholars who wish to expand on our work in this chapter. First, given immigrant context consists of institutional logics differences between countries, further studies can map out in detail the specific differences between each type of logics for the purpose of examining logics differences between specific pairs of countries. For example, scholars interested in examining differences between Taiwan and Australia should delineate logics differences for the seven main types of societal logics (family, market, state, corporation, profession, religion, and community) identified by Thornton et al. (2012). This will pave the way for the foundation of future studies that look at how logic differences may affect Australian migrant family enterprises in Taiwan and Taiwanese migrant family enterprises in Australia.

Second, in this chapter we explore only one type of intent for migrant business family members – transgenerational intent. Other intents can be investigated, such as entrepreneurial intent (Carr & Sequeira, 2007), strategic intent (Riviezzo, Garofano, Napolitano, & Marino, 2015), and business family members' intent with regards to their relationship with the business (Lumpkin, Martin, & Vaughan, 2008).

Third, our framework highlights immigrants' sensemaking of logics differences. Further research can be conducted to investigate the micro processes by which sensemaking of institutional logics take place. In particular, some institutional logics scholars have raised the issue that individuals are not always perceptive of logics differences or contradictions (Voronov & Yorks, 2015). We need a greater understanding of how perception of logics differences takes place and what implications these perceptions have for response strategies.

And finally, we have mentioned identities as important mediators of logics' impact on immigrant business family members' intent. In this regard, we've noted four types: family, business family, entrepreneurial, and mainstream/ ethnic identity. Since all these identities can reside in one person, we suggest that future research can examine how these identities may interact to influence migrant business family members.

NOTE ON FUNDING

This research received sponsorship provided by the Ministry of Science and Technology, Executive Yuan, Taiwan, under grant number [MOST 107-2917-I-214-001].

REFERENCES

Abrutyn, S. & J. H. Turner (2011), "The old institutionalism meets the new institutionalism," *Sociological Perspectives*, **54** (3), 283–306.

Aguilera, R. V., W. Q. Judge, & S. A. Terjesen (2018), "Corporate governance deviance," *Academy of Management Review*, **43** (1), 87–109.

Almandoz, J. (2012), "Arriving at the starting line: The impact of community and financial logics on new banking ventures," *Academy of Management Journal*, **55** (6), 1381–406.

Block, J. H. & M. Wagner (2010), "Necessity and opportunity entrepreneurs in Germany: Characteristics and earnings differentials," *Schmalenbach Business Review*, **62** (2), 154–74.

Blume, K., M. Ejrnaes, H. S. Nielsen, & A. Wurtz (2009), "Labor market transitions of immigrants with emphasis on marginalization and self-employment," *Journal of Population Economics*, **22** (4), 881–908.

Brubaker, R., M. Loveman, & P. Stamatov (2004), "Ethnicity as cognition," *Theory and Society*, **33** (1), 31–64.

Brundin, E., E. F. Samuelsson, & L. Melin (2014), "Family ownership logic: Framing the core characteristics of family businesses," *Journal of Management and Organization*, **20** (1), 6–37.

Burke, P. J. & D. C. Reitzes (1991), "An identity theory approach to commitment," *Social Psychology Quarterly*, **54** (3), 239–51.

Carr, J. C. & J. M. Sequeira (2007), "Prior family business exposure as intergenerational influence and entrepreneurial intent: A theory of planned behavior approach," *Journal of Business Research*, **60** (10), 1090–8.

Carsrud, A. L. (1994), "Meandering of a resurrected psychologist or, lessons learned in creating a family business program," *Entrepreneurship Theory and Practice*, **19** (1), 39–48.

Chao, R. K. (1995), "Chinese and European American cultural models of the self reflected in mothers' childrearing beliefs," *Ethos*, **23** (3), 328–54.

Chrisman, J. J., F. Kellermanns, K. C. Chan, & K. Liano (2010), "Intellectual foundations of current research in family business: An identification and review of 25 influential articles," *Family Business Review*, **23** (1), 9–26.

Christopherson, S. (2007), "Barriers to "US style" lean retailing: The case of Wal-Mart's failure in Germany," *Journal of Economic Geography*, **7** (4), 451–69.

Chua, J. H., J. J. Chrisman, & P. Sharma (1999), "Defining the family business by behavior," *Entrepreneurship Theory and Practice*, **23** (4), 19–39.

Collins, J. (2003), "Cultural diversity and entrepreneurship: Policy responses to immigrant entrepreneurs in Australia," *Entrepreneurship and Regional Development*, **15** (2), 137–49.

Danes, S. M., J. Lee, K. Stafford, & R. K. Zachary Heck (2008), "The effects of ethnicity, families and culture on entrepreneurial experience: An extension of sustainable family business theory," *Journal of Developmental Entrepreneurship*, **13** (3), 229–68.

De Massis, A., J. H. Chua, & J. J. Chrisman (2008), "Factors preventing intra-family succession," *Family Business Review*, **21** (2), 183–99.

De Massis, A., P. Sieger, J. H. Chua, & S. Vismara (2016), "Incumbents' attitude toward intrafamily succession: An investigation of its antecedents," *Family Business Review*, **29** (3), 278–300.

Dencker, J. C., S. Bacq, M. Gruber, & M. Haas (forthcoming), "Reconceptualizing necessity entrepreneurship: A contextualized framework of entrepreneurial processes under the condition of basic needs," *Academy of Management Review*.

Friedland, R. & R. R. Alford (1991), "Bringing society back in: Symbols, practices, and institutional contradictions," in W. W. Powell & P. J. DiMaggio (eds), *The New Institutionalism in Organizational Analysis*, Chicago: University of Chicago Press, pp. 232–63.

Guan, X. & X. Li (2017), "A cross-cultural examination of family communication patterns, parent–child closeness, and conflict styles in the United States, China, and Saudi Arabia," *Journal of Family Communication*, **17** (3), 223–37.

Haveman, H. A. & G. Gualtieri (2017), "Institutional logics," in R. J. Aldag (ed.), *Oxford Research Encyclopedia of Business and Management*, Oxford: Oxford University Press.

Hess, R. D. & G. Handel (1959), *Family Worlds: A Psychosocial Approach to Family Life*, Chicago: University of Chicago Press.

Hwang, K.-K. (2012), *Foundations of Chinese Psychology: Confucian Social Relations*, New York: Springer.

Jaskiewicz, P., K. Heinrichs, S. B. Rau, & T. Reay (2016), "To be or not to be: How family firms manage family and commercial logics in succession," *Entrepreneurship Theory and Practice*, **40** (4), 781–813.

Kagitcibasi, C. (1982), "Old-age security value of children: Cross-national socioeconomic evidence," *Journal of Cross-Cultural Psychology*, **13** (1), 29–42.

Kloosterman, R. & J. Rath (2001), "Immigrant entrepreneurs in advanced economies: Mixed embeddedness further explored," *Journal of Ethnic and Migration Studies*, **27** (2), 189–201.

Kontinen, T. & A. Ojala (2010), "The internationalization of family businesses: A review of extant research," *Journal of Family Business Strategy*, **1** (2), 97–107.

Kontos, M. (2003), "Self-employment policies and migrants' entrepreneurship in Germany," *Entrepreneurship and Regional Development*, **15** (2), 119–35.

Lansford, J. E., J. Godwin, L. P. Alampay, L. M. U. Tirado, A. Zelli, S. M. Al-Hassan, D. Baccini, A. S. Bombi, M. H. Bornstein, L. Chang, K. Deater-Deckard, L. Di Giunta, K. A. Dodge, P. S. Malone, P. Oburu, C. Pastorelli, A. T. Skinner, E. Sorbring, & S. Tapanya (2016), "Mothers', fathers', and children's perception of parents' expectations about children's family obligations in nine countries," *International Journal of Psychology*, **51** (5), 366–74.

Laurence, G. A. (2016), "Is resistance futile? Acculturation and disadvantage theory in immigrant entrepreneurship," *Journal of International Business and Entrepreneurship Development*, **9** (1), 88–101.

Lok, J. (2010), "Institutional logics as identity projects," *Academy of Management Journal*, **53** (6), 1305–35.

Lumpkin, G. T., W. Martin, & M. Vaughn (2008), "Family orientation: Individual-level influences on family firm outcomes," *Family Business Review*, **21** (2), 127–38.

Maitlis, S. & M. Christianson (2014), "Sensemaking in organizations: Taking stock and moving forward," *Academy of Management Annals*, **8** (1), 57–125.

Mann, M. A. (2004), "Immigrant parents and their emigrant adolescents: The tension of inner and outer worlds," *American Journal of Psychoanalysis*, **64** (2), 143–53.

McCall, G. J. & J. L. Simmons (1978), *Identities and Interactions: An Examination of Human Associations in Everyday Life*, New York: Macmillan.

McPherson, C. M. & M. Sauder (2013), "Logics in action: Managing institutional complexity in a drug court," *Administrative Science Quarterly*, **58** (2), 165–96.

Merolla, D. M., R. T Serpe, S. Stryker, & P. W. Schultz (2012), "Structural precursors to identity processes: The role of proximate social structures," *Social Psychology Quarterly*, **75** (2), 149–72.

Meyer, J. W. & B. Rowan (1977), "Institutionalized organizations: Formal structure as myth and ceremony," *American Journal of Sociology*, **83** (2), 340–63.

Meyer, R. E. & G. Hammerschmid (2006), "Changing institutional logics and executive identities: A managerial challenge to public administration in Austria," *American Behavioral Scientist*, **49** (7), 1000–14.

Meyer, R. E. & M. A. Hollerer (2016), "Laying a smoke screen: Ambiguity and neutralization as strategic responses to intra-institutional complexity," *Strategic Organization*, **14** (4), 373–406.

Meyers, B. (1984), "Minority group: An ideological formulation," *Social Problems*, **32** (1), 1–15.

Mutch, A. (2018), "Practice, substance, and history: Reframing institutional logics," *Academy of Management Review*, **43** (2), 242–58.

Ndofor, H. A. & R. L. Priem (2011), "Immigrant entrepreneurs, the ethnic enclave strategy, and venture performance," *Journal of Management*, **37** (3), 790–818.

North, D. (1990), *Institutions, Institutional Change, and Economic Performance*, Cambridge: Cambridge University Press.

Pache, A.-C. & F. Santos (2013), "Embedded in hybrid contexts: How individuals in organizations respond to competing institutional logics," in M. Lounsbury & E. Boxenbaum (eds), *Institutional Logics in Action*, Vol. 39, Part B, Bingley: Emerald Group Publishing, pp. 3–35.

Park, Y. S., B. S. K. Kim, J. Chiang, & C. M. Ju (2010), "Acculturation, enculturation, parental adherence to Asian cultural values, parenting styles, and family conflict among Asian American college students," *Asian American Journal of Psychology*, **1** (1), 67–79.

Pieterse, J. N. (1997), "Deconstructing/reconstructing ethnicity," *Nations and Nationalism*, **3** (3), 365–95.

Pukall, T. J. & A. Calabro (2014), "The internationalization of family firms: A critical review and integrative model," *Family Business Review*, **27** (2), 103–25.

Qin, D. B. & E.-J. Han (2014), "Tiger parents or sheep parents? Struggles of parental involvement in working-class Chinese immigrant families," *Teacher College Record*, **116** (8), 1–32.

Raaijmakers, A. G. M., P. A. M. Vermeulen, M. T. H. Meeus, & C. Zietsma (2015), "I need time! Exploring pathways to compliance under institutional complexity," *Academy of Management Journal*, **58** (1), 85–110.

Redding, G. (2008), "Separating culture from institutions: The use of semantic spaces as a conceptual domain and the case of China," *Management and Organization Review*, **4** (2), 257–89.

Riviezzo, A., A. Garofano, M. R. Napolitano, & V. Marino (2015), "Moving forward or running to standstill? Exploring the nature and the role of family firms' strategic orientation," *Journal of Family Business Strategy*, **6** (3), 190–205.

Robertson, D. W. & P. R. Grant (2016), "Immigrant entrepreneurship from a social psychological perspective," *Journal of Applied Social Psychology*, **46** (7), 394–409.

Ruiter, S. & F. van Tubergen (2009), "Religious attendance in cross-national perspective: A multilevel analysis of 60 countries," *American Journal of Sociology*, **115** (3), 863–95.

Sanders, J. M. & V. Nee (1996), "Immigrant self-employment: The family as social capital and the value of human capital," *American Sociological Review*, **61** (2), 231–49.

Smetana, J. G. (2002), "Culture, autonomy, and personal jurisdiction in adolescent–parent relationships," in R. V. Kail & H. W. Reese (eds), *Advances in Child Development and Behavior*, Vol. 29, Amsterdam: Academic Press, pp. 51–87.

Soleimanof, S., M. W. Rutherford, & J. W. Webb (2018), "The intersection of family firms and institutional contexts: A review and agenda for future research," *Family Business Review*, **31** (1), 32–53.

Stavrou, E. T. & P. M. Swiercz (1998), "Securing the future of the family enterprise: A model of offspring intentions to join the business," *Entrepreneurship Theory and Practice*, **23** (2), 19–39.

Suchman, M. C. (1995), "Managing legitimacy: Strategic and institutional approaches," *Academy of Management Review*, **20** (3), 571–610.

Suddaby, R., A. Bitektine, & P. Haack (2017), "Legitimacy," *Academy of Management Annals*, **11** (1), 451–78.

Thornton, P. H., W. Ocasio, & M. Lounsbury (2012), *Institutional Logics Perspective: A New Approach to Culture, Structure, and Process*, Oxford: Oxford University Press.

Tost, L. P. (2011), "An integrative model of legitimacy judgments," *Academy of Management Review*, **36** (4), 686–710.

Tung, R. L. (2008), "The cross-cultural research imperative: The need to balance cross-national and intra-national diversity," *Journal of International Business Studies*, **39** (1), 41–6.

Verver, M. & J. Koning (2018), "Toward a kinship perspective on entrepreneurship," *Entrepreneurship Theory and Practice*, **42** (4), 631–66.

Voronov, M. & L. Yorks (2015), "'Did you notice that?' Theorizing differences in the capacity to apprehend institutional contradictions," *Academy of Management Review*, **40** (4), 563–86.

Ward, C. & N. Geeraert (2016), "Advancing acculturation theory and research: The acculturation process in its ecological context," *Current Opinion in Psychology*, **8**, 98–104.

Williams, D. W., M. L. Zorn, T. R. Crook, & J. G. Combs (2013), "Passing the torch: Factors influencing transgenerational intent in family firms," *Family Relations*, **62** (3), 415–28.

Witt, M. A., L. R. Kabbach de Castro, K. Amaeshi, S. Mahroum, D. Bohle, & L. Saez (2018), "Mapping the business systems of 61 major economies: A taxonomy and implications for varieties of capitalism and business systems research," *Socio-Economic Review*, **16** (1), 5–38.

Wong, B., B. S. McReynolds, & W. Wong (1992), "Chinese family firms in the San Francisco Bay area," *Family Business Review*, **5** (4), 355–72.

Wright, M., J. J. Chrisman, J. H. Chua, & L. P. Steier (2014), "Family enterprise and context," *Entrepreneurship Theory and Practice*, **38** (6), 1247–60.

Wry, T. & J. G. York (2017), "An identity-based approach to social enterprise," *Academy of Management Review*, **42** (3), 437–60.

Yan, J. & R. Sorenson (2006), "The effect of Confucian values on succession in family business," *Family Business Review*, **19** (3), 235–50.

Zhou, M. (2004), "Revisiting ethnic entrepreneurship: Convergencies, controversies, and conceptual advancements," *International Migration Review*, **38** (3), 1040–74.

Zhou, Y., Q. Hu, J. Yao, & X. Qin (2016), "The determinants of family business owners' intrafamily succession intention: An interplay between business owners and institutional environment," *Chinese Management Studies*, **10** (4), 710–25.

Zucker, L. G. (1977), "The role of institutionalization in cultural persistence," *American Sociological Review*, **42** (5), 726–43.

5. Conflict behavior and emotions in the escalation and de-escalation of intra- and intergenerational conflict in family business

Komala Inggarwati Efendy, Artemis Chang and Roxanne Zolin

INTRODUCTION

Conflict between and among family members working together in their firms is inevitable. Literature has acknowledged this conflict as one of the main factors that cause the failure of family businesses (Beckhard & Dyer, 1983; Harvey, Cosier, & Novicevic, 1998; Merwe & Ellis, 2007). Although conflict does not always negatively impact an organization, it can quickly escalate to a destructive level, which can in turn negatively impact an individual's well-being (Amarapurkar & Danes, 2005), family relationships (Merwe & Ellis, 2007), and business performance (Eddleston & Kellermanns, 2007; Kellermanns & Eddleston, 2007). Yet, little investigation has been conducted regarding the escalation and de-escalation of family business conflict (Benavides-Velasco, Quintana-García, & Guzmán-Parra, 2013; Frank, Kessler, Nosé, & Suchy, 2011). Therefore, family business conflict is a worthwhile topic to be examined.

People respond to a conflict differently, either avoiding, accommodating, competing, compromising, or collaborating (Thomas, 1992). Conflict researchers believe that the use of these conflict-handling styles influences the dynamics of conflict and, in turn, the outcomes of the conflict (Davis, Capobianco, & Kraus, 2004; Deutsch, 2014). For example, Janssen and van de Vliert (1996) suggested that conflict was more likely to de-escalate when the conflicting parties demonstrated stronger concern for each other's goals, which led to a more accommodating, more problem-solving, more compromising, and less forced approach to conflict. Similarly, Medina and Benítez (2011) found that problem solving and accommodation were the most effective behaviors for negotiators to de-escalate a highly escalating conflict between a superior and subordinate. Although conflict literature has long shown the importance of conflict-handling styles in a conflict process, it is surprising that little intensive research has been done on the subject of conflict management within family businesses (Frank et al., 2011; Sorenson, 1999).

Another important factor to consider that has not received sufficient attention in conflict literature is the parties' emotions (Nair, 2008). Emotions are intertwined with conflict (e.g., Brundin & Sharma, 2011; Nair, 2008) and can influence the ability of family members to identify business opportunities (Boyatzis & Soler, 2012), family business strategies and decision making (Bee & Neubaum, 2014), how family members work together (Gonzalo Gómez, Botero, Jose Bernardo Betancourt, & Maria Piedad López, 2014), and family members' intention to work in their firm (Brundin & Sharma, 2011). Although emotions and conflict-handling styles are often displayed in a conflict, only a few studies have addressed how the combination of the parties' conflict-handling styles and emotional reactions affect the escalation and de-escalation of conflict. Such studies in the context of family businesses are even more limited. Family business literature suggests that the way family members respond to an ongoing conflict may be different than those in non-family firms (Loignon, Kellermanns, Eddleston, & Kidwell, 2016, p. 350).

Furthermore, the behavior of conflicting parties influences each other (Thomas, 1992). Previous studies identified two response patterns in interpersonal interaction – reciprocal and complementary (Butt, Choi, & Jaeger, 2005). A reciprocal response refers to a response where individuals respond to the other party in similar ways. A complementary response is when one party elicits different behavior to maintain interactions. In the context of family conflict, previous studies have focused on how family members influence and shape each other's behaviors. For example, Vuchinich (1984) found that family members tended to reciprocate the conflict-handling styles used by their adversaries. Parents tend to respond to children's adaptive emotions regulated with more supportive emotional responses and children's maladaptive emotions regulated with more unsupportive emotional responses (Morelen & Suveg, 2012). The findings of several studies have shown that negative reciprocity can negatively impact family relationships (e.g., Carstensen, Gottman, & Levenson, 1995). This study suggests that individual family members will respond to intra- and intergenerational conflicts differently.

In an effort to understand the dynamics of family business conflict, specifically in intra- and intergenerational relationships, this study employed an inductive qualitative approach to empirically explore the behaviors of family members in dealing with conflicts, including how family members respond to conflict in intra- and intergenerational relationships, how family members respond to each other's conflict behavior, and how family member responses relate to conflict escalation and de-escalation.

To answer these research questions, this study: (a) considered the parties' conflict behavior to be a combination of emotions and conflict-handling styles, as this study suggests that emotions are inextricably inherent to conflict (Jones, 2000), and together with conflict-handling styles, may contribute to or impede conflict and its resolution processes; and (b) analyzed the data in two different familial relationships: intra- and intergenerational relationships.

This study makes several noteworthy contributions to family business literature, as it adds to the understanding of the dynamics of intra- and inter-generational family business conflicts and helps to fill an important gap in knowledge about the escalation and de-escalation of family business conflicts. The findings of this study provide opportunities for family business practi-tioners, including owners, family members, employees, business advisors, and other stakeholders, to effectively manage conflict.

LITERATURE REVIEW

Conflict Escalation and De-escalation

The intensity of a conflict can increase (escalate) or decrease (de-escalate) over time (Wall & Callister, 1995). Conflict escalation and de-escalation refer to the different stages of a conflict (Pruitt, 2009) and observable processes during the conflict. Conflict escalation refers to the process of an increase in the intensity of a conflict and the severity of tactics used during the conflict (Medina & Benítez, 2011; Pruitt & Kim, 2004; Wall & Callister, 1995). Pruitt and Kim (2004) suggested that a conflict is escalated when more participants are involved in the conflict, more resources are allocated to the conflict, more issues are added to the conflict, more extreme tactics are used (e.g., the third party's tactic change from persuasive arguments to threats or violence), and/ or the parties have more extreme goals (for example, the goal of the third party changes from winning the conflict to hurting or getting revenge on another). Conflict is also escalated when the relationship of the disputants is worsened (Janssen & van de Vliert, 1996). In workplace settings, conflict escalation can also be viewed from a variety of aggressive behaviors, such as homicide, theft, sabotage, prosecuting strikers, work slowdown, hostile comments, negative performance evaluations, and so forth (Pruitt, 2012). The concept of conflict de-escalation is related to a decrease in one or more dimensions of conflict escalation, such as the issues are reduced, the relationship of the disputants is improved, and/or the conflict moves towards a settlement.

In the context of family businesses, conflict often occurs due to the overlap between family and business systems, which have contradictory concerns or goals (Gersick, Davis, Hampton, & Lansberg, 1997). Family systems are sub-jective, emotional, and egalitarian, while business systems are objective and meritocratic (Craig & Moores, 2015; Pieper, Astrachan, & Manners, 2013). In a recent study, Schlippe and Frank (2016) suggested that the complexity of family business conflicts is the result of incompatible communication logics, where communication within the family is attachment-oriented and communi-cation within the business is decision-oriented. Furthermore, family business scholars suggest that family business conflicts are likely to escalate due to the interference of emotions and feelings during conflicts (Fahed-Sreih, 2017, p. 55), which could influence the behavior of the parties (Thomas, 1992).

Conflict Behavior

Conflict behavior refers to an individual's reactions to a disagreement. Van der Vliert (1997) defined conflict behavior as "an individual's intended or displayed outward reaction to a conflict issue experienced" (p. 20). This definition marks two components of behavior, intended and displayed, which are also known as conflict resolution approaches and overt conflict (Pondy, 1967). The parties' behavior is an important component of a conflict. Recent work has supported the notion that the outcomes of a conflict are determined by how the parties respond to the conflict (Davis et al., 2004; Deutsch, 2014; Thomas, 1976). For example, Thomas (1976) suggested that the actions taken by one party can influence the subsequent behavior of the other party, which can in turn escalate or de-escalate the conflict. Similarly, Davis et al. (2004) proposed that an individual's responses to a conflict could make the conflict either better (constructive responses) or worse (destructive responses). His study used two conflict theories to examine the behavior of family members in a family business conflict, the conflict management theory and the emotional regulation theory.

Conflict-Handling Styles

A review of the organizational conflict literature found that research on con-flict behavior has primarily focused on conflict-handling styles, which refer to a conflict party's intention to respond to a conflict. The most commonly accepted models of conflict-handling styles are those suggested by Kilmann and Thomas (1977) and Rahim (2002). The first identifies the dual dimensions of assertiveness, which refers to the individual's desire to satisfy his or her own concern, and cooperation, which alludes to the individual's desire to satisfy another individual's need. The latter identifies strategies based on the degree to which a person attempts to satisfy his or her own concerns and the concerns of others. The combination of these two dimensions results in five conflict management styles – competition/dominating, collaboration, compromise, accommodation, and withdrawal.

Conflict literature has highlighted the important roles of conflict-handling styles in conflict escalation and de-escalation. For example, a study by Janssen and van de Vliert (1996) found that a stronger concern for another individual's goals approach would lead to a more accommodating, more problem-solving, more compromising, and less forceful approach to conflict, which can in turn help to de-escalate the conflict. Conflict studies in the context of the workplace have found that problem solving and accommodation are the most effective behaviors for negotiators to de-escalating a highly escalating superior–subordinate conflict (Medina & Benítez, 2011). Meanwhile, another study found that only a problem-solving style could prevent conflict escalation (Leon-Perez, Medina, Arenas, & Munduate, 2015). In the context of a farm family business, Danes, Leichtentritt, Metz, and Huddleston-Casas (2000) examined the relationship between conflict-handling styles and the severity of conflicts, and found that aggression was the most positive important predictor of conflict severity. Despite numerous studies on conflict-handling styles, limited empirical research has been conducted into the conflict-handling styles used by family members and their impact on the intensity of conflicts. A study conducted by Sorenson (1999) examined the impact of conflict management strategies used in family businesses, on business and family outcomes, and found that collaboration, accommodation, and compromise styles lead to better outcomes, for both the family and business, than competitive and avoidance styles.

Some scholars have suggested that the five modes of conflict resolution strategies (conflict-handling styles) may not be enough to accurately describe the behaviors of individuals during a conflict, and considered the concept of conflict behavior to be different from conflict styles (Davis et al., 2004; Deutsch, 2014; Monroe, Borzi, & DiSalvo, 1989; van de Vliert & Euwema, 1994; Van der Vliert, 1997, p. 26). For example, Davis et al. (2004) argued that the dual-concerns model oversimplified the wide variety of individual behaviors displayed during a conflict. Robbins and Judge (2014) argued that conflict styles were non-overt behaviors and referred to individuals' preferences and intentions in coping with conflict situations. Meanwhile, conflict behaviors are overt behaviors that reflect specific discrete actions and statements displayed by individuals during a conflict (Davis et al., 2004; Robbins & Judge, 2014). Therefore, studies that explore a variety of behaviors that emerge during conflict are merited.

Emotions and Conflict

Emotions are often present in a conflict and play a central role in conflict resolution (Nair, 2008). Yet, emotions have not received sufficient attention in conflict literature (Fisher & Shapiro, 2005; Jones, 2000; Nair, 2008; Posthuma, White, Dworkin, Yánez, & Swift, 2006; Thomas, 1976). Emotions, such as anger, frustration, and disappointment, have been identified in either task, process, or relationship conflict (Jehn, 1997). Previous studies found that negative emotions, such as anger, anxiety, and frustration, often emerged in a conflict (Amason, 1996; Jehn, 1995). Positive emotions could lead to more satisfactory outcomes in negotiation and, conversely, negative emotions could make conflicts spiral out of control (Fisher & Shapiro, 2005). A study by Pruitt, Parker, and Mikolic (1997) found that anger was identified as one of an individual's emotional reactions that could escalate conflict. In the specific context of negotiation, a review by Van Kleef, De Dreu, Pietroni, and Manstead (2006) found that positive emotions increased the likelihood that a person would employ cooperative behavior during the negotiation process, and by contrast, a person who experienced negative emotions was urged to behave more competitively. Moreover, previous research has found that having the ability to regulate emotional expressions decreases physical aggression (Garcia-Sancho, Salguero, & Fernandez-Berrocal, 2014) and the use of dominating/competing strategies (Rahim, 2002), which in turn leads to positive outcomes.

Emotions have also been considered an important component in family businesses (Bee & Neubaum, 2014; Boyatzis & Soler, 2012; Gonzalo Gómez et al., 2014), including in family business conflicts (Labaki, Michael-Tsabari, & Zachary, 2013). Conflict that involves negative emotions (relationship conflict) is often a characteristic of family firms and detrimental to family business performance (Eddleston & Kellermanns, 2007; Gersick et al., 1997; Nosé, Korunka, Frank, & Danes, 2017). However, research into the role of emotions in family business conflicts is limited (Gonzalo Gómez et al., 2014; Labaki et al., 2013) and has not directly examined the influence of emotions in managing and resolving family business conflicts.

In summary, a review of existing studies shows that emotions are a part of conflict resolution and that conflicting parties tend to deal with the conflict differently. This supports the argument that effective conflict resolution processes are not only dependent on an individual's conflict-handling styles, but also on an individual's ability to manage her/his emotions (Pietersen, 2014).

RESEARCH METHOD

Design of the Study

This study used a qualitative approach with in-depth interviews, as the study focused on gaining insights from patterns that emerged from the data rather than collecting data to confirm or disconfirm models, hypotheses, or theories (Taylor & Bogdan, 2015, p. 7). A critical incident technique was utilized because it facilitates researchers to relate the context, strategy, and outcome to identify patterns, and because it can be used across multiple family businesses to reveal common themes that increase generalizability (Cassell & Symon, 2004, p. 67).

Procedure

The study involved family business members, including owners, family chief executive officers (CEOs), and non-family employees, who were purposely selected from family businesses in Indonesia where more than 51 percent of the shares were owned by members of a single family and managed by at least two family members. The eligible family businesses were derived from personal contacts and the researcher's workplace, friends, and relative networks. Eligible participants were owners, family members, and non-family executives who had been working in the business for at least two years.

The selection procedure was as follows. A list of eligible family businesses was first drawn up from the author's personal contacts, and workplace, friends, and relative networks. Next, the owners, family members, or non-family executives were contacted and asked if they would be willing to participate in the study. Finally, once they agreed to participate, a convenient date, time, and place was arranged for the interview.

A purposive sampling method was used in this study because (a) there is a lack of family business databases in Indonesia (e.g., Merwe & Ellis, 2007), and (b) family business members tend to be reluctant to discuss their conflicts, as the word "conflict" is often perceived as having a negative connotation and raises sensitive issues. A variety of categories of family businesses were observed to cover a representative sample of the variety population, including business size, generational structure, industry, and location (urban/rural).

Face-to-face interviews were conducted in accordance with the agreed times and places. Interviews began with a brief introduction, including the purpose of the study and that their participation was voluntary, they could withdraw at any time during the interview without penalty, and all information they pro-

Table 5.1   *Data triangulation*

Source(s) of incident	Number of incidents
At least both conflict parties	33 (46.5%)
At least one conflict party and another family business member	21 (29.6%)
Only one conflict party	17 (23.9%)
Total	*71 (100 %)*

vided would be treated as confidential. Each of the participants provided either verbal or written informed consent prior to the interview.

After providing some demographic data, participants were asked to recall at least two major conflicts they had recently experienced or they were experiencing in their family firm, with probes to identify the parties' behavior during the conflict and the escalation and de-escalation of the conflict. Questions were asked about the conflict, such as what the conflict was about, what the conflict parties did during the conflict, the outcomes of the conflict, and so forth. Probing questions and paraphrasing were used to clarify and confirm information provided by participants.

The duration of the interviews varied from 60 to 90 minutes. Twelve out of 60 participants refused to be recorded as a matter of sensitivity. The participants who reported ongoing conflicts (12 incidents) agreed to answer a text message sent to them two weeks after the interviews asking about the progress of the conflict. Data saturation was achieved after interviews with participants from the twentieth company were undertaken. However, interviews were continued with committed participants to determine possible new insights and ensure that data saturation was achieved. In total, 71 work-related conflicts provided sufficient information and were available for analysis.

Furthermore, multiple informants were interviewed for data triangulation (Yin, 2009, p. 116) to minimize individual subjectivity and ensure the validity of the data. However, because interfamilial conflict is a very sensitive issue, it was hard to obtain access to all those involved. To minimize response bias, in that participants may not have felt comfortable discussing their conflicts or may wrongly attribute the behavior of the other parties, other family business members (family and non-family) were also interviewed to triangulate the data and strengthen the findings. Multiple participants were able to be interviewed in 22 (66 percent) of the 29 participant companies. Consequently, most reported incidents were triangulated with other sources of information (Table 5.1).

Data Analysis

Each incident reported during the interviews was transcribed and each participant and their company's name were replaced with a pseudonym (initials P01 for participant 1, P02 for participant 2, and so forth) for purposes of confidentiality and anonymity. The transcripts were analyzed at the incident level using the content analysis procedures outlined by DeCuir-Gunby, Marshall, and McCulloch (2011) to generate themes. This involved reading through the incident descriptions to become familiar with the data set, generating initial codes, and collating similar codes into themes.

The researcher developed an initial set of codes derived from the literature and that emerged through multiple readings of several incidents. New codes were added as other codes emerged during the coding process. The revised codebook was then used to code the conflicts reported through interviews and critical incidents. A random sample of incidents (25 percent) was cross-coded by two colleagues for inter-rater reliability. The reliability of the sample was between 79 and 80 percent, which could be considered conclusive, because it reached more than 70 percent agreement (Hays & Singh, 2012, p. 308). The themes were then further grouped into categories based on common characteristics.

RESEARCH FINDINGS

This study examined family members' behavior and its implications towards conflict escalation and de-escalation in the context of family businesses. An analysis was conducted at the incident level by investigating the reactions of both parties to a conflict within and between generations. The results section begins with a demographic profile of the participants, followed by the primary analysis results, which are presented in six sections. The first section presents the escalation and de-escalation patterns of conflict. The following section discusses the key themes that emerged from the data related to conflicting parties' behaviors in conflict situations. The next two sections discuss family members' behavior towards conflict between and within generations. Examples of incidents and relevant quotes from participants are provided, together with discussions about the impact of the parties' conflict behavior on conflict escalation and de-escalation. This chapter concludes with a discussion, implications, and recommendations for future studies.

Companies and Participants

Table 5.2 shows the demographic characteristics of the firms and participants. Twenty-nine family businesses in Indonesia, including small (n = 2), medium (n = 10), and large-sized (n = 17) firms and from a variety of industries, such as food and beverage, plastic and packaging, property, trading and distribution, and so forth, participated in this study. In terms of the age of the firms, more than 70 percent of the participating firms were 21 years old or more. The number of family members in a business ranged from two to eight people, with an average of 3.6 people.

Family businesses managed by family members of the first and second generations constituted the highest percent (75.9 percent). Only 13 out of 29 family businesses included non-family members in their top management teams. The number of non-family executives in the top management level ranged from one to three executives.

The demographic profile of participants in Table 5.2 shows that 60 participants, including 48 family and 12 non-family members, participated in this study, and most were male (n = 48). Participants ranged in age from 25 to 71 years old, with an average of 47.5 years. In terms of educational background, 37 out of 60 participants held a bachelor's degree, while 14 participants had completed high school or under, and the remaining nine participants were doctoral degree holders. The average tenure for all participants was 17.3 years. Most had been in the firms for more than 10 years. No participants had specifically taken courses in conflict management and resolution; however, seven participants said that they had taken a class in organizational theory and behaviors, which included a section on conflict management theory. In addition, 26 junior family members were working with the senior generation. Seven out of the 26 were doctoral degree holders, while the rest were bachelor's degree holders, and 15 out of the 26 junior family members had completed their studies overseas.

Conflict Escalation and De-escalation

Three main patterns of conflict escalation and de-escalation emerged from the reported incidents: (a) "escalate" (E) conflict (34 incidents), (b) "escalate–de-escalate" (ED) conflict (23 incidents), and (c) a "not-escalated" (NE) conflict (14 incidents). Below is a description of each of these themes, with supporting examples and quotes from the interviews.

Escalate conflict
This refers to a conflict in which the intensity increased, and as an agreement was not reached (either unresolved or unilaterally decided), the intensity remained high. Some incidents led to a broken relationship and ended with one

Innovation, growth, and succession in Asian family enterprises

Table 5.2   *Firm, participant, and incident characteristics*

Firms	Total	Participants	Total	Incidents	Total
Size		**Gender**		Intra-generational	43
Small	2	Male	46	Intergenerational	28
Medium	10	Female	14	*Total*	71
Large	17	*Total*	60		
Total	29				
Firm age (years)		**Age (years)**			
≤ 20	8	≤ 40	19		
21–30	4	Family CEOs	41–50		
31–40	9	51–60	11		
41–50	5	> 60	11		
> 50	3	*Total*	60		
Total	29				
Generations		**Familial ties**			
1st	2	Family CEOs			
2nd	4	Non-family	48		
1st and 2nd	22	executives	12		
2nd and 3rd	1	*Total*	60		
Total	29				
Family members in		**Education**			
the business		High school or			
2	5	under	14		
3	10	Undergraduate	37		
4	10	Postgraduate	9		
≥ 5	4	*Total*	60		
Total	29				
Non-family		**Tenure (years)**			
members in the top		≤ 10	25		
management team		11–20	17		
Yes	13	21–30	7		
No	16	31–40	8		
Total	29	> 40	3		
		Total	60		

party leaving the business and/or the family home. A son who was working with his mother shared his experience:

> I took over the management of our company several years ago. My mother is responsible for controlling the production processes. I wanted to use our profit to restructure and pay back the company's debts, but my mother wanted to use the money to add to the inventory. I tried to explain to her why we should reduce our debt level, but she would not understand. We got into intense arguments and I decided to leave the company. (P31, Incident 69)

Escalate–de-escalate conflict

This pattern refers to a conflict that initially escalated but then decreased and the conflicting parties were able to come to an agreement. A non-family employee described a conflict between two brothers that escalated and then de-escalated, as follows:

> The older brother, who was the marketing director of the company, intended to extend credit terms to help a big loyal customer deal with his liquidation problems. On the other hand, the younger brother, who held the position of financial director, disagreed as this policy could increase the risk of bad debt. They both became very emotional and the younger brother left the meeting. In the following discussion, the younger brother finally agreed, but set several conditions. (P17, Incident 43)

Not-escalated conflict

This refers to a conflict in which the intensity did not increase during the incident and an agreement was reached. A father–daughter conflict is described as an example: "My father often gave special discounted prices to certain customers based on his personal relationships. I preferred to offer special prices to all customers based on different quantities purchased. We discussed this issue in a calm way. He provided me some trade-offs to consider and gave me [the] freedom to make decisions" (P53, Incident 71).

Behavior of the Parties

Two themes and five subthemes related to the behavior of the conflicting parties emerged from the data, including emotional regulation (regulated and unregulated emotions) and style of handling a conflict (cooperation, competition, and avoidance) (Table 5.3). Each theme and their interactions are described in the following subsections, with supporting examples and quotes from the interviews.

Emotional regulation

The first theme relating to the parties' conflict behavior—emotional regulation— refers to the way in which conflicting parties dealt with their

Table 5.3   Key themes in conflict behavior

Categories and subcategories	Description	Examples of participant quotes
Emotional regulation	The way in which conflicting parties dealt with their emotions or feelings in a conflict situation.	
Able to regulate emotions	One's emotions are lessened (such as taking time to cool down) and/or they are able to communicate positive emotions (such as remain calm and talk politely).	"When I said that good employees should be entitled to a bonus, my father said that I was presumptuous, and he was very angry. I said nothing and went home. I avoided a direct conflict. In the next few days, I met him when he was calm" (P01, Incident 1).
		"They have many disagreements and arguments about work. However, they still get along well enough and work with one another. As far as I know, they talk politely, and the son tends to comply with what his father says" (P13, Incident 56).
Unable to regulate emotions	One's emotions are amplified, which often involves verbal and physical aggression.	"At the time of the conflict, my father and my brother were quarrelling. My father broke a chair and my brother hit the wall" (P01, Incident 23).
		"Adriel rose from his seat and shouted: 'It is not your business! What do you want?'" (P3, Company 1).
Styles of handling conflict	Actions taken by conflicting parties to handle their conflict.	
Competition	Parties show a strong intention to achieve one's own desired outcome.	"They both [brothers] did not wish to listen to any explanation. They often strongly believe that their own ideas are always right, and that others' opinions are wrong" (P04, Incident 26).
Cooperation	Parties show a willingness to compromise or collaborate with the other party.	"I involved other shareholders and also non-family executives in the decision-making process in order to make a better decision and to satisfy all shareholders. After considering many aspects, such as the availability of skilled employees and cost implications, we finally delayed the plan" (P26, Incident 54).
Avoidance	Parties ignore any issues that expose conflict.	"Perhaps, my brother wanted to warn me, but I didn't easily accept his comments. We then kept a distance between us and had our own way of doing business" (P09, Incident 4).

emotions or feelings in a conflict situation. During the interviews, it was discovered that conflicting parties tended to experience negative emotions (in 56 out of 60 incidents). At the earlier stage of the conflict, almost all conflicting parties reported that they were more likely to be displeased or annoyed when they were criticized and/or unable to voice their opinions. Two basic emotional reactions were identified from the data: regulated and unregulated emotions. The former refers to a decrease in negative emotions and/or the ability to control emotions, and the latter refers to an uncontrolled expression of negative emotions.

The findings identified 14 incidents where one or both parties were able to control their emotions and communicated positive emotions, such as taking time to cool down, remaining calm, talking politely, and so forth. In contrast, the results of the analysis showed that when conflicting parties stuck to their stand, some were unable to control their emotions. They perceived their counterparts to be selfish, stubborn, and less cooperative, and they often expressed negative attitudes, such as the use of verbal aggression (e.g., harsh words, yelling, screaming, the raising of one's voice), and even physical aggression (e.g., hitting the wall/a table, breaking a chair). Verbal aggression was utilized by at least one party in approximately 37 of the incidents. Physical aggression occurred in 10 out of the 71 incidents.

Styles of handling conflict

Another factor that characterizes conflict behavior is the style of the parties in dealing with a conflict, which refers to how conflicting parties defend their ideas, opinions, or interests. During the process of analysis, three main styles used by conflict parties in handling conflict were observed: (a) competition, (b) cooperation, and (c) avoidance. The first style was labeled a "competition" style, in which conflict parties showed strong intentions to achieve or to impose their own goals or needs. They often ignored the other's needs. A "cooperation" style was indicated by the willingness of the parties to compromise or search for integrative solutions. In order to resolve a conflict, conflict parties were willing to talk openly about their disagreement, give in to some of their needs, and/or to consider the other's opinions, ideas, or interests. The third style identified from the data was "avoidance." The findings showed some parties ignored or avoided/withdrew from the conflict by terminating the conversation or leaving, avoiding each other, or pretending that there was no conflict.

Typology of Conflict Behavior

This subsection discusses the typology of conflict behavior as a product of conflict-handling style and emotional regulation (Table 5.4). The interac-

Table 5.4   Typology of conflict behavior and its characteristics

Emotional regulation	Conflict-handling styles		
	Competition	Cooperation	Avoidance
Regulated emotions	*Assertive-persuasive* Effort to influence others' opinions in an acceptable manner (respectful, not easily contentious).	*Collaborative* Willing to work together to get the best solution for the company or reach mutually agreeable solutions and keep the relationship positive.	*Passive* Desire to please others. Does not argue. Wants to maintain long-term relationships.
Unregulated emotions	*Aggressive* Pursues own needs/goals. Verbally and/or physically threatening. Refuses to cooperate.	*Collaborative-aggressive* Willing to cooperate but more aggressive about their opinions/goals. Often communicates aggressively (e.g., defensive or angry).	*Passive-aggressive* Does not argue, but shows non-verbal actions with aggression. Gives an angry look.

tion between conflict-handling style (Table 5.4, columns) and emotional regulation (Table 5.4, rows) resulted in six types of conflict behavior: assertive-persuasive (competition – regulated emotions), aggressive (competition – unregulated emotions), collaborative (cooperation – regulated emotions), collaborative-aggressive (cooperation – unregulated emotions), passive (avoidance – regulated emotions), and passive-aggressive (avoidance – regulated emotions).

Assertive-persuasive

This refers to the behavior of conflicting parties where the parties insist on achieving their own goals peacefully by persuading or influencing the other party to accept, or approve, their perspectives or ideas. The following incident shows the assertive-persuasive behavior of a son who insisted on replacing an old machine with a new one, even though his idea had been refused by his father several times. He spent months trying to convince his father that the company needed to buy a new machine, and stated:

> I intended to replace an old machine with a new automatic machine to increase the production capacity and efficiency. My father did not approve it. He argued that the current machine was still good enough. I did not give up. I avoided confrontation but kept persuading him. I talked to him when he was calm and feeling well. Finally, after several months, he gave his approval. (P51, Incident 21)

An assertive-persuasive behavior was also clearly shown by a son when handling a conflict with his father. The son was able to control his emotions and avoided a frontal confrontation.

> When I said that good employees should be entitled to a bonus, my father said that I was presumptuous, and he was very angry. I said nothing and went home. I avoided direct conflict. In the next few days, I met him when he was calm and explained the idea of a bonus scheme for managers. After several discussions, finally we resolved it. (P01, Incident 1)

Aggressive

In aggressive behavior, conflicting parties show aggressive efforts to impose their own desires, accompanied by strong emotions, which often involve verbal and/or physical aggression. This behavior is also characterized by a win–lose, intimidation, or adversarial relationship. The two incidents below illustrate how a father and his daughter demonstrated aggressive behavior during their conflicts. They pursued their own ideas and lacked control over their emotions.

> The daughter was working in another company when her father asked her to work in his [family] company. With her previous work experience, she wanted to make some changes in the way the company operated. For example, she believed that the company required a division of labor. Therefore, she changed the organizational structure, created several new divisions, such as an accounting division and a human resources division, and planned to hire several administrators. Her father rejected this idea as it would increase the number of employees and, eventually, salary expenses. He asked his daughter to stop making changes within the company. He wanted the business to run as usual. (P40, Incident 34)

> Another incident simultaneously occurred when the daughter wanted to replace a tax consultant who had been working with her father for more than 10 years with another one. Her father refused to accept Susan's plan. They got involved in strong arguments where voices were raised. They were drawn into a prolonged disagreement. Finally, Susan decided to leave the company. (P40, Incident 35)

Collaborative

In this study, collaborative behavior is conceptualized as actions taken by conflicting parties to work together to find the best solution for the company and maintain a positive relationship. The following example shows how conflicting parties held a series of discussions to resolve their disagreement and were able to regulate their emotions.

> There was a disagreement between my sister and I over a plan to relocate our production lines. I involved other shareholders [passive shareholders] and also non-family executives in the decision-making process in order to make a better decision and satisfy all shareholders. After considering many aspects, such as laborers and cost implications, we finally agreed to delay the plan. (P26, Incident 54)

Collaborative-aggressive

This refers to the actions taken by conflicting parties to settle a conflict, where the intention was to get much of what they wanted. Therefore, they often communicated aggressively, such as being defensive, angry, and disrespectful, as shown in the incident below.

> Hans, one of the founding shareholders, asked his brother, Evan, who was currently responsible for the business, to employ his eldest son, David, in the business. Evan was very receptive and gave David a position as a purchasing manager. However, this did not last long, as David showed a lack of commitment and expected flexible working hours, something that was not usual practice at the company. On the other side, David claimed that he did his job right. A heated argument took place between Evan and David, and later David was fired from the company. Hans was actively involved in the disagreement between Evan and David. The conflict between Evan and David became a conflict between Evan and Hans. After some discussions, they agreed to resolve their conflict. Evan let David work in his other company, and Hans accepted it even though it was not what he wanted. (P19, Incident 6)

Passive

This behavior refers to responses where conflicting parties pretend that there is no disagreement or conflict among them, or avoid things that they disagree about and accept it as it is. The following incident shows how four family members who ran a big jewelry store committed to preventing conflict by ignoring any disagreements that might arise among them. During the interview, one of them stated:

> We [four siblings] have been working together for more than 30 years after the death of our father. Yes, we have experienced conflicts, but they were in the beginning years. We prefer to prevent conflict by promoting mutual understanding and respect. For example, one of us might buy a customer's jewelry at the wrong price [too expensive]. Others might disagree with the decision. But we have committed that each of us has the same authority to make decisions, and we will not blame each other. So, we [have] laid aside our disagreements to maintain family harmony. (P47, Incident 19)

Passive-aggressive

This refers to the behavior of conflicting parties who admit that there is a conflict but avoid it and do not want to discuss or resolve it. Conflict parties who show passive-aggressive behavior usually have intense emotions themselves. The two following incidents show that some parties demonstrated passive-aggressive behavior by terminating or leaving a conversation. A family CEO said, "I wanted to implement an automatic packaging system. There were constraints but I thought we could handle it. My brother disagreed with me. I have tried to talk to him several times, but he would always leave the conversation" (P15, Incident 42). Similarly, another family CEO revealed his experiences,

> When our father told us his succession plan, my brother left the meeting without responding. I knew he disagreed with it, but he didn't want to argue with his father. After that meeting, my brother avoided to meet with and talk to my father. He expressed his anger by intentionally not going to work or not doing his tasks. (P20, Incident 8)

Conflict Behavior and Escalation and De-escalation of Intergenerational Conflict

This subsection discusses the possible contributions of conflict behavior to the escalation or de-escalation of an intergenerational family business conflict. There were 43 intergenerational conflicts reported in this study. Most of those incidents (42 incidents) were conflicts between family members of the first and second generations. Only one incident was a conflict between family members of the second and third generations. Table 5.5 shows how family members behaved in intergenerational conflicts (43 incidents). As can be seen, senior members were most likely to behave aggressively (32 out of 43 conflicts) and were only willing to collaborate in seven incidents. Furthermore, there were three incidents and one incident in which senior members showed passive and passive-aggressive behaviors, respectively. In contrast, junior family members exhibited aggressive behavior during a conflict with their senior members in 17 out of 43 incidents, while there were 10 incidents in which junior members behaved assertive-persuasively. Junior members' collaborative-aggressive, collaborative, and passive-aggressive behaviors were identified in six, four, and three incidents, respectively.

Conflicting parties' behavior and conflict escalation and de-escalation are presented in Table 5.6. From the results, the majority of the behavior was shown by family members in intergenerational conflicts, in which seniors tended to respond aggressively and juniors were more likely to behave aggressively and assertive-persuasively. Thus, the data presented in Table 5.6 show that when both senior and junior parties demonstrated aggressive behavior (in all 13 incidents), an intergenerational conflict was most likely to escalate.

This behavior included aggressive efforts to impose their own desires accompanied by strong emotions, such as anger, frustration, and so forth. This behavior was also characterized by threats to others through verbal and physical aggression, such as raised voices, the use of harsh words, hitting the wall, and so forth, which in turn led to an adversarial relationship (e.g., refusing to talk, leaving a meeting without explanation, and avoiding direct communication). Incidents 34 and 35, described in the subsection above, were

Table 5.5   Senior and junior family members' conflict behavior in intergenerational conflict (n = 43)

		Junior					
		Assertive-persuasive	Collaborative	Passive	Aggressive	Collaborative-aggressive	Passive-aggressive	Total
Senior	Assertive							
	Collaborative	3	2		2			7
	Passive		2		1			3
	Aggressive	10			13	6	3	32
	Collaborative-aggressive							
	Passive-aggressive				1			1
	Total	13	4		17	6	3	43

Table 5.6   Senior and junior family members' conflict behavior and conflict escalation or de-escalation

		Junior						
		Assertive- persuasive	Collaborative	Passive	Aggressive	Collaborative-aggressive	Passive-aggressive	Total
Senior	Assertive-persuasive							
	Collaborative	NE = 1 ED = 2	NE = 2		NE = 1 ED = 1			7
	Passive		E = 2		ED = 1			3
	Aggressive	E = 1 NE = 2 ED = 7			E = 13	ED = 2 E = 4	E = 3	32
	Collaborative-aggressive							
	Passive-aggressive				ED = 1			1
	Total	13	4		17	6	3	43

Notes: ED = "escalate–de-escalate"; NE = "not escalated"; E = "escalate".

examples of escalated conflicts, where conflicting parties (father and daughter) insisted on pursuing their own goals and lost control of their emotions. Their conflicts continuously escalated until the daughter decided to stop working in the family firm. Conflicts also escalated when senior and junior members displayed aggressive and passive-aggressive behaviors (e.g., Incidents 8 and 42 described above) or passive (e.g., Incident 19 described above) and collaborative behaviors (e.g., Incident 54 described above).

Conversely, the findings indicate that when junior members behaved assertive-persuasively in dealing with aggressive senior members (nine out of 10 incidents), an intergenerational conflict was more likely to de-escalate. This can be seen from Incidents 1 (father–son conflict in company 1) and 21 (father–son conflict in company 23) described above. In those conflicts, the sons tried to influence their fathers, who handled their conflicts aggressively and persuasively. In both incidents, the sons intended to implement ideas that were refused by their fathers. Instead of confronting their fathers directly, they tried to persuade and convince their fathers that their plans needed to be implemented. Although the conflicts initially escalated, those parties were able to resolve their conflicts peacefully. Moreover, it seemed that the likelihood of intergenerational conflicts would not escalate or de-escalate when one or both parties were able to manage their emotions.

Conflict Behavior and Escalation and De-escalation of Intra-Generational Conflict

There were 28 intra-generational conflicts reported in this study, with six of these incidents occurring between family members of the first generation and the rest (22 incidents) between those of the second generation. Table 5.7 shows that, in most incidents (20 out of 28 incidents), family members exhibited similar behavior, such as collaborative versus collaborative (nine incidents), aggressive versus aggressive (eight incidents), passive versus passive (two incidents), and passive-aggressive versus passive-aggressive (one incident).

Table 5.8 shows the behavior of the conflicting parties and the intensity of the conflict. The number of incidents was insufficient to indicate the relationship between each combination of conflict behavior and conflict escalation or de-escalation. However, by giving attention to the more frequent conflict behavior, it seemed that when both parties were aggressive, intra-generational conflicts were more likely to escalate (all eight incidents). Moreover, the results show that when the conflict was handled collaboratively, the likelihood of an intra-generational conflict to not escalate or de-escalate increased.

In summary, the intensity of a family business conflict may not escalate, escalate, or escalate but then de-escalate. The findings indicate that, to some extent, the escalation or de-escalation of a conflict was influenced by the

Table 5.7   *Family members' conflict behavior in intra-generational conflict (n = 28)*

| | | Party 1 | | | | | |
		Assertive-persuasive	Collaborative	Passive	Aggressive	Collaborative-aggressive	Passive-aggressive
Party 2	Assertive-persuasive						
	Collaborative		9			6	1
	Passive			2			
	Aggressive				8		1
	Collaborative-aggressive						
	Passive-aggressive						1

Table 5.8   Family members' conflict behaviors and the escalation and de-escalation of intra-generational conflict

		Party 1					
		Assertive-persuasive	Collaborative	Passive	Aggressive	Collaborative-aggressive	Passive-aggressive
Party 2	Assertive-persuasive						
	Collaborative		ED = 3 NE = 6			ED = 6	E = 1
	Passive			NE = 2			
	Aggressive				E = 8		E = 1
	Collaborative-aggressive						
	Passive-aggressive						E = 1

conflict behavior of both parties, which varied according to the emotional regulation and conflict-handling styles of the parties. The first refers to the ability of conflicting parties to manage their emotions during a conflict (regulated and unregulated). The second explains the way parties handled a conflict (cooperation, competition, and avoidance). A combination of the party's emotional regulation and conflict-handling styles was conceptualized to result in the following behaviors: (a) assertive-persuasive, (b) collaborative, (c) passive, (d) aggressive, (e) collaborative-aggressive, and (f) passive-aggressive. The findings also indicate that conflicting parties behaved differently in intra- and intergenerational conflicts, and the escalation or de-escalation of a family business conflict was influenced by the conflict behaviors exhibited by both parties.

CONCLUSION AND DISCUSSION

This study presents the common conflict behaviors displayed by family members in dealing with intra- and intergenerational conflict in their family firms, how family members respond to each other's conflict behaviors, and how those conflict behaviors relate to escalation or de-escalation of the conflict. The findings of the current study suggest that conflict-handling styles should be implemented in conjunction with emotional regulation.

A benefit of this study is that it makes conflict behavior more understandable by analyzing the interactions between two conflict behavioral dimensions (emotional regulation and conflict-handling style) and categorizing them into six conflict behaviors: assertive-persuasive, collaborative, passive, aggressive, collaborative-aggressive, and passive-aggressive. To some extent, this typology is quite similar to that described in the conflict literature, such as four personal responses to conflict: aggressive, assertive, passive, and passive-aggressive (Doherty & Guyler, 2008, pp. 147–9), as well as five conflict-handling styles: collaborating, accommodating, compromising, competing, and avoiding (Rahim, 2002). However, by considering the parties' emotional reactions and conflict-handling styles, this study found that the competing style could involve various forms of aggressive (verbal and physical) and persuasive approaches. In the current study, these behaviors were identified as independent responses and labeled as aggressive (competing style with aggressive approaches) and assertive-persuasive (competing style with persuasive approaches). Similarly, some family members may also express negative emotions (communicate aggressively and are more insistent about their own opinions) while working with one another to find a solution. This behavior was labeled collaborative-aggressive, which is different from collaborative behavior.

The current study found that family members tend to behave differently in inter and intra-generational conflicts and the behavior of family members could lead to conflict escalation or de-escalation. In intergenerational conflict, senior family members (mostly parents) are likely to be aggressive when facing a disagreement with junior family members (mostly sons or daughters). This could be understood in the context of Indonesian culture, which is a collectivist culture that emphasizes values such as respect and obedience to the elderly. Children are expected to be respectful to their parents and obey them without question. Therefore, when junior family members demonstrate different ideas, they are viewed as disrespectful against their parents' will and could easily incite their seniors' anger. Consequently, aggressive responses of junior family members (competition and unregulated emotions) were more likely to escalate a conflict. Conversely, an assertive-persuasive approach seemed to be more effective in dealing with a conflict with senior family members. An assertive-persuasive approach could persuade senior members to approve or accept junior members' opinions or goals without being offensive.

It is somewhat surprising that there were a significant number of juniors who displayed aggressive behavior in conflicts with their senior family members. The findings indicate that junior members felt their seniors did not recognize or appreciate their work. For example, a father cancelled remuneration schemes implemented by his son, or overrode the outcomes of a meeting conducted by his daughter. Moreover, junior members' aggressive behavior may also indicate a shift in values among junior family members that may be a result of their higher levels of and Western-oriented education. Juniors may want to be treated as equal partners in the decision-making process, whereas total parental authority is a characteristic of Indonesian culture.

In an intra-generational conflict, family members are more likely to be collaborative, aggressive, or collaborative-aggressive in their behavior. Intra-generational conflicts are more likely to escalate when both parties are aggressive or passive-aggressive. The findings of this study support and extend the results of previous studies (e.g., Janssen & van de Vliert, 1996; Medina & Benítez, 2011), suggesting that a conflict is more likely to escalate when conflicting parties are more self-concerned and show lower concern for others (competing/forceful styles). Accommodating, compromising, and avoiding styles could be a shortcut to ending the conflict and avoiding a prolonged conflict. These styles may produce an acceptable, if not agreeable, resolution. However, the present results show that although conflicting parties insisted on pursuing their own goals (competing style), a conflict could have positive outcomes if they pursued their goals persuasively.

Regardless of the small amount of data, it seems that the combination of passive-aggressive behavior, and any other conflict behaviors, in both intra- and intergenerational conflicts, resulted in conflict escalation. As noted earlier, a passive-aggressive individual tends to avoid conflict or avoid directly discussing the issues at hand but continues to have negative emotional feelings, which often creates hostility toward others and fuels the conflict. This finding may help explain why the avoidance conflict-handling style is related to relatively negative business and family outcomes (Sorenson, 1999).

One of the interesting findings is the tendency of how family members responded to each other's behavior. In this study, it seemed that senior family members tended to reciprocate juniors' aggressive and assertive-persuasive responses. Senior members tended to respond to the juniors' aggressive behavior with more aggressive actions (e.g., raised voices, throwing something) and responded to the juniors' persuasive behavior with a more supportive behavior (e.g., approved the son's plans). Meanwhile, some junior members tended to react more reciprocally, and others reacted more complementary (by behaving assertively-persuasively) to aggressive senior members. Meanwhile, in intra-generational conflicts, the findings showed reciprocal patterns of interactions between siblings. In this type of conflict, family members tended to respond to the other party by demonstrating similar behavior, such as collaborative behavior being met with collaborative responses, aggressive behavior being met with aggressive responses, and collaborative-aggressive behavior being met with collaborative-aggressive responses. This reciprocal behavior was probably because family members within a generation have relatively equal power.

This study fills some of the gaps and provides original findings about family members' conflict behavior and contributes to family business and conflict management literature in several ways. First, it shows that family members behave differently in intra- and intergenerational conflicts. In intergenerational conflicts, the results of this study highlight the important role that junior family members play in soliciting seniors' responses. Meanwhile, in intra-generational conflicts, family members tended to reciprocate the other parties' behavior. Second, this study shows that the conflict resolution process involves both rational and emotional factors. While most studies have emphasized conflict resolution methods as a rational process (Montes-Berges & Augusto, 2007; Nair, 2008), this study highlights the significant role of emotion in conflict. The findings confirm that a person may display different emotional reactions and conflict-handling styles in conflict situations, and the combinations of those two factors can promote specific conflict resolution behaviors that can have different impacts on the escalation and de-escalation of family business conflicts. Finally, by studying family businesses in Indonesia, this study also contributes to knowledge about both family business and conflict research in a collectivist culture and developing countries, which is rare (Kozan & Ergin, 1999). The findings expand the understanding of how family members behave in dealing with conflict in their family firm in this context, and how their behavior may escalate or de-escalate the conflict more generally.

As conflict is inevitable and can potentially harm individual well-being, family relationships, and the future of the business, it is important for family members to find a way to prevent their conflicts from escalating or to de-escalate an escalated conflict. The findings from this study suggest that, since the actions taken by a family member in responding to a conflict play an important role in influencing whether or not the conflict escalates, family members need to learn how to deal with a conflict more effectively. First, they should be able to regulate their emotions, and then work cooperatively through the disagreement to reach a mutually accepted solution. Family members may improve their skills by gaining mutual understanding and managing their strong emotions. Second, junior family members should be aware that aggressive behavior may lead to a negative spiral of reciprocal interactions, which can escalate a conflict to become destructive. Junior members with a more assertive-persuasive behavior may be able to diminish the aggressive behavior of senior members, de-escalate the situation, and resolve the conflict. Third, family members should exhibit a more cooperative style with more regulated emotions in dealing with intra-generational conflicts, as other parties may reciprocate this positive behavior.

This study may be limited in its generalizability to other cultural contexts because it was conducted in Indonesia, where family ties are strong, the father is usually dominant, and being of a senior generation in the family is respected. This may be different from Western patterns of relationships, as well as from some other Eastern countries. As the findings are reported based on the participants' stories, the results of this study may in some sense be argued to be biased towards a certain perspective. Participants may have different feelings about escalated, unresolved, or well-managed conflicts.

The use of a different methodology, such as a network analysis, a longitudinal study, or employing a different level of analysis, may increase the understanding of conflict in family firms. Previous research has mainly focused on father–son or father–daughter dyad conflicts (Haberman & Danes, 2007) and has not paid much attention to the interpersonal relationships between team members. As family top management teams have a complex pattern of interactions, communication, and informal behaviors, it may be important to expand the unit of analysis from a dyad to a triad, or a network, to allow for a more accurate diagnosis of family business conflict, where better conflict management strategies can be developed.

REFERENCES

Amarapurkar, S. S., & Danes, S. M. (2005). Farm business-owning couples: Interrelationships among business tensions, relationship conflict quality, and spousal satisfaction. *Journal of Family and Economic Issues, 26*(3), 419–41.

Amason, A. C. (1996). Distinguishing the effects of functional and dysfunctional conflict on strategic decision making: Resolving a paradox for top management teams. *Academy of Management Journal, 39*(1), 123–48.

Beckhard, R., & Dyer, W. G., Jr. (1983). SMR forum: Managing change in the family firm – issues and strategies. *Sloan Management Review (pre-1986), 24*(3), 59.

Bee, C., & Neubaum, D. O. (2014). The role of cognitive appraisal and emotions of family members in the family business system. *Journal of Family Business Strategy, 5*(3), 323–33. doi:10.1016/j.jfbs.2013.12.001

Benavides-Velasco, C., Quintana-García, C., & Guzmán-Parra, V. (2013). Trends in family business research. *Small Business Economics*, 1–17. doi:10.1007/s11187-011-9362-3

Boyatzis, R. E., & Soler, C. (2012). Vision, leadership and emotional intelligence transforming family business. *Journal of Family Business Management, 2*(1), 23–30. doi: 10.1108/20436231211216394

Brundin, E., & Sharma, P. (2011). Love, hate, and desire: The role of emotional messiness in the business family. In A. L. C. M. Brannback (Ed.), *Understanding Family Businesses* (pp. 55–71). New York: Springer.

Butt, A. N., Choi, J. N., & Jaeger, A. M. (2005). The effects of self-emotion, counterpart emotion, and counterpart behavior on negotiator behavior: A comparison of individual-level and dyad-level dynamics. *Journal of Organizational Behavior, 26*(6), 681–704. doi:10.1002/job.328

Carstensen, L. L., Gottman, J. M., & Levenson, R. W. (1995). Emotional behavior in long-term marriage. *Psychology and Aging,* 10, 140–9. doi:10.1037/0882-7974.10.1.140

Cassell, C., & Symon, G. (2004). *Essential Guide to Qualitative Methods in Organizational Research.* Thousand Oaks, CA: Sage.

Craig, J. B., & Moores, K. (2015). The A-GES framework: Understanding the family business difference. In S. L. Newbert (Ed.), *Small Business in a Global Economy: Creating and Managing Successful Organizations* (pp. 123–54). Santa Barbara, CA: Praeger.

Danes, S. M., Leichtentritt, R. D., Metz, M. E., & Huddleston-Casas, C. (2000). Effects of conflict styles and conflict severity on quality of life of men and women in family businesses. *Journal of Family and Economic Issues, 21*(3), 259–86.

Davis, M. H., Capobianco, S., & Kraus, L. A. (2004). Measuring conflict-related behaviors: Reliability and validity evidence regarding the conflict dynamics profile. *Educational and Psychological Measurement, 64*(4), 707–31. doi:10.1177/0013164404263878

DeCuir-Gunby, J. T., Marshall, P. L., & McCulloch, A. W. (2011). Developing and using a codebook for the analysis of interview data: An example from a professional development research project. *Field Methods, 23*(2), 136–55. doi:10.1177/1525822X10388468

Deutsch, M. (2014). Cooperation, competition, and conflict. In M. Deutsch, P. T. Coleman, & E. C. Marcus (Eds), *The Handbook of Conflict Resolution: Theory and Practice* (3rd ed., pp. 3–28). San Francisco, CA: Jossey-Bass.

Doherty, N., & Guyler, M. (2008). *The Essential Guide to Workplace Mediation and Conflict Resolution: Rebuilding Working Relationships* (Vol. 1). London: Kogan Page.

Eddleston, K. A., & Kellermanns, F. W. (2007). Destructive and productive family relationships: A stewardship theory perspective. *Journal of Business Venturing, 22*(4), 545–65. doi:10.1016/j.jbusvent.2006.06.004

Fahed-Sreih, J. (2017). *Conflict in Family Businesses: Conflict, Models, and Practices.* Cham: Palgrave Macmillan.

Fisher, R., & Shapiro, D. (2005). *Beyond Reason: Using Emotions as You Negotiate.* New York: Penguin.

Frank, H., Kessler, A., Nosé, L., & Suchy, D. (2011). Conflicts in family firms: State of the art and perspectives for future research. *Journal of Family Business Management, 1*(2), 130–53. doi:10.1108/20436231111167219

Garcia-Sancho, E., Salguero, J. M., & Fernandez-Berrocal, P. (2014). Relationship between emotional intelligence and aggression: A systematic review. *Aggression and Violent Behavior, 19*(5), 584–91. doi:10.1016/j.avb.2014.07.007

Gersick, K. E., Davis, J. A., Hampton, M. M., & Lansberg, I. (1997). *Generation to Generation: Life Cycles of the Family Business.* Boston, MA: Harvard Business School Press.

Gonzalo Gómez, B., Botero, I. C., Jose Bernardo Betancourt, R., & Maria Piedad López, V. (2014). Emotional intelligence in family firms. *Journal of Family Business Management, 4*(1), 4–23. doi:10.1108/JFBM-08-2013-0020

Haberman, H., & Danes, S. M. (2007). Father–daughter and father–son family business management transfer comparison: Family FIRO model application. *Family Business Review, 20*(2), 163–84.

Harvey, M., Cosier, R. A., & Novicevic, M. M. (1998). Conflict in family business: Make it work to your advantage. *Journal of Business and Entrepreneurship, 10*(2), 610–12.

Hays, D. G., & Singh, A. A. (2012). *Qualitative Inquiry in Clinical and Educational Settings.* New York: Guilford Press.

Janssen, O., & van de Vliert, E. (1996). Concern for the other's goals: Key to (de-) escalation of conflict. *International Journal of Conflict Management, 7*(2), 99–120.

Jehn, K. A. (1995). A multimethod examination of the benefits and detriments of intra-group conflict. *Administrative Science Quarterly, 40*(2), 256–82.

Jehn, K. A. (1997). A qualitative analysis of conflict types and dimensions in organizational groups. *Administrative Science Quarterly, 42*(3), 530–57.

Jones, T. S. (2000). *The Language of Conflict and Resolution.* Thousand Oaks, CA: Sage.

Kellermanns, F. W., & Eddleston, K. A. (2007). A family perspective on when conflict benefits family firm performance. *Journal of Business Research, 60*(10), 1048–57. doi:10.1016/j.jbusres.2006.12.018

Kilmann, R. H., & Thomas, K. W. (1977). Developing a forced-choice measure of conflict-handling behavior: The "Mode" instrument. *Educational and Psychological Measurement, 37*(2), 309–25. doi:10.1177/001316447703700204

Kozan, M. K., & Ergin, C. (1999). Third party role in conflict management in Turkish organizations. *Human Organization, 58*(4), 405–15.

Labaki, R., Michael-Tsabari, N., & Zachary, R. K. (2013). Emotional dimensions within the family business: Towards a conceptualization. In K. Smyrnios, P. Poutziouris, & S. Goel (Eds), *Handbook of Research on Family Business* (2nd ed., pp. 734–64). Cheltenham, UK and Northampton, MA, USA: Edward Elgar Publishing.

Leon-Perez, J. M., Medina, F. J., Arenas, A., & Munduate, L. (2015). The relationship between interpersonal conflict and workplace bullying. *Journal of Managerial Psychology*, *30*(3), 250–63. doi:10.1108/JMP-01-2013-0034

Loignon, A. C., Kellermanns, F. W., Eddleston, K. A., & Kidwell, R. E. (2016). Bad blood in the boardroom: Antecedents and outcomes of conflict in family firms. In F. W. Kellermanns & F. Hoy (Eds), *The Routledge Companion to Family Business*. New York: Roudledge.

Medina, F. J., & Benítez, M. (2011). Effective behaviors to de-escalate organizational conflicts in the process of escalation. *Spanish Journal of Psychology*, *14*(2), 789–97. doi:10. 1037/0022-3514.66.4.674

Merwe, S. P. v. d., & Ellis, S. M. (2007). An exploratory study of some of the determinants of harmonious family relationships in small and medium-sized family businesses. *Management Dynamics*, *16*(4), 24–35.

Monroe, C., Borzi, M. G., & DiSalvo, V. S. (1989). Conflict behaviors of difficult subordinates. *Southern Communication Journal*, *54*(4), 311–29. doi:10.1080/10417948909372765

Montes-Berges, B., & Augusto, J. M. (2007). Exploring the relationship between perceived emotional intelligence, coping, social support and mental health in nursing students. *Journal of Psychiatric and Mental Health Nursing*, *14*(2), 163–71. doi:10.1111/j.1365-2850.2007.01059.x

Morelen, D., & Suveg, C. (2012). A real-time analysis of parent–child emotion discussions: The interaction is reciprocal. *Journal of Family Psychology*, 26, 998–1003. https://doi.org/10.1037/a0030148

Nair, N. (2008). Towards understanding the role of emotions in conflict: A review and future directions. *International Journal of Conflict Management*, *19*(4), 359–81. doi:10.1108/10444060810909301

Nosé, L., Korunka, C., Frank, H., & Danes, S. M. (2017). Decreasing the effects of relationship conflict on family businesses: The moderating role of family climate. *Journal of Family Issues*, *38*(1), 25–51. doi:10.1177/0192513X15573869

Pieper, T. M., Astrachan, J. H., & Manners, G. E. (2013). Conflict in family business: Common metaphors and suggestions for intervention. *Family Relations*, *62*(3), 490–500. doi:10.1111/fare.12011

Pietersen, C. (2014). Interpersonal conflict management styles and emotion self-management competencies of public accountants. *Mediterranean Journal of Social Sciences*, *5*(7). doi:10.5901/mjss.2014.v5n7 p273

Pondy, L. R. (1967). Organizational conflict: Concepts and models. *Administrative Science Quarterly*, *12*(2), 296–320. doi:10.2307/2391553

Posthuma, R. A., White, G. O., III, Dworkin, J. B., Yánez, O., & Swift, M. S. (2006). Conflict resolution styles between co-workers in US and Mexican cultures. *International Journal of Conflict Management*, *17*(3), 242–60.

Pruitt, D. G. (2009). Escalation and de-escalation in asymmetric conflict. *Dynamics of Asymmetric Conflict*, *2*(1), 23–31. doi:10.1080/17467580903214501

Pruitt, D. G. (2012). Conflict escalation in organizations. In C. K. W. De Dreu & M. J. Gelfand (Eds), *The Psychology of Conflict and Conflict Management in Organizations* (pp. 245–62). Hoboken, NJ: Erlbaum Psych Press.

Pruitt, D. G., & Kim, S. H. (2004). *Social Conflict: Escalation, Stalemate, and Settlement*. New York: McGraw-Hill.

Pruitt, D. G., Parker, J. C., & Mikolic, J. M. (1997). Escalation as a reaction to persistent annoyance. *International Journal of Conflict Management*, *8*(3), 252–70. doi:10.1108/eb022798

Rahim, M. A. (2002). Toward a theory of managing organizational conflict. *International Journal of Conflict Management, 13*(3), 206.

Robbins, S. P., & Judge, T. (2014). *Organizational Behavior* (Vol. 16). Boston, MA: Pearson.

Schlippe, A. v., & Frank, H. (2016). Conflict in family business in the light of systems theory. In F. W. Kellermanns & F. Hoy (Eds), *The Routledge Companion to Family Business*. New York: Roudledge.

Sorenson, R. L. (1999). Conflict management strategies used by successful family businesses. *Family Business Review, 12*(4), 325–39. doi:10.1111/j.1741-6248.1999.00325.x

Taylor, S. J., & Bogdan, R. (2015). *Introduction to Qualitative Research Methods: A Guidebook and Resource* (4th ed.). Hoboken, NJ: Wiley.

Thomas, K. W. (1976). Conflict and conflict management. In M. D. Dunnette (Ed.), *Handbook in Industrial and Organizational Psychology*. Chicago, IL: Rand McNally.

Thomas, K. W. (1992). Conflict and conflict management: Reflections and update. *Journal of Organizational Behavior (1986–1998), 13*(3), 265.

Van der Vliert, E. (1997). *Complex Interpersonal Conflict Behaviour: Theoretical Frontiers*. Hove: Psychology Press.

Van de Vliert, E., & Euwema, M. C. (1994). Agreeableness and activeness as components of conflict behaviors. *Journal of Personality and Social Psychology, 66*(4), 674–87. doi:10.1037/0022-3514.66.4.674

Van Kleef, G. A., De Dreu, C. K. W., Pietroni, D., & Manstead, A. S. R. (2006). Power and emotion in negotiation: Power moderates the interpersonal effects of anger and happiness on concession making. *European Journal of Social Psychology, 36*(4), 557–81. doi:10.1002/ejsp.320

Vuchinich, S. (1984). Sequencing and social structure in family conflict. *Social Psychology Quarterly, 47*(3), 217–34. www.jstor.org/stable/3033819

Wall, J. A., & Callister, R. R. (1995). Conflict and its management. *Journal of Management, 21*(3), 515–58. doi:10.1177/014920639502100306

Yin, R. K. (2009). *Case Study Research: Design and Methods* (Vol. 4). Thousand Oaks, CA: Sage.

6. Toward an e-commerce strategy: Impact of family dynamics

Salvatore Tomaselli, Yong Wang, Donella Caspersz and Rong Pei

INTRODUCTION

There has been interest in understanding how technology has affected business organizations since the mid-1950s when information technology (IT) was first applied to the business process (Markus & Robey, 1988). However, the phenomenal growth of e-commerce and the growing application of e-commerce to business processes has changed the nature of business transactions, and the way in which a business derives its value, making e-commerce initiatives increasingly important from a strategic point of view (Chang, Jackson, & Grover, 2002).

Early scholars mostly considered e-commerce as *a way of selling a company's products over the internet* (Herbig & Hale, 1997) by utilizing their websites for advertising, public relations, and customer service access (Griffith & Krampf, 1998). Today, it is clear that e-commerce influences all sectors and all markets and *is related to the total strategy and operations of enterprise*, by connecting these operations with networks that exceed the limits of enterprise (Haig, 2001) to share business information, maintain business relationships, and conduct business transactions by means of telecommunications networks (Lagrosen, 2005).

Nowadays, the literature tends to consider e-commerce as "a business model in which transactions take place over electronic networks, mostly the Internet. It includes the process of electronically buying and selling goods, services, and information … is not just about buying and selling; it also is about electronically innovating, communicating, collaborating, and discovering information. It is about e-learning, e-customer service, e-government, social networking, problem-solving, and much more" (Turban et al., 2018, p. v).

While this new economic environment offers potential benefits to societies and creates opportunities for businesses, it also poses a threat to traditional businesses, especially to family-controlled businesses. Family business is a popular form of business across the globe. According to the Family Firm Institute, family businesses represent two thirds of the businesses worldwide and contribute 70–90 percent of the global gross domestic product and 50–80 percent of the employment in the majority of the economies.[1] Yet like their non-family counterparts, family businesses are vulnerable to challenges stemming from the external context. The disruption deriving from the smart development of e-commerce, and, in general, the internet-based economy and the digital economy can be one of these.

Although there are some debates about the precise definition of a family business, it is generally accepted that a family business is one where the family has a controlling interest and – unlike in non-family firms – the family is dominant in the strategic decision making of the business (Chua, Chrisman, & Sharma, 1999; Chrisman, Chua, & Sharma, 2005; Dyer, 2003), and its influence is fundamental and enduring (Whetten, Foreman, & Dyer, 2014). The exploration of such influence has been the field of analysis of the line of research on "familiness," a construct elaborated by Habbershon and Williams (1998).

In this chapter, we explore the effects of such family influence on the design and implementation of e-commerce strategy. To this aim we analyze three family businesses in China. Two of these cases have also been analysed in other works (Caspersz et al., 2017; Caspersz et al. 2019). We concentrate our attention on China as, on the one hand, it has experienced a dramatic growth of e-commerce over the last years,[2] and, on the other hand, family businesses are the dominant form of business among privately owned companies.[3]

We also make a conceptual contribution when discussing the implications of our findings on the e-commerce strategy of the firms in our study, proposing the inclusion of the family among the factors that influence the e-commerce adoption process, and suggest that dynamic capabilities may be useful in analyzing how the influence of the family contributes to configure the e-commerce business strategy by a family business.

We begin with reviewing the literature about studies on e-commerce strategy of family businesses. We then describe the approach that we have taken and report the findings from the case studies. Subsequently we discuss the implications of the findings, propose our conceptual contribution, and provide a brief commentary on our future research agenda.

CORPORATE STRATEGY AND E-COMMERCE IN FAMILY BUSINESSES: REVIEW OF THE LITERATURE

The involvement of the family in the strategy creation and implementation is largely recognized as the central, enduring, and distinctive feature that distinguishes a family from a non-family business (Whetten et al., 2014). Thus the systemic influence of family (Habbershon & Williams, 1999) and its psychological characteristics (adaptability, rigidity, cohesion, and the like) also affect the strategy creation process and the strategies adopted by the business (Chua et al., 1999; Brunninge, Nordqvist, & Wiklund, 2007; Astrachan, 2010) as "it creates patterns of goals, strategies, and structures that are often formulated, designed and implemented in ways that can be radically different from non-family firms" (Salvato & Corbetta, 2014).

Although it can be a source of competitive advantage in strategic change (Zellweger, Eddleston, & Kellermans, 2010), family influence may result in conflicts in priorities and goals for the business (Schulze, Lubatkin, Dino, & Buchholtz, 2001), decision making, control (Koeberle-Schmid & Caspersz, 2013), and, ultimately, continuity of the business (Miller, Steier, & Le Breton-Miller, 2003).

Literature on strategic processes in family businesses has highlighted that the role of key family business actors and the actions they perform are central in determining the dynamism of otherwise relatively inertial entities such as organizational routines and capabilities, and that to understand how stability and change can be mutually determined and become a duality attention can be directed towards the subjectivity, agency, and power exerted by key actors, which have power to leverage and reinterpret deeply rooted values, beliefs, and action patterns (Salvato & Corbetta, 2014).

König, Kammerlander, and Enders (2013) argue that the differences that family influence injects into the business system significantly affect when and how firms adopt discontinuous innovations and, thus, provide a new explanation for why incumbent firms, contrary to the prevailing paradigm, differ in their responses to discontinuous change.

The adoption of e-commerce strategy falls into the category of discontinuous innovation, asking for strategic innovation, since it calls for fundamental reconceptualization of the business model and the reshaping of existing markets (by breaking the rules and changing the nature of competition) to achieve dramatic value improvements for customers and high growth for companies (Schlegelmilch, Diamantopoulos, & Kreuz, 2003).

Under the new context created by the dramatic development of e-commerce transactions, there are a series of questions waiting to be addressed, such as how family influence adapts to the new environment, given that control is often a core concern of family businesses (Miller & Le Breton-Miller, 2005); how family businesses adjust their resources and processes to align with the e-commerce business model; what education and training should family businesses adopt for their key actors to ensure effective strategic thinking in the e-commerce context; how do family businesses sustain and further develop their socioemotional (Berrone, Cruz, & Gomez-Mejia, 2012) and financial wealth; and how do family businesses adjust their resources and processes to develop competitive advantages under the new climate. These questions are crucial to the development of family businesses in the new era.

We reviewed the literature on corporate strategy and e-commerce in family businesses, primarily drawing upon academic articles published in academic journals (see also Caspersz et al., 2019). Since our focus is on family businesses we reviewed those journals specifically devoted to this field of study – *Family Business Review* and *Journal of Family Business Strategy* – and extended our analysis to *Entrepreneurship Theory and Practice*, which is considered one of the journals relevant to family business research (De Massis, Sharma, Chua, & Chrisman, 2012). However, we did not find any contribution that directly and explicitly dealt with e-commerce, and e-commerce strategy in family businesses in any of these journals. So, we extended our search to other academic journals. The search was conducted using Google Scholar, and with the terms "e-commerce," "family business," and "strategy" in the fields of title, keywords, and abstract. We sourced 22 references, where, in most cases, family business was associated with small to medium-sized enterprises (SMEs).

Since our focus of interest is on (a) e-commerce corporate strategy in family businesses and (b) the impact of the family on the decision and the process of adopting e-commerce, we concentrated our review on those articles dealing with this topic. We then added 23 more references that were cited in the 22 previous references, reaching the total number of 45 references, 28 of which are journal articles. Even though this list of references is not exhaustive, we are confident that this is an appropriate representation of the literature thus far.

A general overview of the literature shows that even though only a few journals published articles on this topic, no journal has published more than one article in the same year, there has been an absence of interest in the topic within the key scholarly journals addressing family business studies, and it seems that the interest of scholars in the issue is also sporadic. Finally, it was interesting to notice that among the 45 references, only one (Chang et al., 2002) included "corporate strategy" in its title. We thus conclude that there is an absence of relevant scholarly research that addresses our topic.

However, from the overall analysis of the collected literature, main topics and areas of research regarding the adoption of e-commerce in SMEs emerge and are reported in Figure 6.1.

Chang et al. (2002) conducted a study that focused on the *integration between corporate strategy and e-commerce*. They adopted Narver and Slater's (1990) conceptualization of market orientation focusing on customer orientation and competitor orientation and identified the most relevant components of these two dimensions.

Drew (2003) analyzed different areas of the strategic uses of e-commerce by SMEs in the east of England highlighting that the most important *driving*

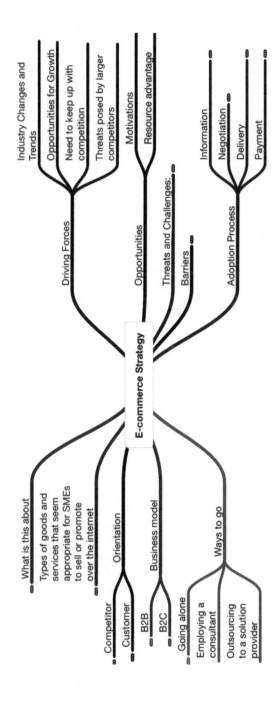

Figure 6.1   Main topics and areas of research regarding the adoption of e-commerce in SMEs emerging from the literature review

forces for the adoption of e-commerce include industry changes and trends, opportunities for growth, the need to keep up with competition, and threats posed by larger competitors.

Levenburg and Magal (2005) made an effort to identify small firms' *motivations for engaging in e-business*, suggesting that motivations fall into different categories, which can be synthesized as follows. (1) *Marketing-related*, including the desire to increase sales (Access Markets International Partners, 2001; Griffith & Krampf, 1998; Levenburg, Schwarz, & Dandridge, 2002; Pratt, 2002; Gadish, 2009; Huang, 2008), either by reaching new customers and markets (Bernroider, 2008) and/or by retaining customers' loyalty (Access Markets International Partners, 2001; Barua, Konana, Whinston, & Yin, 2001; Chordas, 2001; Zank & Vokurka, 2003; Levenburg & Magal, 2005; Huang, 2008); alleviating time constraints placed on staff by providing customer service in person (Pool, Parnell, Spillan, Carraher, & Lester, 2006; Samanta & Kyriazopoulos, 2009; Levenburg & Klein, 2006); accomplishing advertising, promotion, and public relations (Access Markets International Partners, 2001); enhancing the firm's image (Stephenson, Lockwood, & Raven, 2003); improving customer satisfaction (Chordas, 2001); and improving customer retention (Zank & Vokurka, 2003). (2) The desire to *develop and strengthen a relationship with key constituents* (Access Markets International Partners, 2001; Barua et al., 2001; Chordas, 2001; Zank & Vokurka, 2003), mainly (but not exclusively) suppliers and customers, obtained thanks to the possibility to use the potential of the internet to cater for customers' needs, wants, and preferences. (3) Aiming to *improve financial performance* through operational efficiencies (Gadish, 2009; Bernroider, 2008; Chang et al., 2002), enabling a reduction in cost of operations for the company (Gadish, 2009; Samanta & Kyriazopoulos, 2009); reduced accounts receivable (Zank & Vokurka, 2003); reduced transaction costs (Surjadjaja, Ghosh, & Antony, 2003); reduced costs of sales and delivery fulfillment (Access Markets International Partners, 2001); reduced direct or administrative costs (Levenburg et al., 2002); reduced inventory (Zank & Vokurka, 2003); across-the-board cost reductions (Chordas, 2001; Pratt, 2002); increased profits (Levenburg, Schwarz, & Dandridge, 2002; Pratt, 2002); increased income (Samanta & Kyriazopoulos, 2009); better return on investment (Huang, 2008); increased profits (Levenburg et al., 2002; Pratt, 2002). (4) The desire to *obtain information*, mainly gaining supply chain sourcing information (Pool et al., 2006; Levenburg & Magal, 2005). (5) *Buying reasons*, mainly by reaching new suppliers (Bernroider, 2008) and improving supplier relationships (Access Markets International Partners, 2001; Barua et al., 2001; Chordas, 2001; Zank & Vokurka, 2003; Levenburg & Magal, 2005; Huang, 2008).

Huang (2008) identified the e-commerce development strategy dimensions by business as being pursued to gain resource advantage, competitive advantage, and performance advantage. Whereas competitive and performance advantage include most of the elements included in the classification offered by Levenburg and Magal (2005), resource advantage mainly consists of improving professional management capabilities (Huang, 2008) and increasing the likelihood of adopting a double-loop form of organizational learning which can lead to new core competencies and competitive advantage (Chaston, 2001; Huang, 2008).

While the interest towards the advantages and opportunities stemming from e-commerce seem to be dominant, some scholars have also highlighted that e-commerce can generate threats emerging from increased competition, intensified price competition, power shifting down along the distribution channel to the final customer, and the emergence of new buying behavior. E-commerce acts as an accelerator in the multiplication of customer options (Chang et al., 2002; Bernroider, 2008), reduction in customers' search, reduction in switching costs, distribution of information on new products, access to new sales channels, and reduction in entry barriers (level capital requirements) (Chang et al., 2002).

The study of barriers to the development of e-commerce has been the field of interest of a number of scholars who have grouped these into external barriers – that is, supply (Hadjimanolis, 2000; MacGregor, & Kartiwi, 2010), demand (Hadjimanolis, 1999; MacGregor & Kartiwi, 2010), and environmental (Hadjimanolis, 1999; MacGregor & Kartiwi, 2010; Jennex, Amoroso, & Adelakun, 2004; Chiware & Dick, 2008; Cloete, Courtney, & Fintz, 2002; Zhao, Wang, & Huang, 2008; Mukti, 2000; Dedrick & Kraemer, 2001; Oshikoya & Hussain, 2007; Drew, 2003; Markus & Soh, 2002; Jennex et al., 2004; Chepaitis, 2002) – and internal barriers – related to resources (Hadjimanolis, 1999; MacGregor & Kartiwi, 2010; Mutula & Van Brakel, 2007; Zhao et al., 2008; Jennex et al., 2004) and systems.

The process followed to adopt e-commerce – initiate, decide, implement – has been studied by Molla, Heeks, and Balcells (2006). They expanded the technology-organizations-environment framework developed by Tornatzky and Fleischer (1990), by including managerial factors and grouping the factors affecting e-commerce adoption into four categories: contextual, organizational, managerial, and e-commerce specific.

Based on the analysis of two successful and renowned Chinese e-businesses – CCEC and Alibaba – Zhao et al. (2008) built a model describing the four phases of transactional process: information, negotiation, payment, and delivery. In summary, the broader literature has identified different aspects of corporate strategy in e-commerce. It has proposed definitions of e-commerce and tried to identify the types of goods and services that seem more appropriate for SMEs to sell or promote over the internet. It has also described strategic orientation toward competitors and customers, the different pathways followed, and the various business models that can be adopted. Furthermore, the literature has identified the most important driving forces and factors influencing the development of e-commerce, the motivations that influence the decision to adopt e-commerce, the main opportunities and threats faced by SMEs in engaging in e-commerce, and analyzed the e-commerce adoption process. A visual synthetization of our review is represented in Figure 6.2, reporting the main lines and areas of research emerging in the literature. Also, in the appendix, we offer a literature table (Table 6A.1) integrating the list of academic articles included in our review.

Despite this extensive canon, we did not find any contribution devoting attention to the role played by the family in deciding to adopt e-commerce and designing and implementing e-commerce strategies in family businesses. The literature diffusely reports how much e-commerce represents a true challenge to the traditional way of doing business for any company.

We hypothesize that in the case of a family business, given its grounding in tradition and the values of the family, and the central role of key family business actors and the action they perform in determining the firm's dynamism, such a dramatic change might find the family either as a supporter or as a detractor of such a shift, depending on the attitude of key family actors. Similarly, the adoption of e-commerce models can have positive and negative repercussions on the family side.

This proposition is consistent with the generally accepted idea that family is dominant in the strategic decision making of the business (Chua et al., 1999; Dyer 2003; Brunninge et al., 2007; Astrachan, 2010), and that such dominance comes out from the distinctive bundle of resources a firm develops as a result of family involvement and influence, namely familiness (Habbershon & Williams, 1998). Chrisman, Chua, and Litz (2003, p. 468) refined the concept and described familiness as "resources and capabilities related to family involvement and interactions."

Pearson, Carr, and Shaw (2008) analyzed the behavioral and social resources that constitute familiness, as well as its antecedents and outcomes, through the lenses of social capital perspective. They highlighted that resources fall into three dimensions – structural (i.e. network ties, appropriable organization), cognitive (i.e. shared vision, shared language), and relational (i.e. trust, norms, obligations, identification) – and that the idiosyncratic combination of such dimensions of resources determines the family firm capabilities, made of information access (i.e. efficient action and exchange) and associability (i.e. collective goals, collective actions, and emotional support). Also, they identified the antecedent conditions that help create familiness: time, that is the durability and stability of the relationship; closure, or the boundaries of the social networks and the uniqueness of the social capital context; interdependence; and interaction.

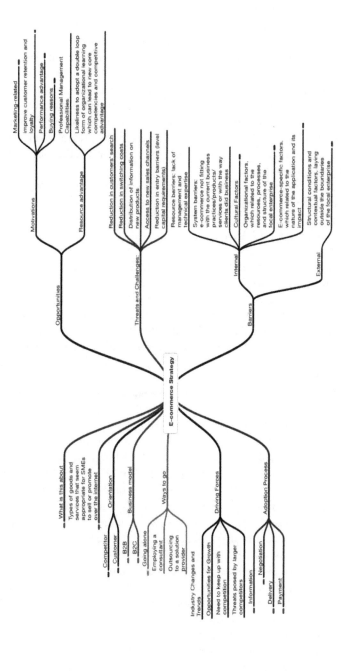

Source: Caspersz et al. (2019).

Figure 6.2   A visual synthesis of the main lines and areas of research on e-commerce strategy emerging in the literature

Ensley and Pearson (2005) focused their study on the on top management teams, reaching the conclusion that the unique dynamics created by the social aspects of the family-owned firm will result in higher cohesion, potency, task conflict, and shared strategic consensus than those top management teams with less familiness.

In another study (Caspersz et al., 2019) – relying on two of the three cases analyzed in this chapter, but focusing on organizational identity – we found support for the proposition that e-commerce has an influence on the organizational identity of family businesses. Our interest in the present chapter is to complement this by investigating how family relations affect the e-commerce strategy in family businesses.

In this way we try to contribute to the acquisition of more knowledge about e-commerce strategy adoption in family businesses.

RESEARCH APPROACH

Our research followed an exploratory and qualitative approach. Although the development of an accurate family business definition is still ongoing, researchers generally agree that family businesses refer to those where family holds significant ownership of the business and has remarkable impact on business management (DeMassis, Frattini, Pizzumo, & Cassia, 2015). As also reported in our previous work (Caspersz et al., 2019), we selected family businesses based on three criteria, supported by academic literature: (a) more than 50 percent of the voting shares are controlled by one family, and/or a single family group effectively controlling the business (Westhead, Cowling, & Howorth, 2001; DeMassis et al., 2015), (b) the company is perceived by its chief executive as a family business (Westhead et al., 2001); and (c) the chief executive anticipates passing the business to the next generation of family members (Astrachan & Kolenko, 1994). Moreover, we decided to incorporate SMEs in our study (based on the definition provided in the SME Promotion Law of China in 2003). By focusing on companies of a similar size, we avoided the risk of distracting heterogeneity as a result of difference in company size (De Massis et al., 2015). Where data collection was concerned, we relied on our contacts in the Beijing Institute of Technology and Hebei University of Technology. The two universities owned multi-dimensional connections with businesses because of their education and research activities. Via the connections, we sought to obtain a balanced sample of case companies taking into account both homogeneity and heterogeneity (cf. Merriam, 1988). We conducted field research in two diverse regions in China, namely Beijing, where many high-technology firms were located and was the capital of the country with well-developed market infrastructure, and the western inland Xinjiang autonomous region, which overall lagged behind other provinces in technology and market infrastructure but was rich in nascent opportunities for new and entrepreneurial activities. By doing this, we considered regional heterogeneity as well as data accessibility. In addition, owing to the nature of this research, we embraced companies that had embarked on the e-commerce platform, and this was to ensure homogeneity and cross-case comparability. As a result, our study finally involved three family businesses, two of which were located in Beijing and one in Xinjiang. E-commerce recently commenced to demonstrate its dynamism in the Chinese economic landscape, particularly after the naissance of companies such as Alibaba Group and Tencent. The mesmerizing effect that these companies have created has either attracted followers that would attempt to maximize their utility via the online springboard, or imposed e-commerce on disadvantaged market players to maintain their legitimacy in the market.

We used semi-structured interviews with key informants in the firms, initially with the founder of each case company, in conjunction with a plan of further data collection from key family members and employees in management and non-management positions. We undertook visits to the headquarters of the three companies and interviews were conducted during the visits. Each interview commenced with a brief introduction explaining the purpose, process, and implications of the research. The interview questions were open-ended and focused on business history, business resources, as well as corporate and e-commerce strategies. The intention of this approach was to allow interviewees on the one hand to concentrate on our research foci, whilst on the other hand to bring in their own theses which were perceived relevant. Tables 6.1 and 6.2 show the profiles of the case companies and interviewees.

Before the interviews, we identified a number of themes from the literature review that may be connected to e-commerce strategy. The purpose of this review was to form the foundation of our theoretical perspective, guiding us in the data collection and analysis. These themes were incorporated into our questionnaire design. Each interview lasted on average two to three hours. All interviews were conducted in Mandarin and were recorded and transcribed for detailed analysis. We obtained ethics approval for our research. The transcripts of the interviews vary from 23 to 40 pages.

We took an interpretative approach to data analysis, mainly because of the qualitative nature of the study in general, and the descriptive nature of the data in particular (Creswell, 1994). For each transcript we used coding to understand data; whenever information was ambiguous or further explanation was needed, we made telephone calls to case companies to clarify and confirm. Then we compared the transcripts of the case companies, highlighting similar comments and grouping them until final themes were developed. The narratives containing the final set of themes were organized accordingly.

Table 6.1   Case company profile

Case	Region	From	Main activities	Generation in control	Owned by
LM	Beijing	2001	Health medication and cosmetic products manufacturing	First	Founder
JY	Beijing	2010	Online training in accounting	Second	Founder and his son
WD	Xinjiang	1998	Vehicle parts sales and service	First	Founder and family and non-family staff members

Table 6.2   Interviewee profile

Case	Interviewee	Gender	Age	Education
LM	Founder	Female	70+	University degree education
JY	Owner-manager (second generation)	Male	40+	University degree education
WD	Founder	Female	Early 50s	University degree education

FINDINGS

This section of the chapter reports the main findings of our research. For each of the three cases, it reports the business background, the e-commerce strategy, and the influence of the family on the e-commerce strategy.

Case 1: LM

Business background

LM was a healthcare medication product manufacturing company founded in 2001 by the founder who had recovered from cancer; the business initially adopted a direct sales model. In 2016, the business recorded 500-million-yuan worth assets and 6 billion yuan annual sales, employing approximately 1,000 employees in Beijing and Shanghai. However, from 2011 the model started to be challenged by a series of changes in economic environment, including radical development of high technologies and e-commerce. Young talented people in the business were attracted by novelty of the technology and the opportunities it offered for career development. This put the business on the edge of losing its human capital. The founder finally decided to embark on e-commerce.

E-commerce strategy

At the beginning, the founders attempted to integrate the existing offline direct marketing with the new online channels. But the model did not work, and the result was less optimistic than expected. The online and offline teams had different views and perspectives and could not understand each other. This drove the founder to separate the offline and online commerce to two parallel businesses, each one with its own team, market segmentation and associated performance tasks. To sustain this strategy with adequate financial resources, the founder further decided to go public, float one third of the company on the stock market, as well as engage in charity activities. The expectation was that the company would no longer be perceived as a traditional manufacturing firm, but a cutting-edge business equipped with new technology, strategic wisdom, capital market operation, and social responsibility orientation. The founder named this as "3 +1 strategy", a sustainable long-term strategy, focusing on health medication products manufacturing, e-commerce, capital market operation, plus charity activities.

In this context, health medication products manufacturing was perceived as the foundation of the firm. e-commerce was used as an auxiliary tool, opening a new trading platform for the firm, in addition to traditional offline trading. The adoption of e-commerce also created an impact on the corporate vision. Whereas in the past it had a single focal point, health medication, the adoption of e-commerce allowed the company to provide products that could offer customers and employees greater, better and more quality life.

Influence of the family on e-commerce strategy

E-commerce adoption in LM can be viewed as a result of family relationship balancing. E-commerce adoption was initiated by the founder's son, along with a group of young and talented managers. After being lobbied from various angles, the founder finally accepted the concept that e-commerce could offer the firm opportunities in optimizing its operations and performance. But she and her son viewed differently the impact of e-commerce on the business. The founder's stance was conservative, with the belief that the business' competitive advantage was originated from the manufacturing and e-commerce could only assist in extending marketing capacity. The son, however, saw e-commerce as a tool to reform the organization's foundation.

After intensive debates, the founder made her final decision, "in the company, I am the empress and he is the subordinate. He can make suggestions … whether I take the suggestions is a matter of myself… company is different from family and we pay attention to rules and governance." The son was eventually assigned to be in charge of the e-commerce division, but e-commerce was configured to serve as a marketing strategy, not an overarching strategy.

The appointment of the son was to keep him identified with the firm, as well as satisfying his desire for independency.

Case 2: JY

Business background

JY was founded in 2010, relying on the experience of a certified accountant who had experiences in preparing candidates for the exams as certified accountant. The business was established as a partnership between the lecturer's son, who had resigned from a computer programming company, and a friend of his, who was an IT specialist. Later on, the father joined the partnership and the equity became equally shared by the three.

The company dedicated to digital education was located in Beijing, providing services related to preparing candidates for examinations in accounting for qualifications as junior and senior accountants and certified accountants. The training targeted examinations set up by national professional institutions and was delivered via online videos, online live lectures, and face-to-face interaction. By doing so, the founder adopted a user-friendly flexible approach that differed from conventional training. The business had grown since inception and in 2016 it employed about 50 people.

E-commerce strategy

The e-commerce adoption strategy of JY was organic, unlike LM. The father of the incumbent executive (the founder) was a university lecturer specialized in accounting. Because of his distinguished teaching, accreditation bodies frequently invited him to train practitioners for their qualifications or specialty licenses. It was on this basis, coupled with the son's IT knowledge, that in 2010 they decided to found JY, one of the earliest online accounting education firms. The business delivered accounting courses online to students desiring for accounting certificates issued by professional institutions. JY adopted a B2C business model, creating a direct connection with customers. Online activities were the core of the business, supported by staff members working offline.

E-commerce was rooted in JY's operations, since the courses in accounting and the supplementary services were delivered via online live lectures, online videos, as well as supplementary face-to-face interaction. Despite being one of the first movers to the field and the utilization of the most advanced technology, the company confronted emulation pressure from competitors. This pushed the founder to further diversify. In the son's words, "If we only know software and e-commerce, without expertise in this specific field, we cannot be successful. e-commerce is only a medium for us, but can enable us to extend."

Influence of the family on e-commerce strategy

JY built up its competitive advantage through the combination of the first generation's subject expertise, the son's knowledge, and online technology. In this context, e-commerce became an overarching strategy as a result of a natural process, enabled by harmonious relationship between the two generations. The two generations were able to appreciate strengths and weaknesses of each and had the wisdom to combine them in an original way. The interaction between the two generations was constructive, encouraging a more rounded and bespoke decision to be taken. Eventually, e-commerce was adopted as a corporate strategy, as this lay within the boundary of the son's expertise. Additionally, the son believed the services buttressed by e-commerce would become a sun-rising arena, supporting future business development. Early entry into this field would only benefit, not undermine, the business long-term survival.

Case 3: WD

Business background

The car component retailing business WD was launched by two sisters in early 1998 in Xinjiang, selling car components such as belts, filters, gearboxes, and plugs. With a funding of 100,000 yuan sourced from their savings and sponsorship from their parents, they started the retailing service in the center of Urumqi, the capital of Xinjiang. Today, the company has 21 franchising branches in a range of cities throughout Xinjiang (the geographical size of Xinjiang is equivalent to Iran; due to the massive area Xinjiang covered, the company set up an array of branches to deliver the service). Towards the end of 2016, WD started to merge with an e-commerce company located in Beijing that aimed to construct an overarching online platform to integrate a range of car component retailing companies at the provincial level. In 2016, WD employed 55 people and had annual sales of 40 million yuan and registered assets of 5 million yuan.

E-commerce strategy

WD engaged in e-commerce in 2016 as a consequence of environmental shifts. With the ownership of 21 franchising branches across Xinjiang, WD in the past was perceived by competitors as a competitive force in the market. Yet, this competitiveness was difficult to sustain, due to the oversupply of similar products and competition from online platform companies. The risk of business decline in the short to medium term, if no strategic adjustment was taken, was apparent. The founder explained,

> We are in a difficult position. On the one hand, many small companies are selling similar products. Quality wise, customers are not easy to differentiate good or bad, unless they are specialists. On the other hand, recently online platform companies enter into this sector. Through acquiring competent retailing companies, they buy in not only high quality assets but sector knowhow. Given their technological superiority and sponsorship from venture capitalists, they swiftly extend their market share, pushing us towards the corner.

After a period of brainstorming and family debates, WD finally decided to team up with an online platform design company located in Beijing, and initiated a merging process. The agreement was that after the merger, the family would hold shares of the corporate firm and maintain their control over operations in the Xinjiang region. According to the grand plan, the online platform company would acquire a range of retailing companies akin to WD at the provincial level so that competitive advantages of both parties could be maximized. That is, the online platform company specializing in designing e-commerce interfaces would focus on technological aspects, whilst retailing companies that own customer bases, including garages, car repairing companies, and other direct customers, would concentrate on the development of distribution channels and logistics. The collaboration would offer efficient, accurate, and economic services to a broader group of customers.

During the merger, WD paralleled the online selling to their traditional offline trading, where e-commerce played a complementary role, similar to that in LM. Ultimately, e-commerce would become an overarching strategy for the entire integrated corporate firm. In this context, e-commerce was prominent not only because it acted as a vehicle, offering support to the corporation; more importantly, the scenario shed light on the possibility that e-commerce, as a technological mechanism, might catalyze restructuring and reconfiguration in the entire sector. More interestingly, if this occurred in the car component retailing sector, it would not be surprising if a similar scenario occurred in other sectors, especially service-related sectors.

Influence of the family on e-commerce strategy

E-commerce adoption for WD was a matter of strategic adjustment, not a consequence of family interest, like LM. Between the two sisters, the younger sister (the founder) consistently showed superior business talent and wisdom and was more powerful in personality. Most of the strategic decisions were made by her, whilst in the process the older sister often actively participated, interacted with other stakeholders, and offered her perspective whenever necessary.

E-commerce adoption in the case of WD was rather passive. Neither of the two sisters was familiar with the online technology, nor were they prepared for the effect e-commerce had caused to the sector, which was a traditional field that had little association with high technology. When they realized that new technology was shaking the foundation of the family business, they had no way but to face the reality. Under these circumstances, interpersonal trust, stewardship, and family cohesion, the attributes woven in the family business fabric, came to the fore. Strategic actions such as exploration of technological partners, negotiation on collaborations, and agreement on the merger all occurred in a short time period, which won time for WD and placed it in an advantageous position.

Table 6.3 reports a synthesis and synoptic comparison of the three cases, synthesizing the main aspects of the business background, the business e-commerce strategy, and the family influence on the adoption of e-commerce.

DISCUSSION

Our research addressed how e-commerce strategy affects the family business organization. This impact is reflected in two aspects in our study: the first is on business operations (i.e. industrial impact) and the second is on family relationships (i.e. familial impact). Therefore, our study makes a contribution in that it highlights not only the business issue (e-commerce reshapes business operations) but also the influence of the family on the adoption of e-commerce.

While change in any organization can be planned (top down), emergent (bottom up), contingent on the context in which the organization is embedded, or by management choosing how to respond to their environment (Todnemby, 2005), organizations must manage these changes for the purpose of their business survival and long-term success. In sum, in today's dynamic environment business organizations must be adaptable and respond quickly to change. If not, organizations may be outpaced by competitors, and their overall business value proposition will be threatened.

In our case studies, we noted how the pressure of wider trends influenced the companies to adopt, to a greater or lesser extent, e-commerce practices. This was especially notable in the cases of LM and WD, although deepening their e-commerce engagement was inevitable for JY given the nature of the business. The main motivation for the businesses to adopt e-commerce was related to their search for competitive advantage (Drew, 2003; Phan, 2003; Porter 1990; Bernroider, 2008; Huang, 2008; Levenburg & Magal, 2005), even though in the case of LM there was also the desire to reinforce the relationship with younger-generation employees, considered as key constituents of the business (Access Markets International Partners, 2001; Barua et al., 2001; Chordas, 2001; Zank & Vokurka, 2003). Thus, e-commerce "forced" a change in all three companies, as they restructured to keep up with market trends. However, maintaining and further extending competitive advantages that an organization has in the marketplace are also crucial. Thus, while embracing the opportunity afforded to them by applying e-commerce to their business practices, in weaving e-commerce into the corporate strategy and reconfiguring resources and their operational model accordingly, the case companies engaged in an evolutionary process as described by Molla et al. (2006).

The evidence suggests that the case companies were mindful that e-commerce could either complement or dominate their business value proposition (Samanta & Kyriazopoulos, 2009). When e-commerce was perceived as playing a dominant role as in the case of JY, the business founder organized logistic support and ensured that all the services that the company was offering were lined up with e-commerce. Alternatively, when the use of e-commerce was not deemed as delivering the mainstream organizational value as in the case of LM, the company founder readily "side-lined" e-commerce in their business processes. This posture of the founder was forced to change by the disruptive impact of e-commerce, and she finally reconsidered both the role of e-commerce in the business's corporate strategy and the position of the son in the business strategy design. Notably, the founder's change of perspective was stimulated by her relationship with her daughter who persistently asked her to experience e-commerce from a buyer's perspective. Once she understood the importance of e-commerce for clients, she changed her mind in respect to its role in the business, and the confidence to be attributed to her son.

Finally, in the case of WD, both resource and system barriers (Hadjimanolis, 2000; MacGregor & Kartiwi, 2010) emerged in respect to the unprepared corporate culture and synchronizing of e-commerce with the business practices of the time.

Clearly, the case companies demonstrated agility to engage with e-commerce. With the emergence of IT, market competition has become intensified. In this competitive environment, where the competitive territory is shifting, managers cannot expect to develop long-term solutions or routines for business operations, but to consider nurturing or further developing their agility to continuously reconfigure their resources and resketch strategies to address market changes (Zahra, Sapienza, & Davidsson, 2006): e-commerce presented the case companies with this opportunity.

The case studies also offer some insight on the influence of the family relationship in the adoption of e-commerce, showing the existence of synergies among the family firm's behavioral and social resources and the resulting capabilities that represent the heart of family firm social capital, namely, familiness (Habbershon et al., 2003). The three stories confirm the imperfect imitability of family history (each of the three cases has a different family

Table 6.3   *Synoptic comparison of the three cases*

Business background		
LM	**JW**	**WD**
Health medication products with plants in Beijing and Shanghai.	Online training company specializing in accounting. Began in Beijing as an online training company specializing in accounting in 2010, when the founder	Selling car components such as belts, filters, gearboxes, and plugs.
Initiated e-commerce engagement in 2011, as a result of market transition.	resigned from a computer programming company and commenced the business with his father, an experienced	At the end of 2016, started to merge with an e-commerce company located in Beijing that aimed to construct an overarching online platform to integrate
Risk of losing its human capital, as the younger-generation employees, especially those well educated, often identified themselves with modern business operations, not traditional business routines.	accounting lecturer, and a friend who was an IT specialist.	a range of car component retailing companies at the provincial level.
	User-friendly, flexible approach that differed from conventional training.	In 2016, WD employed 55 people and had annual sales of 40 million yuan and registered assets of 5 million
Approximately 1000 employees in Beijing and Shanghai, and in 2016, 500 million yuan in assets and 6 billion yuan in annual sales.	50 staff members; annual sales around 16 million yuan in 2016.	yuan.
		21 franchising branches in a range of cities.

E-commerce strategy

LM	JW	WD
Initial attempt to combine existing offline selling with the online channels.	The e-commerce adoption approach was organic since startup in 2010.	Engagement in e-commerce in 2016 as a consequence of environmental shifts.
Outcomes far below expectations.	One of the earliest online accounting education firms, founded on the basis of the father's accounting-focused expertise and the son's ICT knowledge.	Challenge: oversupply of similar products and competition from online platform companies.
Adjustment, by making offline and online trading independent, parallel to each other: each with its own team, market segmentation, and associated performance task.	E-commerce as an outcome of natural selection, attributable to the company's online features and available resources.	Decision to team up with an online platform design company located in Beijing, and initiate a merging process.
Expectation: to make the image of the company evolve from that of a traditional manufacturing firm to that of a cutting-edge business equipped with new technology, strategic wisdom, capital market operation expertise, and social responsible orientation.	The courses were delivered via online live lectures, online videos, as well as supplementary face-to-face interaction. E-commerce in this case was rooted into the business operations.	Online platform company specializing in designing e-commerce interfaces focusing on technological aspects, while retailing companies would concentrate on the development of distribution channels and logistics.
Health medication and cosmetic products manufacturing as the foundation of the firm and e-commerce used as an auxiliary tool, opening a new trading platform for the firm, in addition to traditional offline trading.	Challenge in differentiating its service from its competitors, as the founder realized that most of their competitors were offering training by using similar teaching materials and the same curriculum set up by accreditation bodies.	Initially, e-commerce played a complementary role.
At the second stage, the adoption of e-commerce produced a relevant impact on the corporate vision, generating a focus change from health medication, to a wider model of providing any product that could give customers and employees greater, better, and a more quality life.		Ultimately, e-commerce would become an overarching strategy for the entire integrated corporate firm.

Impact of the family on e-commerce strategy

LM	JW	WD
E-commerce adoption as a result of family relationship balancing between the founder and her son.	Intergenerational relationship harmonious and pleasant.	The relationship between the two sisters was sound and well balanced
The founder believed that business survival ought to rely on manufacturing, while e-commerce may help in extending marketing capacity.	Although he was not a specialist in management, the father was happy to contribute and offer his own perspective to his son for reference.	The younger sister (the founder) consistently showed superior business talent and wisdom and was more powerful in personality. Most strategic decisions were made by her.
The son perceived e-commerce as a mechanism to restructure the organization fundamentally.	This was helpful to the son when the decision on e-commerce was made, since the interaction was constructive, encouraging a more rounded and bespoke decision to be taken.	The older sister often actively participated, interacted with other stakeholders, and offered her perspective whenever necessary.
Since the founder considered herself as "the empress" and the son as "subordinate," the son was eventually assigned to be in charge of the e-commerce division, but e-commerce was configured to serve as a marketing strategy, not an overarching strategy.	Eventually, e-commerce was adopted as a corporate strategy as this laid within the boundary of the son's specialty knowledge.	E-commerce adoption was rather passive: a matter of strategic adjustment, not a consequence of family interest compromising.
The appointment of the son was mainly to keep him identified with the firm, as well as satisfying his desire for independence.	Additionally, the son believed services buttressed by e-commerce would become sun-rising sectors, supporting future business development.	Neither of the two sisters was familiar with online technology, nor were they prepared for the effect e-commerce would have on the sector.
In the coming years, e-commerce would only play a supplementary role.	Early entry into this field would only benefit, not undermine, the business's long-term survival.	When they realized that new technology was shaking the foundation of the family business, they had to face reality.
The ability of the son to work behind the scenes, actively advocating e-commerce and proposing the new strategy, determined the smooth but substantial transformation of the business strategy, without challenging his mother's leadership.		Interpersonal trust, stewardship, and family cohesion, the attributes woven into the family business fabric, came to the fore.
A significant change in the founder's attitude towards e-commerce happened when her daughter introduced her to online shopping.		Strategic actions such as exploration of technological partners, negotiation on collaboration, and agreement on the merge occurred in a short time period, which gained time and placed the company in an advantageous position.

history), the social complexity of informal decision making, and the casual ambiguity created by family routines (Pearson et al., 2008).

They also show the existence of a dynamic relationship between structural, cognitive, and relational dimensions, that generates the conditions of strategic alignment indispensable to adopt a dramatically innovative strategic decision, such as the one to enter e-commerce.

In JY and WD, e-commerce was brought in relatively easily where the family relationship was harmonious and mutually respectful. The father and son in JY and the two sisters in WD were stewards, who shared common interests and had a common understanding of business operations and the strategic position. Where e-commerce adoption was concerned, teamwork, an equal relationship, and collaboration at the top management level were available, and this further motivated non-family employees to take collective action. Although e-commerce was finally positioned at different levels in JY and WD, there was a spirit of unanimity shared by family members, resulting in a comfortable settling in of the new technology.

The situation in LM differed, where the intergenerational relationship was more like principal versus agent. Intergenerational conflict in this case existed where the founder was more autocratic and demanded compliance from the younger generation. In China, the underlying philosophy of Confucianism creates highly paternal, hierarchical structures in which respect to the senior generation is demanded (Goel, He, & Karri, 2011). In this context, intergenerational conflict that may be dealt with openly in the West is unlikely to be aired, let alone solved. In LM, e-commerce was to a certain extent adopted as a compromising strategy to minimize agency behavior. Nevertheless, the disruptive impact of e-commerce induced a change in the founder's attitude when she finally understood its relevance for the long-term survival of the business. And such an attitude was favored by the influence of a family member (the daughter) who had no official and factual engagement with the business, but (perhaps just because of this) was able to make the founder open her mind and consider e-commerce from a different perspective. This is consistent with Pearson et al.'s (2008) suggestion that in a family firm, the family and the business do not exist as distinct entities, but, instead, are enmeshed with one another, creating a complex, interactive web of relationships encompassing both the family and the firm, and that familiness arises from the synergies among the behavioral and social resources contained within the system.

The literature has highlighted that among the many sources of motivation that drive family businesses to engage in e-commerce is a search for resource advantage through developing and strengthening the relationship with key constituents (Access Markets International Partners, 2001; Barua et al., 2001; Chordas, 2001; Zank & Vokurka, 2003). Our cases highlight that in addition to suppliers, customers, and other stakeholders – such as workers in the case of

LM – the family has to be recognized as a key constituent in family businesses, and one that stands in a very influential position (Sharma, Chrisman, & Chua, 1997; Chua et al., 1999; Dyer 2003).

IMPLICATIONS, PROPOSED CONCEPTUALIZATION, AND FUTURE RESEARCH AGENDA

Our findings suggest that in applying e-commerce to the business process, the peculiar characteristics of family businesses create unique challenges to corporate strategy design and implementation.

Our research supports the proposition that e-commerce has an impact on the culture of the organization. That is, because e-commerce disrupts both the structure and operations of an organization, the organizational culture in particular is the locus of control. In family businesses, the locus of control is highly significant, and this is usually the family (in many cases, the founder). Thus, our contribution lies in providing a preliminary illustration that an e-commerce strategy disrupts the family in the family business. This, of course, has long-term implications for the continuity of the family business.

All the case study companies seem to support the proposition that along with other enabling and constraining factors that are identified in the literature, the family should also be considered as a crucial element in strategic changes. Thus, our exploratory research has identified the family as a key variable in addition to those identified by Molla et al. (2006) as specifically influencing corporate strategy and e-commerce adoption in family businesses (see Figure 6.1). We therefore adjust the original model proposed by Molla et al. (2006) to include the family and its dynamics as being among the influencing factors affecting e-commerce and corporate strategy in family businesses (Figure 6.3).

In considering our findings, we suggest that the concept of dynamic capabilities may be relevant in respect to the agility of family businesses to continuously reconfigure their resources and resketch strategies to address not only market changes (Zahra et al., 2006), but also internal challenges related to the relationship between family members. Originally, the term dynamic capabilities referred to a firm's ability to integrate, build, and refigure external and internal competencies to take advantage of rapidly changing environments (Teece, Pisano, & Shuen, 1997). In China, the concept has been usefully applied to understanding how the broader environment that frames business operations (Li & Lui, 2014) and the relational environment within firms them-selves (Lin, Su, & Higgins, 2016) influences the dynamic capability of firms to embrace management innovations. Thus, while Li and Lui (2014) found that environmental dynamism within the broader environmental context is a driver for the adoption of dynamic capabilities that can contribute to the firm performance, Lin et al. (2016) found that the relational capability of managers themselves acted as a dynamic capability that, in turn, influenced the propensity to adopt management innovations such as in e-commerce applications.

This conceptualization seems relevant to the findings from our case studies. We thus suggest that this conceptualization of dynamic capabilities – particularly the relational capability – may be useful in analyzing how the influence of the family contributes in configuring the fitting of e-commerce into the corporate strategy of family businesses. That is, when perceived as a dynamic capability that is influenced by both the broader environmental dynamism in which a firm operates, as well as the internal affect-related relationships in a firm, the choice of the e-commerce business model may well be explained as one that balances the need of effectiveness and efficiency that satisfies market interests, and that manages the influence of the family over the business and maintains efficacy in decision making.

Our research contributes to the suggestion by Astrachan (2010) that further research is needed in examining how family dynamics affect strategic issues such as innovation. Nevertheless, we are unsure whether this finding is unique to the Chinese context, or perhaps an emerging economy phenomenon, and we recognize the need for further research to understand the dynamics that we report here.

Our findings give a positive answer to both the question of whether the adoption of e-commerce has an influence on family businesses, and whether family dynamics influence e-commerce strategy in family businesses.

Nevertheless, a number of gaps and controversies need to be overcome to advance our understanding of the impact of e-commerce on family businesses. Further research is needed to answer such questions as how family influence accommodates to the new environment, given that control is often a core concern of family businesses. How do family businesses adjust their resources and processes to align with the e-commerce business model? What education and training should family businesses adopt for their key actors to ensure effective strategic thinking? How do family businesses sustain and further develop their socioemotional (Berrone et al., 2012) and financial wealth? How do family businesses adjust their resources and processes to develop competitive advantages in the new climate?

Our future research agenda will investigate some of these aspects further. We hope to develop a longitudinal study drawing on our case studies and other firms to monitor how the family and the business reciprocally influence the process of e-commerce adoption and corporate strategy. Further, as the topic has only been qualitatively investigated, it needs validation through quantitative studies. We hope to develop reliable and valid instruments of analysis to this aim. These instruments form the foundation of the quantitative study and their relationships with e-commerce adoption and family influence can then be tested. We further hope that we may be able to utilize an action-research

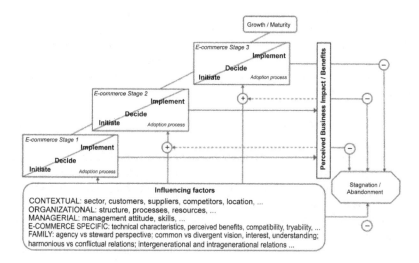

Figure 6.3   *Conceptual model for e-commerce adoption process in family businesses*

agenda in implementing studies. However, given the limitations that we describe below of working with firms in the research site, we will have to consider our methodological approach carefully. Nonetheless, the importance of being able to undertake this research is that we will garner a rich canon of research that will inform us how these dynamics affect continuity as a family business. The significance of family businesses not only in China but also worldwide makes this a worthwhile endeavor.

LIMITATIONS OF THE STUDY

This study is not short of limitations, one of which is related to the research environment. First, family business as a business entity is relatively new in China. Family businesses sporadically emerged in China after the economic reform in 1979. Family firms as a whole do not feel comfortable with the family icon, due to ideological and historical reasons. Though the three companies involved accepted our research invitation, the extent of revelation of family-related issues or interactions between family and business was limited. In fact, two companies repeatedly queried the research purpose and the potential usage of research findings at the beginning of the interviews, and one even made it clear that she would strategically answer the questions, depending on the research purpose. Given the concerns that entrepreneurs have, it is less likely that researchers portray a comprehensive picture of the businesses studied. Second, Ralston et al. (1996) recognized wide-ranging variations among businesses from different regions of China. While the level of regional economy influences business operations, technological infrastructure and sociocultural factors may have an impact on businesses. The three companies scrutinized in the current study were from two regions, Beijing and Xinjiang, which only capture limited indigenous features of China.

CONCLUDING REMARKS

Research on e-commerce adoption and the impact of family dynamics is scarce in the field of family business studies, though the significance of the research focus is potentially remarkable. The current study provides empirical evidence that irrespective of the way e-commerce is maneuvered in businesses – either as an overarching platform or an auxiliary tool – there can be significant consequences on family dynamics, rather than simply on business matters. We suggest that future research in this field will further benefit from cross-cultural comparison and longitudinal investigation. Indeed, the whole realm has remarkable space for future development and warrants substantial effort before one can expect to develop domain-specific theories.

NOTES

1. www.ffi.org/page/GlobalDataPoints.
2. In China, there has been a compound annual growth rate of 120 percent since 2003 in the e-commerce market. Further, e-commerce transactions from China commanded 5–6 percent of total world retail sales in 2012, compared to the United States share of 5 percent (Dobbs, Chen, Orr, Manyika, & Chang, 2013).
3. It is estimated that of the country's 10 million privately owned companies, 80 percent are family businesses (All China Federation of Industry and Commerce as quoted in "The Chinese family business in transition," http://blog.msc -entrepreneurship.com/the-chinese-family-business-in-transition/).

REFERENCES

Access Markets International Partners (2001). Analysis of the US small business internet environment. January. Washington, DC: US Small Business Administration.

Astrachan J. H. (2010) Strategy in family business: Toward a multidimensional research agenda. *Journal of Family Business Strategy*, 1, 6–14.

Astrachan, J. H., & Kolenko, T. (1994). A neglected factor explaining family business success: Human resource practices. *Family Business Review*, 7, 251–62.

Barua, A., Konana, P., Whinston, A., & Yin, F. (2001). Driving e-business excellence. *MIT Sloan Management Review*, Fall, 36–44.

Bernroider, E. W. N. (2008). E-marketing utilisation, endogenous situation and organizational performance in small Austrian software businesses. *International Journal of Internet Marketing and Advertising*, 4(2–3), 262–80.

Berrone, P., Cruz, C., & Gomez-Mejia, L. R. (2012). Socioemotional wealth in family firms: Theoretical dimensions, assessment approaches, and agenda for future research. *Family Business Review*, 25(3), 258–79.

Brunninge, O., Nordqvist, M., & Wiklund, J. (2007). Corporate governance and strategic change in SMEs: The effects of ownership, board composition and top management teams. *Small Business Economics*, 29, 295–308.

Caspersz D., Wang Y., Tomaselli S. & Pei R. (2019). Exploring the intersection of e-commerce and context in family business in China: The effects on organisational form and identity, in D'Allura, G.M., Colli, A. and Goel S. (eds), *Family Firms and Institutional Contexts: Business Models, Innovation and Competitive Advantage*, (pp. 304–23). Cheltenham, UK and Northampton, USA: Edward Elgar Publishing Ltd.

Chang, K.-c., Jackson, J., & Grover, V. (2002). E-commerce and corporate strategy: An executive perspective. *Information and Management*, 40(7), 663–75.

Chaston, I. (2001). The internet and e-commerce: An opportunity to examine organizational learning in progress in small manufacturing firms? *International Small Business Journal*, 19(2), 13–30.

Chepaitis, E. V. (2002). E-commerce and the information environment in an emerging economy: Russia at the turn of the century. In P. C. Palvia, S. C. H. Palvia, & E. M. Roche (eds), *Global Information Technology and Electronic Commerce: Issues for the New Millennium* (pp. 53–72). Marietta, GA: Ivy League.

Chiware, E. R. T., & Dick, A. L. (2008). The use of ICTs in Namibia's SME sector to access business information services. *The Electronic Library*, 26(2), 145.

Chordas, L. (2001). Finding the e-payoff. *Best's Review: Technology Supplement*, September, S5–S8.

Chrisman, J. J., Chua, J. H., & Litz, R. (2003). A unified systems perspective of family firm performance: An extension and integration. *Journal of Business Venturing*, 18, 467–72.

Chrisman, J. J., Chua, J. H., & Sharma P. (2005). Trends and directions in the development of a strategic management theory of the family firm. *Entrepreneurship Theory and Practice*, 23(3), 555–75.

Chua, J. H., Chrisman, J. J., & Sharma P. (1999). Defining the family business by behavior. *Entrepreneurship Theory and Practice*, 23, 19–39.

Cloete, E., Courtney, S., & Fintz, J. (2002). Small businesses' acceptance and adoption of ecommerce in the Western Cape province of South Africa. *Electronic Journal of Information Systems in Developing Countries*, 10(4), 1–13.

Creswell, J. (2012). W.(1994). Research design: Qualitative and quantitative approaches. *Thousand Oaks*, 88(2), 207.

De Massis, A., P. Sharma, J. H. Chua, & J. J. Chrisman (2012). *Family Business Studies: An Annotated Bibliography*. Cheltenham, UK and Northampton, MA, USA: Edward Elgar Publishing.

De Massis, A., Frattini, F., Pizzurno, E., & Cassia, L. (2015). Product innovation in family versus nonfamily firms: An exploratory analysis. *Journal of Small Business Management*, 53(1), 1–36.

Dedrick, J., & Kraemer, K. L. (2001). China IT report. *Electronic Journal of Information Systems in Developing Countries*, 6(2), 1–10.

Dobbs, R., Chen, Y., Orr, G., Manyika, J., & Chang, E. (2013). China's e-tail revolution: Online shopping as a catalyst for global growth. McKinsey Global Institute.

Drew, S. (2003). Strategic uses of e-commerce by SMEs in the east of England. *European Management Journal*, 21(1), 79–88.

Dyer, W. G., Jr. (2003). The family: The missing variable in organizational research. *Entrepreneurship: Theory and Practice*, 27, 401–16.

Ensley, M. D., & Pearson, A. W. (2005). An exploratory comparison of the behavioral dynamics of top management teams in family and nonfamily new ventures: Cohesion, conflict, potency, and consensus. *Entrepreneurship Theory and Practice*, 29(3), 267–84.

Gadish, D. (2009). Online marketing of a dental supply e-store on a tight budget. *Journal of Cases on Information Technology*, 11(1), 1–14.

Goel, S., He, X., & Karri, R. (2011). Family involvement in a hierarchical culture: Effect of dispersion of family ownership control and family member tenure on firm performance in Chinese family owned firms. *Journal of Family Business Strategy*, 2(4), 199–206.

Griffith, D. A., & Krampf, R. F. (1998). An examination of the web-based strategies of the top 100 US retailers. *Journal of Marketing Theory and Practice*, 6(3), 12–23.

Habbershon, T. G., & Williams, M. L. (1999). A resource-based framework for assessing the strategic advantage of family firms. *Family Business Review*, 12, 1–15.

Habbershon, T. G., Williams, M. L., & Daniel, J. (1998). *Toward a definition of 'familiness'*. Working Paper. Snider Entrepreneurial Research Center, Wharton School, University of Pennsylvania.

Habbershon, T. G., Williams, M., & MacMillan, I. C. (2003). A unified systems perspective of family firm performance. *Journal of business venturing*, 18(4), 451–65.

Hadjimanolis, A. (2000). An investigation of innovation antecedents in small firms in the context of a small developing country. *R&D Management*, 30, 235–45.

Haig, M. (2001). *The B2B E-commerce Handbook: How to Transform Your Business-to-Business Global Marketing Strategy*. London: Kogan Page.

Herbig, P., & Hale, B. (1997). Internet: The marketing challenge of the twentieth century. *Internet Research*, 7(2), 95–100.

Huang, L. (2008). Bed and breakfast industry adopting e-commerce strategies in e-service. *Service Industries Journal*, 28(5), 633–48.

Jennex, M. E., Amoroso, D., & Adelakun, O. (2004). E-commerce infrastructure success factors for small companies in developing economies. *Electronic Commerce Research*, 4(3), 263–86.

Koeberle-Schmid, A., & Caspersz, D. (2013). Family governance bodies: A conceptual typology. In K. X. Smyrnios, P. Z. Poutziouris, & S. Goel, S. (eds), *Handbook of Research on Family Business*, Second Edition (pp. 125–41). Cheltenham, UK and Northampton, MA, USA: Edward Elgar Publishing.

König A., Kammerlander N., & Enders A. (2013). The family innovator's dilemma: How family influence affects the adoption of discontinuous technologies by incumbent firms. *Academy of Management Review*, 38(3), 418–41.

Lagrosen, S. (2005). Effects of the internet on the marketing communication of service companies. *Journal of Services Marketing*, 19(2), 63–9.

Levenburg, N. M., & Klein, H. A. 2006. Delivering customer services online: Identifying best practices of medium-sized enterprises. *Information Systems Journal*, 16(2), 135–55.

Levenburg, N. M., & Magal, S. R. (2005). Applying importance-performance analysis to evaluate e-business strategies among small firms. *e-Service Journal*, 3(3), 29–48.

Levenburg, N. M., Schwarz, T. V., & Dandridge, T. C. (2002). Understanding adoption of internet technologies. *Proceedings of the 16th Annual USASBE National Conference*, January 17–20.

Li, Da-yuan & Lui, J. (2014). Dynamic capabilities, environmental dynamism, and competitive advantage: evidence from China. *Journal of Business Research*, 67(1), 2793–9.

Lin, Hai-Fen., Su, Jing-Qin., & Higgins, A. (2016). How dynamic capabilities affect the adoption of management innovations. *Journal of Business Research*, 69, 862–76.

MacGregor, R. C., & Kartiwi, M. (2010). Perception of barriers to e-commerce adoption in SMEs in a developed and developing country: A comparison between Australia and Indonesia. *Journal of Electronic Commerce in Organizations*, 8(1), 61–82.

Markus, M. L., & Robey, D. (1988). Information technology and organizational change: causal structure in theory and research. *Management science*, 34(5), 583–98.

Markus, M. L., & Soh, C. (2002). Structural influences on global e-commerce activity. *Journal of Global Information Management*, 10(1), 5–12.

Merriam, S. B. (1988). *Case Study Research in Education: A Qualitative Approach*. San Francisco, CA: Jossey-Bass.

Miller, D., Steier, L., & Le Breton-Miller, I. (2003). Lost in time: Intergenerational succession, change, and failure in family business. *Journal of Business Venturing*, 18(4), 513–31.

Miller, D., & Le Breton-Miller, I. (2005). *Managing for the Long Run: Lesson in Competitive Advantage from Great Family Businesses*. Boston, MA: Harvard Business School Press.

Molla, A., Heeks, R., & Balcells, I. (2006). Adding clicks to bricks: A case study of e-commerce adoption by a Catalan small retailer. *European Journal of Information Systems*, 15(4), 424–38.

Mukti, N. A. (2000). Barriers to putting businesses on the internet in Malaysia. *Electronic Journal of Information Systems in Developing Countries*, 2(6), 1–6.

Mutula, S. M., & Van Brakel, P. (2007). ICT skills readiness for the emerging global digital economy among small businesses in developing countries: Case study of Botswana. *Library Hi Tech*, 25(2), 231–45.

Narver, J. C., & Slater, S. F. (1990). The effect of a market orientation on business profitability. *Journal of Marketing*, 54(4), 20–35.

Oshikoya, T. W., & Hussain, M. N. (1998). Information technology and the challenge of economic development in Africa. *African Development Review*, 10(1), 100–33.

Oshikoya, T. W., & Hussain, M. N. (2007). Information technology and the challenge of economic development. *African E-Markets Information and Economic Development*, 43–76.

Pearson, A. W., Carr, J. C., & Shaw, J. C. (2008). Toward a theory of familiness: A social capital perspective. *Entrepreneurship Theory and Practice*, 32(6), 949–69.

Phan, D. D. (2003). E-business development for competitive advantages: A case study. *Information and Management*, 40(6), 581–90.

Pool, P. W., Parnell, J. A., Spillan, J. E., Carraher, S., & Lester, D. L. (2006). Are SMEs meeting the challenge of integrating e-commerce into their businesses? A review of the development, challenges and opportunities. *International Journal of Information Technology and Management*, 5(2–3), 97–113.

Porter, M. (1990). *The Competitive Advantage of Nations*. Basingstoke: Macmillan.

Pratt, J. H. (2002). E-biz: Strategies for small business success. Small Business Administration Office of Advocacy.

Ralston, D. A., Yu, K. C., Wang, X., Terpstra, R. H., Gustafson, D. J., & Wei, H. (1996). The cosmopolitan Chinese manager: Findings of a study on managerial values across the six regions of China. *Journal of International Management*, 2, 79–109.

Salvato C., & Corbetta G. (2014). Strategic content and process in family business. In L. Melin, M. Nordqvist, & P. Sharma (eds), *The SAGE Handbook of Family Businesses* (pp. 295–320). London: Sage.

Samanta, I., & Kyriazopoulos, P. (2009). The effect of e-marketing in hotel sector in Greece. *International Journal of Knowledge and Learning*, 5(5–6), 490–504.

Schlegelmilch, B. B., Diamantopoulos, A., & Kreuz, P. (2003). Strategic innovation: The construct, its drivers and its strategic outcomes. *Journal of Strategic Marketing*, 11(2), 117–32.

Schulze, W. S., Lubatkin, M. H., Dino, R. N., & Buchholtz, A. K. (2001). Agency relationships in family firms: Theory and evidence. *Organization Science*, 12(2), 99–116.

Sharma P., Chrisman J. J., & Chua J. H. (1997). Strategic management of the family business: Past research and future challenges. *Family Business Review*, 10(1), 1–36.

Stephenson, H. B., Lockwood, D. L., & Raven, P. (2003). The entrepreneur's guide to the strategic use of the internet. Meeting of the Small Business Institute, New Orleans.

Surjadjaja, H., Ghosh, S., & Antony, F. (2003). Determining and assessing the determinants of e-service operations. *Managing Service Quality*, 13(1), 39–53.

Teece, D. J., Pisano, G., & Shuen, A. (1997). Dynamic capabilities and strategic management. *Strategic Management Journal*, 18(7), 509–33.

Todnemby, R. (2005). Organizational change management: A critical review. *Journal of Change Management*, 5(4), 369–80.

Tornatzky, L. G., & Fleischer, M. (1990). *The Processes of Technological Innovation*. Lexington, MA: Lexington Books.

Turban, E., Outland, J., King, D., Lee, J. K., Liang, T.-P., & Turban, D. C. (2018). *Electronic Commerce 2018: A Managerial and Social Networks Perspective*. Cham: Springer International.

Westhead, P., Cowling, M., & Howorth C. (2001). The development of family companies: Management and ownership imperatives. *Family Business Review*, 14(4), 369–85.

Whetten, D., Foreman, P., & Dyer, W. G. (2014). Organizational identity and family business. In L. Melin, M. Nordqvist, & P. Sharma (eds), *The Sage Handbook of Family Business* (pp. 480–97). London: Sage.

Zahra, S. A., Sapienza, H. J., & Davidsson, P. (2006). Entrepreneurship and dynamic capabilities: A review, model and research agenda. *Journal of Management Studies*, 43(4), 917–55.

Zank, G. M., & Vokurka, R. J. (2003). The internet: Motivations, deterrents, and impact on supply chain relationships. *SAM Advanced Management Journal*, Spring, 33–40.

Zellweger, T. M., Eddleston, K., & Kellermans, F. W. (2010). Exploring the concept of familiness: Introducing family firm identity. *Journal of Family Business Strategy*, 1, 54–63.

Zhao, J., Wang, S., & Huang, W. V. (2008). A study of B2B e-market in China: E-commerce process perspective. *Information and Management*, 45(4), 242–8.

Table 6A.1   Literature table

Author	Journal	Purpose of the study/ research questions	Data source	Data location	Method	Findings
Barua, Konana, Whinston, & Yin (2001)	*Sloan Management Review*	Discuss how does a firm achieves operational excellence through e-business.	Approximately 1125 firms in the manufacturing, retail, distribution, and wholesale sectors, that had a corporate website and also used traditional channels of business	USA	Phone and web-based survey, using questionnaire consisted of 39 items for 10 drivers.	Propose an operational model of e-business value creation, rooted in IT business value research, that provides a reference framework for management and offers guidance for e-business strategies.

Author	Journal	Purpose of the study/ research questions	Data source	Data location	Method	Findings
Bernroider (2008)	*International Journal of Internet Marketing and Advertising*	Analyze whether the endogenous situation faced by the firm is interrelated with the applied level of e-marketing initiatives. Develop a generic model of a firm's competitiveness that can be applied to any company of the target group, regardless of the products or services it produces.	141 software firms	Austria	Structured face-to-face interviews based on a stratified and disproportional sample with subgroups according to company size.	Firms that perceive their relative strengths on branding, pricing, product diversity, internationalization, and access to new technologies have adopted more advanced e-marketing support. The results reveal evidence supporting a positive relationship between assessed organizational performance factors and e-marketing utilization, especially in medium enterprises (MEs). The research assumption that a more intense e-marketing usage is connected with a stronger competitive position is supported by the analysis.

Author	Journal	Purpose of the study/ research questions	Data source	Data location	Method	Findings
Chang, Jackson, & Grover (2002)	*Information and Management*	Explore the integration between corporate strategy and e-commerce.	145 Fortune 500 firms	USA	Content analysis of chief executive officer's letter to shareholders.	E-commerce initiatives are important strategic initiatives, and firms with a stronger e-commerce market orientation will be more successful.
Chaston (2001)	*International Small Business Journal*	Fill the gap in empirical evidence in the small firms literature on the relative importance of double- versus single-loop learning and the role of the learning systems required to support the learning process.	188 small manufacturing firms	UK	Focus group with 56 senior managers of small UK manufacturing firms, followed by a large survey emailed to managing directors of 800 small UK manufacturing firms randomly selected. Component analysis, analysis and multivariate analysis of variance performed on data.	A double-loop learning style which can lead to new core competencies and competitive advantage in respect to those competitors adopting a single-loop learning style.

Author	Journal	Purpose of the study/ research questions	Data source	Data location	Method	Findings
Chiware & Dick (2008)	*The Electronic Library*	Assess the current levels of use and the potential of the technologies in increasing information dissemination and increasing enterprises' competitiveness.	197 SME operators and 35 business support organizations	Namibia	Two questionnaires, plus a qualitative assessment of business information services, carried out in 15 business support organizations.	The adoption of e-commerce strategy falls into the category of discontinuous innovation, asking for strategic innovation, since it calls for fundamental reconceptualization of the business model and the reshaping of existing markets (by breaking the rules and changing the nature of competition) to achieve dramatic value improvements for customers and high growth for companies.
Cloete, Courtney, & Fintz (2002)	*Electronic Journal of Information Systems in Developing Countries*	Explore how small businesses in a developing country perceive the potential benefit of e-commerce and look at their consequent adoption of e-commerce activities in their own organizations.	34 small manufacturing businesses	South Africa	Questionnaire to test the perception of e-commerce benefits and e-commerce adoption levels amongst small manufacturing businesses in the Western Cape.	The available technologies are not adopted to the extent that it is necessary for survival in a rapidly changing environment.

Author	Journal	Purpose of the study/ research questions	Data source	Data location	Method	Findings
Dedrick & Kraemer (2001)	*Electronic Journal of Information Systems in Developing Countries*	Report on the state of the art in China on internet, e-commerce, government policy, computer market, software, IT services, and computers production.	Existing literature	China	Review of government reports and documents	There are many barriers that must be surmounted if China is to tap into the potential of the internet and e-commerce, including high telecommunications cost, lack of needed legal guidelines, and some aspects of consumer behavior and business practices.
Drew (2003)	*European Management Journal*	Explore areas of the strategic uses of e-commerce.	200 businesses which (1) had established active websites, (2) appeared to be conducting e-business to some degree, (3) fit the UK definition of an SME, and (4) were independent rather than the subsidiary or branch of another entity.	East of England	Survey based on questionnaire	The most important driving forces for adopting e-commerce are industry changes and trends, opportunities for growth, the need to keep up with competitors, and the threat posed by larger competitors.
Gadish (2009)	*Journal of Cases on Information Technology*	Analyze the marketing strategy of an online store.	Case study of a family-owned and operated dental supply company, serving the local community of dentists.	USA	Case analysis	A decision to modernize sales processes came as revenues from the traditional model started falling and existing clients started ordering dental supplies from competitors.

Author	Journal	Purpose of the study/ research questions	Data source	Data location	Method	Findings
Griffith & Krampf (1998)	*Journal of Marketing Theory and Practice*	Examine the strategic uses of web-based retailing for traditional retailers.	Top 100 US retailers	USA	Comprehensive content analysis of websites.	A majority of retailers are utilizing their websites for advertising, public relations, and customer services access.
Hadjimanolis (1999)	*R&D Management*	Identify the main factors influencing innovativeness in small firms.	140 businesses	Cyprus	Correlation, multiple regression, and multiple discriminant analysis, based on interviews following a 20-page questionnaire.	The main variables affecting innovation include strategy, expenditure on research and development, cooperation with external technology providers, use of technological information sources, and overall performance of the firm. Contrary to literature claims, intensity of competition was not correlated with innovation.

Author	Journal	Purpose of the study/ research questions	Data source	Data location	Method	Findings
Herbig & Hale (1997)	*Internet Research*	Discuss the future of the internet, and its impact on marketing strategies.	Press articles, opinion leader speeches and interviews, and other second-hand data	USA	Summary of press articles.	The computerized information boom has enormous potential to boost economies worldwide. Access to the web is proving to be a much greater resource than traditional means of advertising. The internet can help companies appeal to audiences of all ages, build customer relationships by providing information on products, and allow small businesses to compete with Fortune 500 companies without incurring the costs expected in such an undertaking.

Author	Journal	Purpose of the study/ research questions	Data source	Data location	Method	Findings
Huang (2008)	*Service Industries Journal*	Investigate the B&B adoption of e-commerce strategy, and empirically build a model for the burgeoning B&B industry adopting e-commerce strategies in e-service.	155 B&B businesses	Taiwan	Longitudinal analysis by descriptive statistics, factor analysis, and linear structural relations.	Identified the e-commerce development strategy dimensions by business as being pursued to gain resource advantage, competitive advantage, and performance advantage. Resource advantage mainly consists of improving professional management capabilities and increasing the likelihood of adopting a double-loop form of organizational learning which can lead to new core competencies and competitive advantage.

Author	Journal	Purpose of the study/ research questions	Data source	Data location	Method	Findings
Jennex, Amoroso, & Adelakun (2004)	*Electronic Commerce Research*	Analyze infrastructure factors affecting the success of small companies in developing economies that are establishing business to business e-commerce ventures.	Two case studies	Italy and Ukraine	Action research and case studies of two companies.	There are five main success factors for companies establishing business-to-business e-commerce ventures: people factor, technical infrastructure, client interface, business infrastructure, and regulatory interface. Each factor has several attributes.

Author	Journal	Purpose of the study/ research questions	Data source	Data location	Method	Findings
Levenburg & Magal (2005)	*e-Service Journal*	Demonstrate the value of Importance Performance Analysis as a tool to assess e-business strategy based on underlying motivation, and make resource allocation recommendations. Identify small firms' motivations for engaging in e-business.	Evaluate e-business strategies among small organizations and make resource allocation recommendations.	USA	Importance Performance Analysis	Motivations to engage in e-commerce fall into different categories: (1) marketing-related; (2) desire to develop and strengthen a relationship with key constituents; (3) aim to improve financial performance; (4) desire to obtain information; (5) buying reasons. Results indicate that customer-focused motivations are most important in adopting e-business; improving profitability is least important.

Author	Journal	Purpose of the study/ research questions	Data source	Data location	Method	Findings
Levenburg & Klein (2006)	*Information Systems Journal*	Examine the practices of small and medium-sized enterprises and analyze performance results of adopting selected customer service applications on the internet.	400 SMEs	USA	Six-page self-administered survey questionnaire mailed to sample businesses, selected from the Dun and Bradstreet database. Selected businesses were at least five years old, had five or more employees, and resided in the locale of interest.	Those SMEs that have adopted the internet have experienced significant and positive benefits. Medium-sized organizations (51–250 employees) are more experienced and sophisticated internet users. Offering online ordering capabilities has a positive impact on perceived sales, while online product demonstrations and engaging in email for customer service purposes have positive impacts on perceived net profits.

Author	Journal	Purpose of the study/research questions	Data source	Data location	Method	Findings
MacGregor & Kartiwi (2010)	*Journal of Electronic Commerce in Organizations*	Compare the perception of barriers to e-commerce adoption in developed and developing economies.	247 non-adopters in Australia; 96 non-adopters in Indonesia.	Australia and Indonesia	247 phone interviews in Australia, 330 surveys distributed in Indonesia. The Cronchbach's Alpha test for reliability was applied to both sets of data.	The perception of importance of barriers to e-commerce adoption differs across the two locations. Security is far more critical in developing economies.
Markus & Soh (2002)	*Journal of Global Information Management*	Explore the influence of structural condition on e-commerce activity	Literature	Asia and USA	Review of the literature	Valid explanation of global differences in e-commerce activity requires a careful assessment of relevant structural factors, varying across countries and cultures. Among these factors there are physical, social, and economic arrangements that shape e-commerce business models and that influence individual and organizational uses of the internet.

Author	Journal	Purpose of the study/research questions	Data source	Data location	Method	Findings
Molla, Heeks, & Balcells (2006)	*European Journal of Information Systems*	Explore why and how one small business adopted e-commerce.	Single case study (wine retailing microenterprise).	Spain	Detailed interviews with the owner-manager, accompanied with examination of pertinent internal documentation such as annual reports, financial statements, minutes, web design drafts.	Expand the technology-organizations-environment framework developed by Tornatzky and Fleischer (1990), by including managerial factors and grouping the factors affecting e-commerce adoption into four categories: contextual, organizational, managerial, and e-commerce. Confirm the value of understanding e-commerce adoption in small enterprises through a four-way categorization, encompassing contextual organizational, managerial, and e-commerce factors. Highlights the way in which the adoption of e-commerce involves phases of initiation, decision, and implementation. Offers historical insight into the process of e-commerce adoption.

Author	Journal	Purpose of the study/research questions	Data source	Data location	Method	Findings
Mukti (2000)	*Electronic Journal of Information Systems in Developing Countries*	Identify potential barriers to e-commerce expansion.	50 businesses engaged in e-commerce.	Malaysia	Postal survey.	The most recurrent categories of barriers to e-commerce adoption relate to security, and the uncertain nature of the legal contract between supplier and customer.

Author	Journal	Purpose of the study/research questions	Data source	Data location	Method	Findings
Mutula & Van Brakel (2007)	*Library Hi Tech*	Characterize the ICT sector in terms of, among other things, the skills needs in the sector for the purpose of powering the emerging digital economy. Cover the status of ICT skills for the digital economy in both developed and developing countries.	55 key stakeholders within the ICT sector in Botswana, including Botswana Telecommunication Corporation, Botswana Power Corporation, the business community, academia, researchers, and legal experts.	Botswana	Focus group to collect data from key stakeholders in the ICT sector. Analysis of data using thematic categorization.	Highlights the existence of an acute global shortage of high-skilled and hands-on personnel necessary for steering the emerging digital economy, in both developed and developing countries, including Botswana. There is a serious skills gap for certified specialists to help develop the sophisticated applications necessary to power the digital economy and more so the applications that depend on it.

Author	Journal	Purpose of the study/research questions	Data source	Data location	Method	Findings
Oshikoya & Hussain (1998)	*African Development Review*	Analyze the challenges and developmental issues faced by African countries in respect to ICT.	Literature	Africa	Review of literature.	African countries face a number of critical issues related to development. Integrating Africa into the world of IT with its vast global infrastructure will provide the means that address most of these challenges. To this end, African countries need to upgrade their capabilities in order to increase their connectivity to global information through the improvement of their telecommunication infrastructure and the acquisition of computer and computer-related equipment.

Author	Journal	Purpose of the study/ research questions	Data source	Data location	Method	Findings
Pool, Parnell, Spillan, Carraher, & Lester (2006)	*International Journal of Information Technology and Management*	Discuss the current state of e-commerce development in SMEs, outline the challenges faced by many SMEs, and propose several options for e-commerce integration.	Literature	Developed economies	Review of literature.	E-commerce growth is spawned by the recognition of long-term benefits for SMEs and is achieved when owners, managers, and entrepreneurs acknowledge that proper management and attention to detail is a critical part of internet commerce. When managed effectively, e-business can transform an SME into another market; where customers tend to be younger, well educated, and more affluent. Maintaining an internet presence among SMEs in developed countries has provided access to new customers, while increasing sales and profits. The same can be expected as internet accessibility increases in emerging economies. Strategic growth decisions to develop an integrated approach to e-commerce can help improve customer service while increasing revenues. Proactive channel development can position an SME as a market leader.

Author	Journal	Purpose of the study/ research questions	Data source	Data location	Method	Findings
Samanta & Kyriazopoulos (2009)	*International Journal of Knowledge and Learning*	Identify the impact of business process improvement in the area of e-marketing in the hotel industry in Greece.	30 hotels	Greece	SWAT analysis on a sample of hotels in the city of Athens.	The majority of firms in the hotel industry in Greece use the e-marketing concept to improve their communication strategy and reach market segments. In order to make further use of e-business, there is a need for change of organizational culture, infrastructure, and the strategic planning of use and development of the e-business.

Innovation, growth, and succession in Asian family enterprises

Author	Journal	Purpose of the study/ research questions	Data source	Data location	Method	Findings
Schlegelmilch, Diamantopoulos, & Kreuz (2003)	*Journal of Strategic Marketing*	Trace the notion of strategic innovation in the literature, and offer corporate examples from Amazon and Swatch to illustrate the key drivers and outcome of strategic innovation. Synthesize the insights gained in a Multiple Indicator-Multiple Causes model	Literature and Amazon and Swatch case analysis.	USA and Europe	Literature review, case analysis, and Multiple Indicator-Multiple Causes model application	Four antecedent drivers (i.e. culture, process, people, and resources) and two strategic outcomes (i.e. customer value and competitive positioning) of strategic innovation are identified and synthesized in a formal model that provides guidance for operationalizing the strategic innovation construct.
Surjadjaja, Ghosh, & Antony (2003)	*Managing Service Quality*	Address the determinants essential for building a successful electronic service (e-service) operation. Clarify ambiguities in the boundaries between e-service, e-business, and e-commerce.	Literature.	UK	Review of the literature	A framework recognizing the distinctiveness and commonalities between e-service, e-business, and e-commerce is provided, and a list of 20 determinants is offered. The determinants have been evaluated to gain better insight and understanding so that effective e-service operation can be designed, developed, and deployed.

Author	Journal	Purpose of the study/ research questions	Data source	Data location	Method	Findings
Zank & Vokurka (2003)	*SAM Advanced Management Journal*	Understand the impact of e-commerce on the relationships among supply chain members, specifically manufacturers, distributors, and industrial customers; the importance of e-commerce ability in selecting distributor partners; the perceived benefits of e-business; the perceived barriers to e-business; and the primary role of e-business in a company's overall business strategy.	Of manufacturers, distributors, and industrial customers.	Emerging economies	Survey	E-commerce was perceived as having a slightly positive impact on supply chain relationships but did not affect the selection of supply chain partners. Customers focused on the potential benefits of reducing costs, while manufacturers and distributors tended to emphasize the impact of e-commerce on customer-related issues. All groups cited a lack of standards and technical know-how as potential barriers to e-commerce. Managers should carefully weigh potential costs and benefits before adopting or expanding an e-commerce strategy.

Author	Journal	Purpose of the study/ research questions	Data source	Data location	Method	Findings
Zhao, Wang, & Huang (2008)	*Information and Management*	Develop a conceptual model suitable for analyzing the business-to-business e-market in China, to help in seeking effective strategies in creating an effective e-market in the Chinese business environment.	Two case studies: Alibaba and China National Commodity Exchange Center.	China	Interviews with corporate executives and staff, accompanied by secondary data collection from the websites and peers.	Personalized and customized services, the structure and control of transaction processes, and strategic partners network are found to be critical e-commerce activities. A business-to-business e-market model of e-commerce value creation is proposed. It illustrates the relationship between the components that support the process and the control of complexity, and provides guidelines in identifying the effective strategy, crucial business activities, and value creation opportunities in each of the phases of the e-commerce process. The four phases of transactional process are described as information, negotiation, payment, and delivery.

7. Managerial coaching and its generational differences in Chinese family business: Findings from 12 Chinese cities

Ran Michelle Ye, Rong Pei, Katalien Bollen and Martin C. Euwema

INTRODUCTION

The number of studies on managerial coaching has largely increased in the past 10 years. Specific research attention is given to managerial coaching in terms of its antecedents (Batson & Yoder, 2012), effective coaching behaviors (Jones, Woods, & Guillaume, 2016), its positive effects on work attitudes, personal learning (Kim, Egan, Kim, & Kim, 2013), and employee performance (Ellinger, Ellinger, Bachrach, Wang, & Elmadagbas, 2011; Raza, Ali, & Ahmad, 2018). Meanwhile, scholars have also investigated organizational characteristics that foster managerial coaching (Hamlin, Ellinger, & Beattie, 2008; McCarthy & Milner, 2013) and improve both individual and organizational performance (Agarwal, Angst, & Magni, 2009; Ladyshewsky, 2010; Liu & Batt, 2010).

Currently, empirical research on managerial coaching is argued to be in its infancy (Egan & Hamlin, 2014). One reason refers to the lack of cross-cultural research including on non-Western populations (Beattie et al., 2014; Grant & Zackon, 2004), while another reason is to the lack of research including the effects of contextual and/or demographic variables on managerial coaching (Pousa, Richards, & Trépanier, 2018; Ye, Wendt, Wang, & Euwema, 2012). By studying managerial coaching in China, we fill important research gaps.

First, we include the influence of belonging to a certain generation on managerial coaching. Over the last decade, the traditional task-oriented definition of leadership has been challenged toward a more people-oriented direction (Avolio, Walumbwa, & Weber, 2009; Eagly & Chin, 2010). As a result, managers need to act more and more as coaches (Ellinger, 2013; Ladyshewsky, 2010;

Park, 2007). In China, numerous changes have taken place in fast-growing organizations and businesses, along with rapid technological development and increased global competition. Chinese organizations are facing new challenges associated with attracting, motivating, retaining, and developing their employees (Isenhour, Stone, & Lien, 2012). These new challenges have brought changes in human resources management in organizations. Many practices that were traditionally conducted by human resources professionals are now being transferred to supervisors and line managers (Hagen, 2012; McCarthy & Milner, 2013). Coaching, as one of the managerial practices that focus on employees' professional development and personal advancement, is particularly recognized and highlighted in the workplace in China (Ye, 2014). From the organizations' perspective, they are making significant efforts to build internal capability by expecting managers to coach (Ellinger et al., 2011): supervisors and line managers are now expected to develop their subordinates and to facilitate their learning (Hagen & Gavrilova Aguilar, 2012). By acting as coaches, managers are becoming progressively more responsible for performing human resources development practices on developing employees from excellent to peak performance (Heslin, Vandewalle, & Latham, 2006), which is demanded by the rapidly growing and changing business environment. Given this, we argue that our knowledge of managers' coaching behavior in China will be incomplete if we do not consider whether the organization is a family business or not.

Second, the Chinese managerial workforce is majorly composed of two distinct generational cohorts: post-1970s and Generation Y (post-1980s). Prior cross-cultural studies have reported a generation effect (D'Amato & Herzfeldt, 2008; Sessa, Kabacoff, Deal, & Brown, 2007; Twenge, 2010) in organizations, particularly Generation Y (post-1980s) working as subordinates (Lynton & April, 2012; Zhao & Liu, 2008). The generation in which people are born affects their perceptions of work and values (Weston, 2001), which influences both a manager's willingness to coach (help others) and coaching effectiveness (Heslin et al., 2006). It would be interesting to study whether post-1980s also "manage" and coach differently compared to preceding generations. So, what is the relationship between managerial generations (namely post-1970s and post-1980s) and managerial coaching? It is difficult for family businesses in China to attract more senior or experienced employees due to the lack of job security (Zhang & Ma, 2009). As a result, in family business, young and talented employees may be more quickly promoted to managerial positions and may have more opportunities to practice their leadership behavior than their counterparts working for multi-national companies or state-owned enterprises featured with clearly defined organizational structures and hierarchies. Therefore, the family business context makes it possible to not only investigate post-1980s' managers' specific managerial behavior (managerial coaching) but also to compare generational differences in practicing coaching.

Third, this study integrates theories on managerial coaching, generational effects, and family business. Therefore, the third purpose of this study is to examine whether being a family business or not moderates the effects of generational cohorts on managerial coaching. Such investigation is not only relevant from a theoretical perspective but also important for practitioners who need sound information to prevent them from stereotypical and ethnocentric thinking managerial behavior (Eagly & Chin, 2010).

In the present research, we attempted to answer the following research questions: (a) Do Chinese family and non-family businesses differ with regard to managerial coaching? (b) What is the relation between the generation the manager belongs to (namely post-1970s and post-1980s) and managerial coaching? And (c) how does the type of business (family versus non-family) interact with managerial generations to influence managerial coaching in China?

Theoretically, the present research enhances not only the understanding of the practice of managerial coaching in China, but also promotes the inclusion of coaching literature by introducing the generational influence at the work-place and the family business context in China, which, to our knowledge, until now are rarely connected, or even investigated in existing empirical research on managerial coaching.

Practically, as managerial coaching is not a "one-time, one-way" interaction (London & Smither, 2002), it is important in coaching that the manager has an authentic interest in mutual trust and respect (Hicks & Peterson, 1997). By highlighting, recognizing, and appreciating the generational factors and differences in Chinese family and non-family business, the present research may enhance the understanding of generational effects in terms of unique values, knowledge, and the innate ability to grow, which may eventually help the managers to manage more effectively dyadic, development-focused coaching relationships. For professionals who have limited prior knowledge in managing or evaluating the performance of intergenerational teams in (non-) family businesses in China, our study may provide useful information to opt for a more appropriate benchmark for data analysis and interpretation.

THEORETICAL FRAMEWORK AND HYPOTHESES

Managerial Coaching

An employee may be coached by his manager, peer(s), or by an external professional from outside the organization. The present study focuses on *managerial coaching*, which is conducted by the employee's direct supervisor.

There is a variety of slightly different definitions of managerial coaching. For instance, Greene and Grant (2003) defined coaching as an outcome-focused process which facilitates self-directed learning. Other scholars have recognized the importance of providing relevant development opportunities (Day, 2000) and described managerial coaching as "a day-to-day process of helping employees recognize opportunities to improve" (Ellinger, Ellinger, & Keller, 2003, p. 438). In summary, managerial coaching is generally viewed as managerial behavior intended to improve subordinates' performance and to facilitate their learning and development.

Managerial coaching is traditionally viewed as an "instructional" intervention (Parsloe, 1992). However, more recent studies (Ellinger & Bostrom, 1999; Heslin et al., 2006; Peterson & Little, 2005) have interpreted managerial coaching more from a "facilitation" perspective. Commonly agreed by scholars, managerial coaching is not a one-way directive, and short-term performance driven-only intervention (Agarwal et al., 2009; Anderson, 2013; Ellinger, 2013; Ladyshewsky, 2010). Instead, it is a reciprocal process, during which the manager acts often as "a partner" by listening to the subordinate and pointing out insights rather than simply providing answers and directions (Peterson & Little, 2005, p. 180). To be specific, setting goals and providing performance-related feedback may be considered with instructional norms, but managerial coaching emphasizes more "the manager as a coach" who supports subordinates by the coordination of resources towards the pursuit of such goals and performance (Duff, 2013). Moreover, during the long-term coaching process, in order to act proactively according to subordinates' performance, progress, and development, managers need to lead in a more adaptive manner (Duff, 2013). Last but not least, for any coaching to be effective, the manager–subordinate relationship needs to be characterized by mutual trust and shared values (Egan & Hamlin, 2014) as "the real vehicle for change" (Gyllensten & Palmer, 2007, p. 168).

In this study, we build on definitions from previous research (Ellinger et al., 2003; Heslin et al., 2006) and define managerial coaching as "a process in which managers (direct supervisors) communicate goals, expectations, and feedback, and provide learning opportunities to employees, in order to improve performance and facilitate development." According to Heslin et al. (2006), coaching consists of three components which can be conceptually derived as (1) "Guidance": the communication of clear performance expectations and constructive feedback regarding performance outcomes and performance improvement. (2) "Facilitation": helping employees to analyze and explore ways to solve problems. And (3) "Inspiration": challenging employees to realize and develop their potential.

Managerial Coaching in Chinese Organizations

Significant changes have been taking place in the Chinese labor market since the government endorsed the role and importance of private enterprises in 2002. Instead of offering lifelong job security, employers opted to provide their employees with various development opportunities and more challenging assignments (Li & Nimon, 2008).

The high-speed, market-driven economy had an in-depth influence on employees' experiences, values, and opinions. The employment contract of "job for life" had been broken (Li & Nimon, 2008) and the employees' psychological contract with their employers was no longer centered on the exchange of loyalty (Ng & Feldman, 2009). Consequently, employees needed to take personal responsibility for developing their employability on the future job market. As a consequence, the importance of a learning goal orientation (Dweck & Leggett, 1988) which is associated with a higher motivation to learn (Brett & Vandewalle, 1999) may therefore increase (D'Amato & Herzfeldt, 2008).

The increase of a learning orientation over time has important implications for both Chinese managers and subordinates in managerial coaching. Learning goal orientation and coaching in the workplace have been linked to a number of studies (Godshalk & Sosik, 2003; Grant, 2007; Sosik et al., 2004). To managers, the most relevant learning and development intentions would be centered on sharpening their management skills and building their leadership (D'Amato & Herzfeldt, 2008). Such self-development learning motivation may be optimally satisfied via managerial coaching.

Managerial Coaching in Family Business

A family business may be defined briefly as a business owned and controlled by members of the same family (Zhang & Ma, 2009). This definition includes two components: one is about ownership, the other is about management. It points to the integration of ownership that is controlled by the family business owner, other family members, and external managers (Zhang & Ma, 2009). As China's transition towards a market-oriented economy continues, family businesses emerge as a force to be reckoned with in the national economy.

In the present study, we argue that managers in family businesses may practice more managerial coaching compared with their counterparts in non-family businesses. From the organization perspective, we argue that current Chinese family businesses, by force of the challenges from the business environment featuring intense competition (Chu, Kara, Zhu, & Gok, 2011; Vallejo, 2008), may enhance efforts to promote coaching and development within the organization. In order to maintain the stability and development of the business operations, it is more crucial for a family business to stay competitive in the market, to maintain a high level of flexibility and adaptability to respond to the demanding requirements from the customers, and to maintain a high level of sustainability in their organizations (Carney, 2005; Young, Peng, Ahlstrom, Bruton, & Jiang, 2008). In such circumstances, it would be ideal for a family business to have highly qualified, experienced, or even out-performing employees to cope with such a situation. However, among the problems encountered by entrepreneurs, the most critical three issues were (1) the incompetent and undependable employees working for the organizations, (2) the overcompetitive market, and (3) lack of a development tool (such as management training) in organizations (Chu et al., 2011). Since family businesses are less preferred by experienced employees in China's workforce (Zhang & Ma, 2009), the organization may have no better choice but to pay more attention and effort to develop young high potentials. From this perspective, the practice of managerial coaching, as one of the most effective interventions for poor performance improvement, management skill development, and knowledge and skill transfer (Kim, Egan, & Moon, 2013; Liu & Batt, 2010) may be largely encouraged and promoted in Chinese family business.

On the other hand, managerial coaching, by definition, is congruent with the organizational culture in Chinese family business. The characteristics of coaching are collective goals, relation, self-improvement, learning from others (particularly from seniors), and practice focus (Ellinger, Hamlin, & Beattie, 2008). According to the findings of recent studies using generally accepted theories and theoretical framework in business administration, such characteristics align with cultures and structures prevailing in Chinese traditional cultures, namely neo-institutional and transformational leadership (Pistrui, Huang, Oksoy, Zhao, & Welsch, 2001; Vallejo, 2008). This high level of congruence may, to a large extent, facilitate more practice of coaching in Chinese family businesses.

On the other hand, compared to managers working for a non-family business, the managers in a Chinese family business may not only be encouraged but also be more willing to practice managerial coaching. The benefits of such practice are more salient in family business. Since coaching is an effective intervention encouraged by the organization for talent development and retention, managers' continuous practice of managerial coaching may facilitate managers to enhance their management skills by demonstrating more "guidance," "facilitation," and "inspiration" coaching behavior to improve subordinates' performance. In the long run, it may contribute to maintaining and improving their employability in the job market, which is more crucial for employees working in family business due to a comparably higher level of "job insecurity" and "job uncertainty" in family business (Zhang & Ma, 2009).

Taken together, it is reasonable to argue that under the dual impetuses of the business market and the labor market, based on the effort put forth by both the employers and the employees, compared with non-family business, managerial coaching may be practiced more in a Chinese family business.

H1: In China, managers in family business report more managerial coaching towards subordinates than those working in a non-family business.

H2: In terms of subdimensions of coaching, managers from family business rate themselves higher on "guidance," "facilitation," and "inspiration" when compared with managers working in non-family business.

Generation Cohort Theory, Managerial Generation in China, and Managerial Coaching

Few countries have undertaken such rapid social experimentations for successive age groups in the way that China has. During the past 60 years, China has undergone multiple momentous revolutions and distinct political campaigns. In terms of academic research, a lot of attention has been paid by scholars to distinguishing the differences among these three generations: the Consolidation generation (1951–60), the Cultural Revolution generation (1961–70), and the Social Reform generation (1971–76).

According to Inglehart's (1977, 1990) theory "scarcity hypotheses," a high level of economic hardship, education shortage, and political instability can be defined as the greatest subjective value that may have a profound and lasting impact on attitudes towards education, employment, and lifestyle of the generation born in that age (Feng, 2009).

Following the study of Hung, Gu, and Yim (2007) and considering the relevance to the present study, we chose to focus on the differences of the following two cohorts in this research: post-1970s (born 1970–79) and Generation Y (born 1980–89). Especially, these two generations are a part of today's workforce in China. The generation of post-1960s was excluded in the present study as most of them will leave China's workforce soon.

The period 1977 to 1979 was one of transition in China. Historical events such as the adoption of the "Open Door" policy in 1978 and the reform on the "collective farms" in 1979 are regarded to be the opening of a new era in the eyes of "the broad masses of the people" (Li & Nimon, 2008). These events may also be regarded as a reflection of the socioeconomic chaos of the time (Yi, Ribbens, & Morgan, 2010).

In their childhood, the post-1970s experienced more dramatic social and political changes than others. They came of age during the Cultural Revolution, when China was closed to the outside world and commercial activities came to a halt to give way to social/political class struggles. In addition, after the post-1970s grew up, they become the first generation in China's history that was actively involved in the market economy. The groups that seemingly benefited from the reform are the educated: teachers, researchers, engineers, and other professionals (Li & Nimon, 2008). Many of them obtained very high incomes (Yang, 1997). They are believed to be more attuned to the new lifestyles than the post-1960s, yet a bit more traditional than Generation Y (Yi et al., 2010).

Generation Y (born 1980–89) in China is a generation of approximately 204 million people, also addressed as the "individualistic generation," "ME generation," and/or the "one-child generation." In contrast to the post-1970s who suffered greatly from social upheaval and scarcity of materials during their childhood, Generation Y spent the majority of their youth in a peaceful and stable societal environment. They came of age during the Economic Reform and grew up in a society where the economy was transforming from a centrally planned system stressing egalitarianism to a market system advocating competition and individual accomplishment (Hung, Gu, & Yim, 2007). They are the first high-tech generation and the first to be born into a wired world. They have been growing alongside the ever increasing prosperity of the Chinese economy (Zhao & Liu, 2008).

Generational differences are argued to be apparent in China's workplace (Yi et al., 2010). Among the pioneering attempts to understand Chinese generational differences in the workplace, Egri and Ralston (2004) reported generational differences among Chinese managers on openness to change, self-enhancement, and conservation values. The findings of Western-based studies revealed that the focal manager's willingness to coach may be impacted by the perceptions of work and his or her personal beliefs and/or values (Heslin et al., 2006). In addition, one of the factors influencing a manager's perception of work and values is the generation in which they were born (Weston, 2001).

In terms of managers' coaching behavior, we expect that post-1970s managers would rate themselves higher than post-1980s. So far, there is a lack of research investigating Generation Y's profile in managerial roles, though they are the future leader and backbone of the Chinese workforce. However, after examining their unique growing background, a number of studies have portrayed Generation Y as follows: unlike the Consolidation and post-1970s generations' acceptance of collectivist values, Generation Y is proud of their personality and individualism (Yi et al., 2010). The large supply of resources gives them strong self-confidence and personal wellbeing is more in control of the individual than it was in preceding generations. Accordingly, they adopt a more open and direct communication style and their career choice seems to be based more on interests and personality (Zhao & Liu, 2008). Meanwhile, the socioeconomic changes during their youth may influence Generation Y to have a higher tolerance to differences, including differences in values and lifestyles (Lynton & April, 2012). Also, Shen, Hall, and Fei (2007) reported that the younger Chinese are more future-oriented, forward-looking, and more confident of their ability to achieve career goals by seeking promotions, changing employers, or identifying the roadmap to eventually reach their goals.

In contrast, the post-1970s have witnessed large-scale dramatic and profound social changes since they were born. They may have strong team spirit and value relationship building, trust, mutual respect, and are hardworking for an agreed objective, as with what they've practiced in childhood in an extreme "scarcity" when they must share and cooperate with others in an effective way (Feng, 2009; Yang & Yang, 2014). In a similar vein, the day-to-day coaching process involves behaviors such as a high-level interpersonal exchange on collective goals (McLean, Yang, Kuo, Tolbert, & Larkin, 2005), developing one-on-one strong emotional bonds (Cox, Bachkirova, & Clutterbuck, 2014), helping others succeed, and role modelling (Noer, Leupold, & Valle, 2007). In the present research, we argue that the relationship with coaching behavior aligns more with the important features of post-1970s generations who may practice more managerial coaching in order to help the subordinate to improve his/her performance to have the common goal and tasks accomplished.

At an individual level, post-1970s managers have vivid and enough life experiences to fully recognize the value and importance of life (job) security, learning, and lifelong development. Thus, it is reasonable to argue that post-1970s may have a comparably stronger motivation on continuing to develop themselves in the workplace and to stay employable in the job market. Given this, they may actively practice managerial coaching as it is an effective intervention to enhancing their management skills by demonstrating more "guidance," "facilitation," and "inspiration" coaching behavior while improving his or her subordinates' performance.

Taken together, we propose that these characters, beliefs, and values are more congruent with managerial coaching.

H3: Post-1970s managers rate themselves higher on their coaching behavior than Generation Y managers.

H4: Compared with Generation Y managers, post-1970s managers rate themselves higher on the subdimensions of managerial coaching: "guidance," "facilitation," and "inspiration."

Family Business, Managerial Generation, and Managerial Coaching

The market environment in China is characterized by its rapid change caused by technological progress as well as institutional transitions. Such situations required a family-owned business to be adaptive to the changing environment, both strategically and structurally (Powell, 1992). All these adaptations raise the complexity of daily jobs, thus requiring more specialized managerial personnel in both family and non-family businesses. However, as aforementioned, due to the comparably insecure employment in family business (Zhang & Ma, 2009), family businesses may not be a favorable working place for more senior and experienced professionals. Therefore, young talent (post-1980s) may be entitled to a better chance and faster track in family business to assume greater management and professional responsibilities including people development. Thus, Generation Y in family businesses, compared with their counterparts in non-family businesses, may practice more managerial coaching as an important intervention for performance management and people development. In contrast, post-1970s managers are now older than 40. Based on the current age composition of the Chinese workforce, it is reasonable to argue that they should already occupy a managerial or senior professional position, no matter whether they are in family or non-family businesses. Taken together, working in a family business or not may have less impact on their coaching behavior.

Thus, we propose:

H5: Family business or not moderates the relationship between generation and managerial coaching, such that the relationship is stronger for Generation Y managers (post-1980s) than for post-1970s managers.

METHOD

Data and Sample

First-year MBA students were asked to fill out a survey and to participate in this research assessing their management style. Data were collected from students in 12 cities in China, including first-tier cities such as Beijing, Shanghai, Guangzhou, and other big cities such as Ha'erbin, Nanning, Kunming, Wuxi, and Wuhan. Data were collected during 2013–14 as part of an MBA course in management and leadership. The managerial job levels of participants range from intermediate to executive. Among the 950 surveys collected, 802 complete surveys were obtained to carry out the family business and generational cohort analysis. Of these, 468 (58 percent) are male and 336 (42 percent) are female, and 107 respondents (13.3 percent) are currently working in a family business. The age range of the participants is from 25 to 44 years old, with a mean of 31,41 years old (SD = 3.91).

Measurements

Managerial coaching
In the present study, we used validated measures of coaching developed by Heslin et al. (2006, p. 879). The scale is composed of 10 items to test managerial coaching with three subdimensions: four items for "guidance" (Cronbach α: 0.82), three items for "facilitation" (Cronbach α: 0.75), and three items for "inspiration" (Cronbach α: 0.83). Participants were asked to rate each item on a five-point Likert-type scale with the following introduction: "Indicate for each statement the extent to which it corresponds to your behavior when you coach your direct reports." Please refer to the Appendix for the full scale.

Family business or not
Family business was coded as "1" and non-family business was coded "2."

Generation cohorts
The samples were segmented into generation cohorts based on birth years, resulting in 183 people from the post-1970s generation (born 1970–79) and 619 managers from Generation Y (born 1980–89). The post-1970s generation was coded as 1 and managers from Generation Y as 2.

Control Variables

To test our hypothesis, we controlled for type of industry, job level, and gender.

Language Issues

The items in the complete original instruments, including the coaching items (©MSI), were all translated from English into Chinese by native speakers, using the so-called application mode of translation (Van de Vijver & Tanzer, 2004). The translators (consultants) were trained in the concepts and were familiar with the societies' culture, therefore, their translations represent the concepts adequately.

RESULTS

Hypotheses Testing

Data management and analyses were executed using SPSS 19.0. In line with the data analysis methods in academic research in the field of coaching (Bozer, Sarros, & Santora, 2014; Grant Rynsaardt, 2010; Kutilek & Earnest, 2001), we used mainly multivariate analysis of variance (manova) analyses since

Innovation, growth, and succession in Asian family enterprises

Table 7.1   *Means, standard deviations, and correlations for all variables*

	Means	Standard devia-tions	1	2	3	4	5	6	7	8	9	10
1. Gender	1.42	.49										
2. Job level	1,84	.92	−.09*									
3. Industry	4.10	1.76	.08*	.09**								
4. Family business or not	1.87	0.34	.06	−.25***	−.17***							
5. Gen XY	1.79	0.40	.11***	−.22***	−.07	.20***						
6. Coaching	3.43	0.56	−.07*	.27***	−.07	−.44***	−.36***	α: 0.86				
7. Guidance	3.44	0.64	−.09**	.24***	−.03	−.41***	−.28***	.88***	α: 0.82			
8. Facilitation	3.38	0.66	−.08*	.20***	−.06	−.36***	−.31***	.84***	.64***	α: 0.75		
9. Inspiration	3.48	0.72	−.02	.22***	−.09**	−.35***	−.33***	.81***	.54***	.53***	α: 0.83	

Notes: * $p \leq .05$, ** $p \leq .01$ (two-tailed), *** $p \leq .001$; gender: 1 = male, 2 = female; family business = 1, non-family business = 2; generation post-1970s = 1, generation post-1980s = 2.

our independent variables have a categorical character to test our hypotheses. Table 7.1 shows the means and standard deviations of the research variables.

From Table 7.1 we can see that job level is found to have a significant effect on all variables. The type of industry affects the level of inspiration. Gender was negatively related to coaching ($r = -.07$, $p \leq .05$) including the subdimensions guidance ($r = -.09$, $p \leq .01$) and facilitation ($r = -.08$, $p \leq .05$), indicating that male managers rate themselves higher on coaching than female managers. These findings contradict prior cross-cultural findings on managerial coaching whereby women rate themselves higher on coaching (Ye et al., 2016).

Based on our dataset, being a family business or not is significantly negatively related to coaching ($r = -.44$, $p \leq .001$) and its three subdimensions: "guidance" ($r = -.41$, $p \leq .001$), "facilitation" ($r = -.36$, $p \leq .001$), and "inspiration" ($r = -.35$, $p \leq .001$). Since family business is coded as "1" and non-family business is coded as "2," this implies that managers in family businesses engage more in coaching (and the different aspects of coaching) than non-family businesses. Furthermore, data show a significant relation between

Table 7.2   *Summary of hierarchical regression analysis: generational cohort predicting managerial coaching in family businesses (N =103)*

	Step 1	Step 2
Gender	−.19	−.19* t = (−2)
Job level	.02	−.02 t = (−.15)
Industry	.13	.13 t = (1.36)
Generational cohort		−.22* t = (−2.25)
R^2	.05	.10
Adjusted R^2	.02	.06

Notes: * $p \leq .05$, ** $p \leq .01$, *** $p \leq .01$ (two-tailed).

generations X and Y and coaching ($r = -.36$, $p \leq .001$) and its three subdimensions: "guidance" ($r = -.28$, $p \leq .001$), "facilitation" ($r = -.31$, $p \leq .001$), and "inspiration" ($r = -.33$, $p \leq .001$) with post-1970s managers engaging in more coaching than post-1980s managers.

In order to examine whether family and non-family businesses differ in their level of coaching (H1) as well as the subdimensions of coaching (H2), we ran a one-way manova analysis, with gender, job level, and type of industry as controls. The manova analysis is used to determine whether there are differences between two independent groups (family business versus non-family business) on more than one continuous dependent variable (here, managerial coaching and its subdimensions).

The results indicate that there is a significant effect of family business or not on managerial coaching in general ($F(2, 788) = 148,70$, $p < 0.001$) and its three dimensions: "guidance" ($F(2, 788) = 128,93$, $p < 0.001$), "facilitation" ($F(2, 788) = 89$, $p < 0.001$), and "inspiration" ($F(2, 788) = 78,40$, $p < 0.001$). Our data confirm Hypotheses 1 and 2 by showing that managers in family businesses report more managerial coaching towards subordinates than those working in a non-family business.

To test whether post-1970s managers rate themselves higher on their coaching behaviors than Generation Y managers (H3 and H4), we split the data into two groups (family business versus non-family business) and ran a hierarchical regression analysis. In Step 1 we added the control variables and in Step 2 the independent variables. The results (Tables 7.2 and 7.3) show that the extent to which one engages in managerial coaching depends on the generation the manager belongs to, both in family ($\beta = -.22$ $p < .05$), and non-family businesses ($\beta = -.31$, $p < .001$).

In addition, post-1970s managers do not only score higher on coaching (M = 3.83) than post-1980s managers in general (M = 3.33) but also on its sub-

Table 7.3　　*Summary of hierarchical regression analysis: generational cohort predicting managerial coaching in non-family businesses (N = 683)*

	Step 1	Step 2
Gender	−.01	.02　t = (.55)
Job level	.21***	.15***　t = (4.17)
Industry	−.03	−.04　t = (−1.10)
Generational cohort		−.31***　t = (−8.35)
R^2	.04	.13
Adjusted R^2	.04	.13

Notes: * $p \leq .05$, ** $p \leq .01$, *** $p \leq .01$ (two-tailed).

Table 7.4　　*Summary of hierarchical regression analysis: generational cohort predicting guidance in non-family businesses (N = 683)*

	Step 1	Step 2
Gender	−.03	−.01　t = (−.30)
Job level	.20***	.16***　t = (4.20)
Industry	−.07	−.07　t = (−2.0)
Generational cohort		−.21***　t = (−5.62)
R^2	.04	.09
Adjusted R^2	.04	.08

Notes: * $p \leq .05$, ** $p \leq .01$, *** $p \leq .01$ (two-tailed).

dimensions: guidance, M= 3.79; facilitation, M = 3.78; and inspiration, M = 3.95 compared to post-1980s managers guidance with M= 3.35; facilitation M = 3.27; inspiration M = 3.36 (Tables 7.4, 7.5, and 7.6). For the subdimensions of coaching, we see that the generation the manager belongs to affects all subdimensions in a non-family business setting (guidance: $\beta = -.21$, p < .001, facilitation $\beta = -.23$, p < .001, and inspiration $\beta = -.32$, p < .001).

In a family business, the generation the manager belongs to only affects the dimension of facilitation ($\beta = -.37$, p < .001) while not affecting guidance $\beta = -.16$, p = ns, or inspiration ($\beta = -.02$, p = ns) (Tables 7.7, 7.8, and 7.9).

In order to test whether the type of business (family business or not) moderates the relation between generational cohort and coaching (including its subdimensions), we ran a manova since both our independent variables are categorical assessing their effects on several continuous variables (Table 7.10).

Table 7.5   *Summary of hierarchical regression analysis: generational cohort predicting facilitation in non-family businesses (N = 683)*

	Step 1	Step 2
Gender	−.03	−.00 t = (−.04)
Job level	.14***	.10** t = (2.70)
Industry	−.00	−.02 t = (−.49)
Generational cohort		−.23*** t = (−5.96)
R²	.02	.07
Adjusted R²	.02	.07

Notes: * p ≤ .05, ** p ≤ .01, *** p ≤ .01 (two-tailed).

Table 7.6   *Summary of hierarchical regression analysis: generational cohort predicting inspiration in non-family businesses (N = 683)*

	Step 1	Step 2
Gender	.03	.06 t = (1.77)
Job level	.17***	.11** t = (2.96)
Industry	.02	.00 t = (.08)
Generational Cohort		−.32*** t = (−8.71)
R²	.03	.13
Adjusted R²	.02	.12

Notes: * p ≤ .05, ** p ≤ .01, *** p ≤ .01 (two-tailed).

Table 7.7   *Summary of hierarchical regression analysis: generational cohort predicting guidance in family business (N = 103)*

	Step 1	Step 2
Gender	−.18	−.18 t = (−1.81)
Job level	−.10	−.12 t = (−1.26)
Industry	.12	.12 t = (1.23)
Generational Cohort		−.16 t = (−1.57)
R²	.06	.08
Adjusted R²	.03	.04

Notes: * p ≤ .05, ** p ≤ .01, *** p ≤ .01 (two-tailed).

Table 7.8 *Summary of hierarchical regression analysis: generational cohort predicting facilitation in family businesses (N = 103)*

	Step 1	Step 2
Gender	–.21*	–.21* t = (–2.33)
Job level	.05	–.01 t = (–.06)
Industry	.12	.11 t = (1.26)
Generational cohort		–.37*** t = (–4.04)
R²	.06	.19
Adjusted R²	.03	.16

Notes: * p ≤ .05, ** p ≤ .01, *** p ≤ .01 (two-tailed).

Table 7.9 *Summary of hierarchical regression analysis: generational cohort predicting inspiration in family business (N =103)*

	Step 1	Step 2
Gender	–.08	–.08 t = (.42)
Job level	.10	.10 t = (1.01)
Industry	.08	.08 t = (.84)
Generational cohort		–.02 t = (–.17)
R²	.02	–.01
Adjusted R²	.02	–.02

Notes: * p ≤ .05, ** p ≤ .01, *** p ≤ .01 (two-tailed).

We entered the independent variables as fixed factors and the control variables (gender, job industry, and job level) as covariates. Manova results ($F_{(1,788)}$ = 5.74, $p < 0.05$) indicate an interaction effect for managerial coaching and inspiration ($F_{(1,788)}$ = 15.80, $p < 0.001$), not for guidance ($F_{(1,788)}$ = 3.49, p = ns) and facilitation ($F_{(1,788)}$ = 0.03, p = ns) (Table 7.11). The effect is stronger for generation Y managers (post-1980s) than for post-1970s managers (Figure 7.1). This supports Hypothesis 5.

DISCUSSION, LIMITATIONS, AND FUTURE RESEARCH

The present research provides insights into how Generation Y managers in China's workforce rate themselves in practicing a specific leadership behavior (managerial coaching), which is distinct from existing research focusing more on the preference of new-generation employees in terms of the leadership styles in China (Xie & Chen, 2014; Ren, Xie, Zhu, & Warner, 2018). To our

Table 7.10 *Summary of manova testing the interaction between type of business and generational cohort on managerial coaching and its subdimensions (N = 788)*

	Mean square	F	Sig
Managerial coaching	1.32	5.74	.02
Guidance	1.10	3.50	.06
Facilitation	0.01	.03	.87
Inspiration	6.43	15.80	.00
Error	781		
Total	788		
Corrected total	787		

Notes: * $p \leq .05$, ** $p \leq .01$, *** $p \leq .01$ (two-tailed).

Table 7.11 *Family business, managerial generations, and coaching*

	Family business or not	Coaching mean	Coaching subdimensions		
			Guidance	Facilitation	Inspiration
Post-1970s Post-1980s	Yes	4,18	4,18	4,22	4.14
	No	3.70	3.64	3.61	3.87
	Yes	3.98	4.05	3.80	4.09
	No	3.26	3.27	3.21	3.28

knowledge, no previous projects directly examine new-generation managers' actual coaching behavior while taking the family business and generational cohorts into consideration. It is for this reason that we consider that the current study contributes to the literature and further research on the family business.

By doing this research, we hope to spur other scholars to go beyond our work and have a closer look at the workplace generational differences and the impact on Chinese family businesses. The generations of the post-1960s are not the focus of the present study as most of them would soon become inactive in China's workforce. However, when they are the founders of the family-owned business, the situation can be more complicated as the influence may still be profound and lasting even after their retirement. In the past four decades, the "one-child" policy has changed the Chinese family structure dramatically. For example, nowadays, it is uncommon to find families with multiple heirs in big cities in China. As Generation Y (post-1980s) is the only heir of the family and the successor of the family-owned business, more research may be carried out in Chinese family businesses when they start running the business.

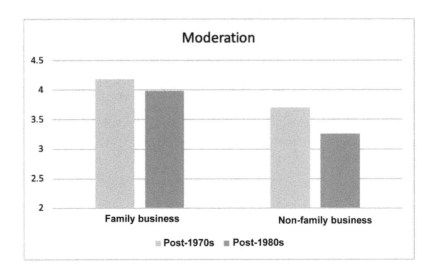

Figure 7.1   *Representation of the interaction between generational cohort and business type (family business or not) on managerial coaching*

For instance: how would they (post-1980s) handle the possible generational clash with the founder of the business (post-1960s) who is also the father/mother in the family? How would they cope with the age/generation-based supervisor–subordinate status incongruence in the family business that may be even more stimulated by the cultural traditions emphasizing seniority both in age and in the hierarchy (Pearce & Xu, 2012)? What would be the effect and effectiveness of such status incongruence on one-on-one managerial practice including managerial coaching? Would they have different perspectives in terms of familism and professionalism in the family business? Would the organizational culture become more learning-oriented and innovative? Would the practice of managerial coaching in Chinese family businesses, as argued by scholars in the Western-based studies (Ellinger & Bostrom, 1999; Beattie et al., 2014), prevail in such an organizational culture?

Practical Implications

One of the future scenarios on leadership and employee engagement holds the prospect that coaching becomes the dominant style globally improving the workplace for employees (Brock, 2009). But the basis of this is to understand the emergence, growth, influences, and contributions of coaching, in order to investigate the dynamic and contextual attributes to customize coaching and better benefit employees being coached.

In Chinese family businesses, there are common features such as smaller organization size, quick business conversion, flexible organization structures, and adaptability to change (Zhang & Ma, 2009). They used to be, for a very long period, not a favorable working place when compared with joint venture companies or state-owned companies.

Nowadays they are still facing many challenges in the areas of talent retention and leadership development as reported in prior research (Chu et al., 2011). Family businesses often struggle between offering an attractive environment for younger employees, while retaining the valuable skills and knowledge of older generations. As previous research has shown, an organizational learning culture in family businesses may be attractive to employees, particularly when it promotes development activities that are more personal, job-related, and career-related (Noe, Wilk, Mullen, & Wanek, 1997). These are exactly what managerial coaching can provide. Clearly, when family businesses understand generation differences in practicing managerial coaching, the organizations could leverage the opportunities to better meet the needs and desires of employees of all ages. Our research highlighted the generation differences in practicing managerial coaching, meanwhile the intent is to suggest that the aforementioned struggle may be resolved by the implementation of generation-specific coaching practice.

Limitations

There are a number of limitations associated with this study. First, our findings are based on the self-reporting of the participants. Due to the lack of subordinates' data, it is impossible to use the subordinates' response to decrease the extent of the error of managers' self-reporting. For instance, it is impossible to control for variables such as subordinates' gender, generation, and education level when we explore and discuss one-on-one managerial coaching in the workplace.

Second, it will always be difficult to make some generalizations without a large satisfied sample size, given the diversity within China. In our sample, participants are studying and working in big cities of China, which might cause a response bias of limiting our sample to urban-educated individuals. Given the size and diversity of the Chinese population, our findings may only be interpreted as a primary attempt to test specific managerial behavior in the cities in which we carried out the present research.

In addition, it is also worth mentioning that since there are ongoing dramatic changes taking place in China, our conclusions need to be kept and explained cautiously, taking the evolving Chinese institutional and social environment into consideration.

Future Research

Understanding generational experiences, values, and perspectives from different generations in the workplace is becoming an essential management skill (Weston, 2001). Given the cross-sectional nature of our data and research, we encourage future longitudinal research to examine the feedback from subordinates in order to assess the causality of the relations tested in a more objective research approach.

As our primary research purpose was to explore the possible difference in managerial coaching between Chinese family and non-family businesses, in the demographic part of the survey, we asked each participant to select whether he or she is currently working in a family-owned business or not, however, without providing a further clarification of his or her role as an owner of the business, a family member, or a professional employed in a family business. We encourage future research with a specific focus on this issue to probe further the participants' roles to achieve a more specific understanding of the practice of managerial coaching in Chinese family businesses.

It is widely accepted by scholars that future practice in business will require more collaboration at the organizational level and new expressions of leadership featuring flexibility, creativity, and adaptability (Balda & Mora, 2011). Accordingly, there is much more that can be done to empirically demonstrate, elaborate, and expound upon managerial coaching considering its positive effects in terms of employees' attitude, communication, performance, and innovation (Ye, 2014). It merits noting that the present study on managerial coaching may shed some light on and promote related research. Thus, it may in the long run contribute to the improvement of employees' wellbeing in the Chinese workplace.

REFERENCES

Agarwal, R., Angst, C. M., & Magni, M. (2009). The performance effects of coaching: A multilevel analysis using hierarchical linear modeling. *International Journal of Human Resource Management*, 20(10), 2110–34.

Anderson, V. (2013). A Trojan horse? The implications of managerial coaching for leadership theory. *Human Resource Development International*, 16(3), 251–66.

Avolio, B. J., Walumbwa, F. O., & Weber, T. J. (2009). Leadership: Current theories, research, and future directions. *Annual Review of Psychology*, 60(1), 421–49.

Balda, J. B., & Mora, F. (2011). Adapting leadership theory and practice for the networked, millennial generation. *Journal of Leadership Studies*, 5(3), 13–24.

Batson, V. D., & Yoder, L. H. (2012). Managerial coaching: A concept analysis. *Journal of Advanced Nursing*, 68(7), 1658—69.

Beattie, R. S., Kim, S., Hagen, M. S., Egan, T. M., Ellinger, A. D., & Hamlin, R. G. (2014). Managerial coaching: A review of the empirical literature and development of a model to guide future practice. *Advances in Developing Human Resources*, 16(2), 184–201.

Bozer, G., Sarros, J. C., & Santora, J. C. (2014). Academic background and credibility in executive coaching effectiveness. *Personnel Review*.

Brett, J. F., & VandeWalle, D. (1999). Goal orientation and goal content as predictors of performance in a training program. *Journal of applied psychology*, 84(6), 863.

Brock, V. (2009). The professional challenges facing the coaching field from an historical perspective. *International Journal of Coaching in Orgnizations*, 7(1), 27–37.

Carney, M. (2005). Corporate governance and competitive advantage in family–controlled firms. *Entrepreneurship theory and practice*, 29(3), 249–65.

Chu, H. M., Kara, O., Zhu, X., & Gok, K. (2011). Chinese entrepreneurs. *Journal of Chinese Entrepreneurship*.

Cox, E., Bachkirova, T., & Clutterbuck, D. (2014). Theoretical traditions and coaching genres: Mapping the territory. *Advances in Developing Human Resources*, 16(2), 139–60.

D'Amato, A., & Herzfeldt, R. (2008). Learning orientation, organizational commitment and talent retention across generations: A study of European managers. *Journal of Managerial Psychology*, 23(8), 929–53.

Day, D. V. (2000). Leadership development: A review in context. *Leadership Quarterly*, 11, 581–613.

Duff, A. J. (2013). Performance management coaching: Servant leadership and gender implications. *Leadership and Organization Development Journal*, 34(3), 204–21.

Dweck, C. S., & Leggett, E. L. (1988). A social-cognitive approach to motivation and personality. *Psychological review*, 95(2), 256.

Eagly, A. H., & Chin, J. L. (2010). Diversity and leadership in a changing world. *American Psychologist*, 65(3), 216.

Egan, T. M., & Hamlin, R. G. (2014). Coaching, HRD, and relational richness: Putting the pieces together. *Advances in Developing Human Resources*, 16(2), 242–57.

Egri, C. P., & Ralston, D. A. (2004). Generation cohorts and personal values: A comparison of China and the United States. *Organization Science*, 210–20.

Ellinger, A. D. (2013). Supportive supervisors and managerial coaching: Exploring their intersections. *Journal of Occupational and Organizational Psychology*, 86, 310–16.

Ellinger, A. D., & Bostrom, R. P. (1999). Managerial coaching behaviors in learning organizations. *Journal of Management Development*, 18, 752–71.

Ellinger, A. D., Ellinger, A. E., & Keller, S. B. (2003). Supervisory coaching behavior, employee satisfaction, and warehouse employee performance: A dyadic perspective in the distribution industry. *Human Resource Development Quarterly*, 14, 435–58.

Ellinger, A. D., Hamlin, R. G., & Beattie, R. S. (2008). Behavioural indicators of ineffective managerial coaching: A cross-national study. *Journal of European Industrial Training*, 32, 240–57.

Ellinger, A. D., Ellinger, A. E., Bachrach, D. G., Wang, Y.-L., & Elmadagbas, A. B. (2011). Organizational investments in social capital, managerial coaching, and employee work-related performance. *Management Learning*, 42(1), 67–85.

Feng, T. (2009). Children Growing Up During the Reform and Opening up: The Post-70 and Post-80's Consciousness of Fairness and Democracy in China [J]. *Youth Studies*, 6.

Godshalk, V. M., & Sosik, J. J. (2003). Aiming for career success: The role of learning goal orientation in mentoring relationships. *Journal of Vocational Behavior*, 63(3), 417–37.

Grant, A. M. (2007). Enhancing coaching skills and emotional intelligence through training. *Industrial and Commercial Training*, 39(5), 257–66.

Grant, A. M., & Zackon, R. (2004). Executive, workplace and life coaching: Findings from a large-scale survey of International Coach Federation members. *International Journal of Evidence Based Coaching and Mentoring*, 2(2), 1–15.

Grant, A. M., Green, L. S., & Rynsaardt, J. (2010). Developmental coaching for high school teachers: executive coaching goes to school. *Consulting Psychology Journal: Practice and Research*, 62(3), 151.

Greene, J., & Grant, A. M. (2003). *Solution-Focused Coaching: Managing People in a Complex World*. London: Momentum Press.

Gyllensten, K., & Palmer, S. (2007). The coaching relationship: An interpretative phenomenological analysis. *International Coaching Psychology Review*, 2(2), 168–77.

Hagen, M. S. (2012). Managerial coaching: A review of the literature. *Performance Improvement Quarterly,* 24(4), 17–39.

Hagen, M., & Gavrilova Aguilar, M. (2012). The impact of managerial coaching on learning outcomes within the team context: An analysis. *Human Resource Development Quarterly*, 23(3), 363–88.

Hamlin, R. G., Ellinger, A. D., & Beattie, R. S. (2008). The emergent "coaching industry": A wake-up call for HRD professionals. *Human Resource Development International*, 11, 287–305.

Heslin, P. A., Vandewalle, D., & Latham, G. P. (2006). Keen to help? Managers' implicit person theories and their subsequent employee coaching. *Personnel Psychology*, 59(4), 871–902.

Hicks, M. D., & Peterson, D. B. (1997). Just enough to be dangerous: The rest of what you need to know about development. *Consulting Psychology Journal: Practice and Research*, 49(3), 171.

Hung, K. H, Gu, F. F., & Yim, C. K. B. (2007). A social institutional approach to identifying generation cohorts in China with a comparison with American consumers. *Journal of International Business Studies*, 38(5), 836–53.

Inglehart, R. (1977). *The Silent Revolution* (Vol. 8). Princeton, NJ: Princeton University Press.

Inglehart, R. (1990). *Culture Shift in Advanced Industrial Society*. Princeton, NJ: Princeton University Press.

Isenhour, L. C., Stone, D. L., & Lien, D. (2012). Advancing theory and research on employee behavior in China. *Journal of Managerial Psychology*, 27(1), 4–8.

Jones, R. J., Woods, S. A., & Guillaume, Y. R. (2016). The effectiveness of workplace coaching: A meta-analysis of learning and performance outcomes from coaching. *Journal of Occupational and Organizational Psychology*, 89(2), 249–277.

Kim, S., Egan, T. M., Kim, W., & Kim, J. (2013). The impact of managerial coaching behavior on employee work-related reactions. *Journal of Business and Psychology*, 28(3), 315–30.

Kim, S., Egan, T. M., & Moon, M. J. (2013). Managerial coaching efficacy, work-related attitudes, and performance in public organizations: A comparative international study. *Review of Public Personnel Administration*, 34(3), 237–62.

Kutilek, L. M., & Earnest, G. W. (2001). Supporting professional growth through mentoring and coaching. *Journal of Extension*, 39(4), 3–13.

Ladyshewsky, R. K. (2010). The manager as coach as a driver of organizational development. *Leadership and Organization Development Journal*, 31(4), 292–306.

Li, J., & Nimon, K. (2008). The importance of recognizing generational differences in HRD policy and practices: A study of workers in Qinhuangdao, China. *Human Resource Development International*, 11(2), 167–82.

Liu, X., & Batt, R. (2010). How supervisors influence performance: A multilevel study of coaching and group management in technology-mediated services. *Personnel Psychology*, 63(2), 265–98.

London, M., & Smither, J. W. (2002). Feedback orientation, feedback culture, and the longitudinal performance management process. *Human Resource Management Review*, 12(1), 81–100.

Lynton, N., & April, K. (2012). Connected but not alike: Cross-cultural comparison of Generation Y in China and South Africa. *Academy of Taiwan Business Management Review*, 8(1), 67–80.

McCarthy, G., & Milner, J. (2013). Managerial coaching: Challenges, opportunities and training. *Journal of Management Development*, 32(7), 768–99.

McLean, G. N., Yang, B.-Y., Kuo, M. H. C., Tolbert, A. S., & Larkin, C. (2005). Development and initial validation of an instrument measuring managerial coaching skill. *Human Resource Development Quarterly*, 16(2), 157–78.

Ng, T. W., & Feldman, D. C. (2009). Age, work experience, and the psychological contract. *Journal of organizational behavior*, 30(8), 1053–1075.

Noe, R. A., Wilk, S. L., Mullen, E. J., & Wanek, J. E. (1997). Employee development: Issues in construct definition and investigation of antecedents. *Improving Training Effectiveness in Work Organizations*, 153, 189.

Noer, D. M., Leupold, C. R., & Valle, M. (2007). An analysis of Saudi Arabian and US managerial coaching behaviors. *Journal of Managerial Issues*, 271–87.

Park, S. (2007). *Relationships among Managerial Coaching in Organizations and the Outcomes of Personal Learning, Organizational Commitment, and Turnover Intention*. Minneapolis, MI: University of Minnesota Press.

Parsloe, E. (1992). *Coaching, Mentoring, and Assessing: A Practical Guide to Developing Competence*. Asbury, IA: Nichols Publishing Company.

Pearce, J. L., & Xu, Q. J. (2012). Rating performance or contesting status: Evidence against the homophily explanation for supervisor demographic skew in performance ratings. *Organization Science*, 23(2), 373–85.

Peterson, D. B., & Little, B. (2005). Invited reaction: Development and initial validation of an instrument measuring managerial coaching skill. *Human Resource Development Quarterly*, 16(2), 179–84.

Pistrui, D., Huang, W., Oksoy, D., Zhao, J., & Welsch, H. P. (2001). Entrepreneurship in China: Characteristics, attributes, and family forces shaping the emerging private sector. *Family Business Review*, 14(2), 141–52.

Pousa, C., Richards, D. A., & Trépanier, C. (2018). Managerial coaching of frontline employees: The moderating role of gender. *Human resource development quarterly*, 29(3), 219–41.

Powell, T. C. (1992). Research notes and communications strategic planning as competitive advantage. *Strategic management journal*, 13(7), 551–8.

Raza, B., Ali, M., Ahmed, S., & Ahmad, J. (2018). Impact of Managerial Coaching on Organizational Citizenship Behavior: The Mediation and Moderation Model. *International Journal of Organizational Leadership*, 7, 27–46.

Ren, S., Xie, Y., Zhu, Y., & Warner, M. (2018). New generation employees' preferences towards leadership style in China. *Asia Pacific Business Review*, 24(4), 437–58.

Sessa, V. I., Kabacoff, R. I., Deal, J., & Brown, H. (2007). Generational differences in leader values and leadership behaviors. *Psychologist Manager Journal*, 10(1), 47–74.

Shen, Y., Hall, D. T., & Fei, Z. (2007). The evolution of career success: Doing well in China. Paper presented at the Academy of Management, Philadelphia.

Sosik, J. J., Godshalk, V. M., & Yammarino, F. J. (2004). Transformational leadership, learning goal orientation, and expectations for career success in mentor–protégé relationships: A multiple levels of analysis perspective. *The Leadership Quarterly*, 15(2), 241–61.

Twenge, J. M. (2010). A review of the empirical evidence on generational differences in work attitudes. *Journal of Business and Psychology*, 25(2), 201–10.

Vallejo, M. C. (2008). Is the culture of family firms really different? A value-based model for its survival through generations. *Journal of Business Ethics*, 81(2), 261–79.

Van de Vijver, F., & Tanzer, N. K. (2004). Bias and equivalence in cross-cultural assessment: An overview. *Revue Europeenne de Psychologie Appliquee*, 54(2), 119–35.

Weston, M. (2001). Coaching generations in the workplace. *Nursing Administration Quarterly,* 25(2), 11–21.

Xie, Y., & Chen, J. (2014). Influence of Need for Employee Involvement on New Generation Employees' Leadership Preference. *Chinese Journal of Management*, (9), 9.

Yang, D. (1997). Generational conflicts and the one child generation. *Youth Studies*, 12.

Yang, D., & Yang, L. (2014). Organizational pressure dimensions measuring of "post-80s" employees and its implications for talent strategy. Open Journal of Social Sciences, 2(12), 13.

Ye, R. M. (2014). *Managerial Coaching in a Changing World: The impact of Gender and Societal Culture in China and Abroad.* Leuven: University of Leuven Press.

Ye, R. M., Wendt, J. H., Wang, X.-H., & Euwema, M. C. (2012). Gender differences in managerial coaching across cultures. Paper presented at the IACMR international conference, June 24–26, Hong Kong.

Ye, R., Wang, X. H., Wendt, J. H., Wu, J., & Euwema, M. C. (2016). Gender and managerial coaching across cultures: female managers are coaching more. *The International Journal of Human Resource Management,* 27(16), 1791–1812.

Yi, X. , Ribbens, B., & Morgan, C. N. (2010). Generational differences in China: Career implications. *Career Development International*, 15(6), 601–20.

Young, M. N., Peng, M. W., Ahlstrom, D., Bruton, G. D., & Jiang, Y. (2008). Corporate governance in emerging economies: A review of the principle-principle perspective. *Journal of Management Studies*, 45, 196–220.

Zhang, J. J., & Ma, H. (2009). Adoption of professional management in Chinese family business: A multilevel analysis of impetuses and impediments. *Asia Pacific Journal of Management*, 26(1), 119–39.

Zhao, E. D., & Liu, L. W. (2008). China's Generation Y: Understanding the workforce. Paper presented at the Management of Innovation and Technology.

APPENDIX: QUESTIONNAIRE ON MANAGERIAL COACHING

Managerial coaching (Heslin et al., 2006, p. 879) is defined as "a process in which managers practice guidance, facilitation and inspiration approaches in the communication of goals and expectations, providing constructive feedbacks and offering resources, opportunities, and challenges to the employees to improve employees' performance and facilitate their development."

Indicate for each statement the extent to which it corresponds to your behavior when you coach your direct reports.

Table 7A.1   Coaching behavior items

	Not at all	Rarely	Sometimes	Regularly	To a greater extent
(1) As a manager, I provide guidance to my subordinates regarding performance expectations.	1	2	3	4	5
(2) As a manager, I help my subordinates to analyze their performance.	1	2	3	4	5
(3) As a manager, I provide constructive feedback to my subordinates regarding areas for improvement.	1	2	3	4	5
(4) As a manager, I offer useful suggestions regarding how my subordinates can improve their performance.	1	2	3	4	5
(5) As a manager, I act as a sounding board for my subordinates to develop their ideas.	1	2	3	4	5
(6) As a manager, I facilitate creative thinking to help my subordinates solve problems.	1	2	3	4	5
(7) As a manager, I encourage my subordinates to explore and try out new alternatives.	1	2	3	4	5
(8) As a manager, I express confidence that my subordinates can develop and improve.	1	2	3	4	5
(9) As a manager, I encourage my subordinates to continuously develop and improve.	1	2	3	4	5
(10) As a manager, I support my subordinates in taking on new challenges.	1	2	3	4	5

Source: Heslin et al., 2006, p. 879.

8. Paternal aunts as matriarchs in Taiwanese family businesses: An anthropological observation

Min-ping Kang and Hung-bin Ding

INTRODUCTION

The research on women in business has been gaining traction in recent years (Bianco et al., 2015; Campopiano et al., 2017; Jimenez, 2009; Zhang et al., 2013; Wright et al., 2014; Bettinelli et al., 2019). Such growth may be attributed to the increasing participation and presence of women in entrepreneurship, corporate boards, and family businesses. A survey by *Fortune* magazine reported that family firms have had a higher percentage of women in a leadership position in recent years (Moran, 2015). Another global survey by EY (formerly Ernst & Young) predicted that there would be even more women leaders in family businesses in the future (Ernst & Young, 2015). A more recent study of EY clients shows that on average, there are 1.14 women in leadership roles. This number is smaller than the 3.5 average of non-family women in the C-suites of family firms (Hall, 2019). The same EY study also reports that only a quarter of women leadership positions in family firms are occupied by women from the owner families. In other words, women of a family business rarely assume the leadership roles in their family firms. The number may be small, but their significances and contributions clearly cannot be measured by their business titles.

There are generally three approaches by which a woman gets involved in the family business of her family: entrepreneurship, succession, and career change (Campopiano et al., 2017). However, women's influence and contributions to their family business are not limited to their professional capacity. It has been well documented that the mother of a family business plays an essential role in developing the family (Kaslow, 1998; Bonner and Bonner, 2012; Smith, 2014). The husband and even the older children may be the wealth creators, but the mother keeps the family together by cultivating a supporting and stable environment. She develops the family culture and passes this culture to the younger generations. When necessary, she may be asked to join the family firm with the expectation that she will do whatever is needed. Of course, women are not always confined to a supporting role. They are also capable of starting their family business. Certain cultural traditions also encourage women entrepreneurship (Welsh et al., 2013; Overbeke et al., 2013, 2015). With the support of their families, women entrepreneurs are more likely to achieve work–life balance thus contributing to their marriage successes (Wu et al., 2010).

A subset of the women in family business research studies the impact of matriarchs on the family business and the family. The power of the matriarch, including the source and the exercise of such power, is the central concern of this literature (Smith, 2014). A family business ruled by a matriarch or a patriarch is different from other businesses due to the former's emphasis on the integration of family and business. Although the patriarch-ruled family business has a higher level of business–family integration than non-family firms, a matriarch is more capable of integrating business and family at every level and in everyday life (Sanday, 1998, 2002). The matriarch can create a tighter business–family connection because she is much more involved in the development and growth of family than the men in the family. Women are the "dominant partner" outside of work in most cultures (Straus, 2008). Their expertise in the family and close association with members of the family can enable them to effectively govern both family and the family business (Martin, 2001).

However, while a woman may gain economic power from her entrepreneurial success or succession, she does not necessarily hold the controlling position in her family. For example, a daughter may succeed in her father's business as chairman/chief executive officer but the father remains the leader of the family. In addition, culture and family traditions may determine if the wife, daughter, or daughter-in-law are eligible to control both the family and the business. Many cultures subscribe to the perspective that women are homemakers and men are breadwinners (Smythe and Sardeshmukh, 2014; Wang, 2010). Despite the improvements, empirical evidence continues to show that daughters and daughters-in-law are much less likely to take control of the family business (Marotz-Baden and Mattheis, 1994; Overbeke et al. 2013, 2015; Smythe and Sardeshmukh, 2014; Wang, 2010). Our examination of the corporate governance data also shows that 28 percent of the family members involved in the family business are women. It is not the majority but this national average is much higher than that of the women family member participation at the Linyuan group, the largest family business group in Taiwan. The Linyuan group is a third-generation family business. Almost 80 percent of the male family members are involved in the family business yet there are no women.

As our understanding of the modern family and the structure of family by and large build on the paternal perspective (Smith, 2014), business researchers seldom take part in the intellectual discussions on the effects of family roles assumed by members of a family. However, the familial roles and their impact on families have been a prominent topic of interest in other social science disciplines. Early anthropological observations of non-western societies have highlighted the significance of uncles and aunts in the upbringing of children (Hsu, 1965; Levi-Strauss, 1969). History and family studies have also shed light on how family members interact with each other (e.g., grandparents and grandchildren) in western society (Ruiz and Silverstein, 2007; Thomas, 2001). These early findings motivate later studies on the impact of specific family roles on families in different cultural and social contexts. For example, a kinship theory study examines the contributions of grandparents, parents, brothers, and sisters to the caring of a woman giving birth. Their quantitative analysis suggests a relationship between the family role assumed by an individual and how he/she contributes to caring for the birth-giving woman. The same research has also underlined contribution differences between the newborn's paternal and maternal sides of uncles, aunts, and grandparents (Huber and Breedlove, 2007; Meyer and Kandic, 2017).

Building on the kinship literature, the purpose of this chapter is to explore the roles of adult women who are born to the family (paternal aunts) in the Chinese culture. Taiwanese society is a branch of the broadly defined modern Chinese culture. Patrilineality practices and values are not as profound as they were decades ago but are still common in Taiwan. Daughters are rarely part of the family business as they become "non-family" after marriage in the Chinese cultural tradition. However, it is not a rare practice to place adult daughters in key business positions in Taiwanese family businesses. Using secondary data and interviews, we analyze the uniqueness of daughters in the family and argue that daughters are more important than daughters-in-law for family businesses. The role of the adult daughters is not limited to their potential ability to expand their family's external network (Redding, 1991). The daughters can also make substantial contributions to care for their families and family businesses. We attest that the unique position of paternal aunts places these adult daughters in an advantageous position in the families and the businesses.

This chapter makes two major contributions. First, it expands the discussions of daughter-in-family business by examining the adult daughters' (paternal aunts) participation to the businesses managed and owned by their families. Second, our research on the paternal aunts' family business participation enhances our understanding of the interactions between different family roles in Chinese family businesses. The rest of this chapter is organized as follows. We review the anthropological literature on women in Chinese family businesses in the second section. The third section presents a descriptive statistical analysis of women in the top 100 Taiwanese business groups. The fourth section presents a case study of a leading furniture manufacturer whose matriarch is a parental aunt, followed by discussions and a conclusion.

WOMEN IN FAMILY BUSINESS

The research on women's participation in the family business generally has two subjects of concern. The first is the role of women in the family business. This school is most interested in the motivations and drivers of women participation (Overbeke et al., 2013, 2015; Hytti et al., 2017). The second school focuses primarily on how women participate in the family business and the impact of their participation. The wife (or mother) and daughter are the family female roles often highlighted in these studies (Jimenez, 2009; Campopiano et al., 2017).

The wife's participation in a family business is mostly informal and supportive. They operate in the shadow of the family. The wife is a central figure of the family economy and finance (Rowe and Hong, 2000). In addition, the wife is the primary caregiver in the family. An important task of a wife is to maintain the harmony of her family. Given the unique role of the wife in preserving the cohesion and harmony of her family, a wife can be viewed as a chief emotional officer (Lyman, 1988; Ward, 1987). Their role as cohesion and harmony creators are particularly critical in times of internal conflict (Campopiano et al., 2017; Jimenez, 2009; Smith, 2014).

The roles of founders' daughters are quite different from their mothers. Such a difference is reflected in the topics of research on the family business daughter. A major concern of daughters is family business succession. Based on his comparison of the father–son succession and father–daughter succession, Jimenez (2009) suggested that the transition between generations is smoother in the scenario of father–daughter successions. The smoothness of the father–daughter transition may be attributed to the three roles of a daughter (Dumas, 1990; Jimenez, 2009). First, a daughter is the caregiver of her father. The father becomes dependent on the daughter. Second, she is the owner of her father's wealth; thus, a daughter is sometimes considered "the taker of the gold." The daughter has obtained independence from her father. Finally, the daughter can be the guardian of the wealth or the "caretaker of the king's gold." In this scenario, the father and the daughter are codependent on each other. The father is still the owner of the wealth yet the daughter plays an active role in safeguarding the wealth. These three types of roles are the daughter's identities regarding her relationship with her father. These identities affect the nature of the father–daughter relationship and the decision making of the family business. Dumas (1990) argued that the codependence relationship is unique because it only appears in the father–daughter relation. This codependence relationship is key to the relatively smooth ownership transition/succession from fathers to daughters.

Despite the unique advantage of daughter succession, the family business succession is primarily a reconversion strategy (Curimbaba, 2002) through which the incumbent family leaders pick the fittest candidate to continue the legacy of the family. A small number of studies have pointed out that the intent to prolong the family legacy makes the sons preferred choices over daughters. Based on the interviews of Italian women family business successors, Curimbaba (2002) concludes that the family's inability to identify and/or to persuade a family male is the key reason for daughter succession. Similarly, the increasing daughter succession in Chinese family businesses is a direct result of the one-child policy adopted by the Chinese government. If a business family only has a daughter and no other children, the daughter will be the primary choice of succession (Deng, 2015).

While many studies have acknowledged daughters' unique roles in family businesses, there is still much to learn about their impact on family businesses. The literature is mostly interested in the leadership and personal traits of women in family businesses (Campopiano et al., 2019) or their transitions between jobs (Curimbaba, 2002). Women in a family business have been stereotyped as caregiving and gentle characters. There are few discussions on women's role as authorities or as influential leaders. Additionally, many studies on women in family businesses focus primarily on mothers and daughters within a family. There is almost no discussion on paternal aunts or the relationship between adult daughters (second generation of the family) and the third generation of the family.

FAMILY AND LINEAGE IN CHINESE SOCIETY

A woman's role in a Chinese family is defined by two related but different social structures, the lineage and the family. A lineage is a group of people who have the same ancestor. The core of a Chinese family is similar to that of a western nuclear family. However, a Chinese family can also expand to include all the descendants of a living parent (or grandparent). A lineage structure is designed to expand the influence of a paternal bloodline. The members of a lineage would trace their origin to an ancestor from a long time ago to expand the boundary of the lineage as broad as possible. A woman is a member of her lineage until she is married to someone outside of her paternal lineage. On the other hand, a daughter is a member of her original family even after she gets married. However, unlike her male siblings, a daughter does not have the right to inherit her parents' (i.e., her father's) wealth. Women in general also have very limited or no role in the business and are not economically independent in traditional Chinese society. Daughters are largely excluded from family business successions (Wang, 2010). Of course, many Chinese families have moved away from this tradition and opened opportunities for family women (Friedman, 2006; Liu, 2004; Topley, 1975). Despite the exclusion of parental wealth inheritance, there is no doubt that a daughter is part of her family of origin. Her life-long membership to her original family is signified by her inclusion of family memorial services in which the entire family mourns the loss of family members and pays respect to the deceased family elders. On the contrary, a woman severs the affiliation with her father's lineage when she marries somebody outside of the lineage. She has no obligation nor is allowed to worship the distant common ancestors from her father's side (Fei, 1939; Freedman, 1966).

A Chinese lineage is designed to maximize the reach of paternal lineage, which can go back centuries (Ebrey and Watson, 1986). However, it is only natural that people of the same ancestor will grow apart after only one or two generations. A lineage holds people of the same lineage together through the planning, organization, and participation of ancestral memorial services. These memorial services are significant rituals to keep the lineage together (Overmyer, 2009). They signify the common roots of lineage members and are instrumental in developing a sense of belonging within the lineage. It should be noted that the ancestral lineage services require economic commitments from its members. The lineage needs financial means to support activities such as the construction of ancestral halls and scheduled religious services. It may be relatively easy to collect random donations when the lineage is small in size and the members live nearby. However, donations are not a stable nor a reliable source of income in the long run. To ensure that the ancestral services are fully funded over time, many lineages create their common resource pools to generate revenues for the common purpose. A more structured example of this mechanism is Ancestral Memorial Property (AMP), which is the undivided economic assets owned by the lineage. An AMP can be managed by the lineage itself or by a trusted third party (Huang, 2016).

A Chinese lineage can be seen as a structure for people remotely related by blood to stay together and stay strong. The "equal division among sons" is a long tradition of family wealth succession in Chinese society (Zheng, 2010). This practice divides all of the father's assets equally among his sons when intergenerational wealth transfer occurs. The practice of equal divisions was developed and codified nearly 2000 years ago to increase the tax income of the central government. However, the enforcement of equal division dilutes family wealth and assets over time. Unless there is a surge of new wealth creation in later generations, the share of wealth passed down to each male offspring will be much smaller in just two to three generations (Fei, 1939; Freedman, 1966).

Although daughters are not eligible to succeed in their parents' business in the Chinese family as defined by lineage, daughters do receive benefits from family wealth in the form of dowry. A daughter receives dowry when getting married or a small wealth set aside if not married. It is very common for wealthy families to provide considerable dowries when their daughters get married. The dowry is, therefore, an endowment for the married daughters from her parents. This gift can also be viewed as her parent's buy-out of her right of inheritance. Another characteristic of Chinese society is that sons are expected to make periodic payments to their parents once they start working. These payments are the sons' contribution to the family. Nonetheless, the unmarried daughters are exempted from this family duty. The daughters can keep all of their incomes. The savings before marriage and the dowry constitute major sources of a daughter's wealth in Chinese society. She can use this personal wealth to help her husband or to start her own business. But the traditional practice prohibits a married daughter from succeeding in her parents' business unless she has no brothers.

Kinship scholars have accepted that patrilineality is the foundation of Chinese family relationships (Freedman, 1965; Chen, 1985). Members of a paternal family are cohabitants under a patriarch. Women are generally considered secondary or supporters in this cultural tradition. But there are two types of women in a Chinese family, the daughters born to this patriarchal family (affiliated by birth) and the daughters born to other patriarchal families (affiliated by marriage). They are both members of a paternal family, but these two groups have different roles in the family. The first category includes daughters, sisters, and paternal aunts. The second category includes daughters-in-law, wives, and mothers. These two different categories of women have different roles in a family. Women affiliated with the family by marriage assume the responsibility of reproduction. On the other hand, women affiliated with the family by birth are tasked to connect her biological family to society (Numazaki, 2000). Married daughters make significant contributions to the expansion of the external networks of their biological families (Fortes, 1969; Fox, 1967).

A different perspective to understand the roles of women in their families is through the lens of a uterine family (Wolf, 1972). The core of a uterine family is the mother who gives birth to sons and daughters. This perspective draws the boundary of a family by the mother. Only the children from the same mother are part of the family. The membership of a uterine family can be broader or narrower than a paternal family. The main difference between a paternal and a uterine family is the familiness of daughters-in-law. A daughter-in-law is not part of the uterine family to which her husband belongs. A young wife is a peripheral member of her husband's multigenerational family. However, a wife can evolve to the role of matriarch as her own children grow up and get married (Johnson, 1983). The family business literature has been a subscriber to the paternal family perspective.

In summary, the family and the lineage serve different purposes in the traditional Chinese society. Both are important pillars of the patrilineage tradition. However, a family performs the functions of care providers and production for its members. It starts to branch off through wealth division and marriage when the patriarch dies. A family will not grow indefinitely. The primary purpose of a lineage is to worship the common ancestors. This organization has the potential to grow indefinitely. In fact, many Taiwanese families are able to trace their lineages to centuries ago.

PATERNAL AUNTS IN THE CHINESE FAMILY BUSINESS

The breakup of families is an important topic of interest in the kinship anthropology. While the common practice is that a family and its wealth are equally divided among sons when their father dies, the breakup can occur before the death of the patriarch. The wife of the son (the daughter-in-law) plays an important role in her husband's breakaway decision. A daughter-in-law is part of the family but only her husband and her children are truly the families from her perspective (Wolf, 1972). In addition, the dowry she received from her original family may reduce or even eliminate her and her husband's economic dependence on the husband's parents and brothers. The breakup may occur sooner than later when a married son is completely economically independent from his original family (Cohen, 1976).

While the daughters-in-law may facilitate the division or breakup of a family, the daughter serves a different role. A daughter is a potential "outsider" from the lineage's perspective. She is not entitled to inherit her father's wealth. But she is clearly a member of her mother's uterine family, just like her brothers. Therefore, a woman occupies an ambiguous position in her original family. She has three identities in her family, a daughter, a sister, and a paternal aunt to her brothers' children. The paternal aunt identity is particularly unique because the brothers' children are not part of her uterine family. Second, the third-generation children and their paternal aunts are seldom very close. This lack of interaction places the paternal aunts in a neutral position among second-generation siblings. She does not inherit anything from her parents so she does not have a strong economic incentive to favor any of her brothers or their children. Third, although the dyad of a paternal aunt and her brothers' children is a structural equal to the dyad of a maternal uncle and his sisters' children, the nature of these two pairs of relationships is very different (Levi-Strauss, 1969). While the maternal uncle dyad is characterized as a "joking relationship" and is labeled as a male mother (Radcliffe-Brown, 1971), the paternal aunt dyad is characterized as a serious and respectful relationship. Therefore, a paternal aunt is also labeled female father by kinship researchers

(Hsu, 1965; Radcliffe-Brown, 1971). The female father can be a substitute for a severe and disciplinary father figure to her brothers' children when her brother is absent. In short, a paternal aunt is a neutral, authority figure in the eyes of her brothers' children. Building on the findings from kinship research, we argue that the paternal aunts can assume the role of family matriarch if she is involved in the family business owned and managed by her original family. Therefore, we propose the following:

P1: The paternal aunt can be a matriarch of the family business due to her neutral position in her original family.

P2: The relationship stated in P1 is more likely to occur when the paternal aunt's male siblings are involved in the family business.

Kinship research suggests the uniqueness of parental aunts in Chinese family businesses. Although there have not been many empirical efforts to systematically examine the roles of parental aunts in family businesses, our propositions can be underscored by limited-scale data collections. In the following section, we will use secondary data and case interviews to illustrate our argument. Please note this is not an effort to support the propositions, but to give examples of the empirical relevance of our propositions.

TWO OBSERVATIONS

We are going to provide two empirical examples in this chapter. The first is the secondary data of the top 100 business groups from Taiwan. The second example is a case study of a paternal aunt matriarch in a Taiwanese family business group. The case is selected through the executive education program of one of the co-authors' affiliated institutions. The secondary data gives an overview of women's participation in family businesses in Taiwan. The case interview provides more details about how a paternal aunt becomes the matriarch in her family.

Although the case may be considered "convenient" data, the co-authors consider it appropriate for the exploratory nature of this study. There are two reasons to study Chinese family businesses using data from Taiwan. First, Taiwanese society is a branch of Chinese culture, yet corporate governance is more transparent in Taiwan than in China. Taiwan is certainly not an authentic representation of traditional Chinese culture but the modernized version of many guiding principles derived from transitional Chinese families is still being practiced in Taiwan. There are not many identifiable paternal aunt matriarch cases in a Chinese family business group. However, the interviewee is fully cooperating with the research team under the condition of anonymity.

For the exploratory nature of this study, this convenient case should be an appropriate window of observation to gather new insights about the role of paternal aunts.

The Collection of the Family Business Group Data

We are interested in women's participation and their positions in Taiwanese family business groups. There are two service providers of corporate govern-ance data in Taiwan. China Credit Information Services (CRIF Taiwan) pub-lishes corporate profiles of Taiwanese business groups annually. Based on the raw data, CRIF ranks the business groups by size. It also publishes the family trees of ranked family business groups and the non-profit organization (NPO), holding companies affiliated with the family in the CRIF corporate profiles. Although the family trees published by CRIF are sometimes incomplete, they are an important starting point to identify core family members. The second data publisher is the *Taiwan Economic Journal* (TEJ). It translates the cor-porate governance information disclosed by listing companies in spreadsheet formats.

The secondary data collected for this research spans from 2009 to 2014. We collected data from all top 100 Taiwanese business groups over the six years. Eighty-two business groups were ranked on the top 100 list from 2009 to 2014. A business group satisfying any one of the following three criteria is considered as a family business group in this study: (1) the leadership positions of the business group are occupied by members of founding families (CRIF, 2014); (2) more than half of the shares are controlled by a family and the chairman/chief executive officer positions are occupied by members of this family; and (3) a business co-controlled by two and more groups yet one of the co-controlling group is a family. We also use information reported in the media to cross-reference the information published by CRIF and TEJ.

Many family business participants hold other positions outside of their family business. It is important to determine the qualifications of these individ-uals. As our focus is on women in a family, we Google searched the profiles of the names identified by CRIF and TEJ to obtain additional information on their work experience. The major sources of work experience information include, but are not limited to, Wikipedia, the corporate homepage, and other major business publications in Taiwan. We also used the names of these indi-viduals to search for their board involvement in the past from the government registries of Taiwan.

Findings from the Secondary Data

The outcome of the secondary data collection results in a dataset of 60 families controlling 55 family business groups. Table 8.1 summarizes the participation of daughters and daughters-in-law from different generations to family businesses. The first generation represents the founding generation. There are a few observations. First, the first-generation daughters-in-law have the highest participation frequency across generations. This group represents the wives of the male family business founders or are sometimes labeled as mothers. They are essentially the co-founders of family businesses or strong supporters of the businesses started by their husbands. Second, while women's participation in a family business is no longer rare in Taiwan, some families continue to deny women's participation in the family business decision making. These families even keep women out of the management/governance of family foundations. This practice implies that the family is where women can have active roles. However, the daughters of founders have higher participation in the family business than daughters-in-law in the second and third generations. The daughters are more likely to work in the family business groups or to succeed in the family business than the daughters-in-law. Third, sons-in-law can play a significant role in the family business group owned/ managed by their wives' families. The first generation son-in-law refers to a man married to a woman entrepreneur. This is a relatively rare situation as few women were large family business founders in Taiwan until the last decades of the twentieth century. Table 8.1 shows only four first-generation son-in-law participations and three of them are essentially working for their spouses as executives in the family business; one of them succeeded his spouse and became the leader of the family business. Son-in-law participation increases drastically in the second generation. Out of 32 sons-in-law involved in the family business group, 23 (72 percent) of them hold positions within the family business group. This number and percentage are higher than those of daughters-in-law and daughters.

We broke down the participation of mother, daughter, and daughter-in-law by generations and reported the results in Table 8.2. We identified 400 women (mother, daughter, and daughter-in-law) affiliated with the top family business groups. These 400 individuals occupied 570 positions because one person may hold multiple positions. Since these groups are all multi-generational family businesses, the mother (the wife of the founder) is either retired or deceased. This explains the very low counts of mother involvement in the family business group. Table 8.2 broke down family business participation into four categories. The first is holding a leadership position in the core business or heading a subsidiary. The second is holding a non-leadership position in the family business. The third is starting up a new business or NPO. The fourth

Table 8.1   *Women in top 100 family business groups in Taiwan (60 families, 55 family business groups)*

	Wife participation				Daughter participation				Son-in-law participation		
Gener- ation	Positions in group	Succ- ession	New ven- tures	Family Found- ation	Positions in group	Succ- ession	New ven- tures	Family Found- ation	Positions in group	Succ- ession	New ven- tures
1st[1]	8	1	2	5	NA	NA	NA	NA	3	1	0
2nd[2]	5	0	1	6	11	7	8	5	18	3	4
3rd[2]	2	1	0	0	6	1	2	0	2	1	0
Total	15	2	3	11	17	8	10	5	23	5	4

Notes: [1] First-generation wife refers to the founder or cofounder. A married woman who founded a business by herself or cofounded a business with her husband will be considered a first-generation woman. The first-generation son-in-law refers to the male brothers-in-law of the founder; [2] second- and third-generation wife participation refers to daughter-in-law participation in the family business.

category of participation is holding a board directorship of the family business group. Our data have shown that the corporate board directorship is the more popular path taken by both daughters and daughters-in-law to participate in their family business. However, it appears that the daughters are more involved in the management of the family business group than the daughters-in-law.

One explanation of the women's participation in the business owned by her family of origin can be attributed to the lack of male siblings (Deng, 2015). This notion suggests that daughter participation is at least partially driven by the need to continue the family legacy or to keep the business in the family. However, our data show that the percentage of daughter participation is higher when the daughters have male siblings in Table 8.3. There are 182 daughters from the 60 family studies in this research. Twenty-three of them have no male siblings. The family business participation of these 23 daughters is fairly equally split as 12 of them participated in their family business and 11 of them did not. However, daughters' participation in the family business is much stronger when they have brothers. We divided the brothers into two subcategories, with children and without children. Among 159 daughters with male siblings, 54.72 percent of the brothers have children and 45.28 percent do not. Across these two groups, about 70 percent of the women with male siblings are involved in their family business. Daughters acquire the identity of "paternal aunts" when their brothers become parents. Next we zero in on daughters' family business participation and divide the group into "sisters" and "paternal aunts" groups. The sister group refers to daughter participation when her brothers don't have any children. The paternal aunt group refers to daugh-

Table 8.2   *Women participation to family businesses*

Generations		No. of family women with names listed in a family tree	Participation in the family business group		Participation in a family foundation	Startup outside of the family business	Board membership		
			Executive position	Work in the group	Holds the title of CEO		Family business group	Family foundation	Family investment arm
M*		2	0	0	0	0	0	0	1
W	1st	73	7	2	3	4	26	26	20
W	2nd	114	9	4	9	17	43	30	56
W	3rd	35	2	1	1	9	8	6	14
W	4th	2	0	0	0	0	0	0	0
W		224 297 (job titles)	18 (8.0%)	7 (3.12%)	13 (5.8%)	30 (13.4%)	77 (34.4%)	62 (27.7%)	90 (40.1%)
D	1st	5	0	0	0	0	1	1	0
D	2nd	113	15	12	8	15	46	42	42
D	3rd	56	14	3	1	6	25	14	27

Generations	No. of family women with names listed in a family tree	Participation in the family business group		Participation in a family foundation	Startup outside of the family business	Board membership		
		Executive position	Work in the group	Holds the title of CEO		Family business group	Family foundation	Family investment arm
	174							
D	272	29 (16.6%)	15 (8.6%)	9 (5.1%)	21 (12.0%)	72 (41.4)	57 (32.7%)	69 (39.6%)
	400							
Total	570 (job titles)	47	22	22	51	149	119	160

Notes: * M refers to the mother of the founder; W refers to the wife of the founder. A first-generation wife represents the wife of the founder. A second-generation wife represents the daughter-in-law of the founder; +D refers to daughters. A first-generation daughter represents the sister of a founder. The second-generation daughter represents the daughter of the founder.

Table 8.3   *Women in her original family and participation in the family business*

No. of family women	Born to the family	With brothers	Brothers' children	Percentage	Family business participation	Percentage
		No: 23			12(Y)*	52.17
					11(N)+	47.82
410	182		No children: 87	54.72%	61(Y)*	70.11
		Yes: 159			26(N)+	29.88
			Yes children: 72	45.28%	49(Y)*	68.05
					23(N)+	31.94

Notes: * Represents the number of family business participating daughters in this category; + represents the numbers of non-participating daughters in this category.

ter participation when her brothers have children. We found similar levels of family business participation in both groups. This result is quite different from the need-based proposition.

Case Interview with the Matriarch of FT

FT corporation is a third-generation family business group in Taiwan. It was started by two brothers of the Lin family from a rural village in central Taiwan. They left their home town to seek better opportunities in the early 1970s. One of the Lin brothers went to a sandcast foundry to work as an apprentice. He later completed his training and started a business of his own. This new venture is the forerunner of the FT corporation. The founder of FT quickly recruited his other brothers and a sister who also left the home town to help out. Forty years later, the founder and his brother passed away. Now the sister who joined the business in the early days is in charge. FT is a major furniture supplier to IKEA. This manufacturer is also one of the very few Taiwanese businesses certified by the IWAY standard, the social responsibility standard of IKEA. Ms. Lin, the younger sister among the siblings, has assumed the chairmanship of the FT group. In addition, she is the matriarch of the entire Lin family. She grew up with four other siblings. The cofounders of the FT group were her oldest and second oldest brothers. Both of them were survived by their widows and children. Ms. Lin also has an older sister and a younger brother, who is the general manager of the FT group. The older sister is not involved in the family business. Chairman Lin is the paternal aunt of her brothers' children. As she is in control of both the business and the family, she is sometimes viewed as the "tiger" aunt in the eyes of her brothers' children.

Ms. Lin expressed that the governance of the family is the area where she puts in the most effort. She implemented policies to ensure equity between family and non-family employees. However, her role as the parental aunt plus the chairmanship places her in an unbiased, neutral, and powerful position to keep the family together. There are several measures to ensure the togetherness of the family. First, there is a Lin education fund for all of her brothers' children. This is essentially an annual stipend to all. However, Ms. Lin strictly requires all of the family branches to fulfill the monthly, seasonal, and yearly ancestral memorial rituals to be eligible for such a stipend. The children are also required to visit their grandmother (i.e., Ms. Lin's mother) and to perform monthly family chores. Second, the family employees receive a salary and bonus from the FT group. However, the family employees do not have the full discretion to use the bonus money. The bonus has to be pooled together by the branch and used for capital investment such as buying a new home for a grown-up child or paying for the seed capital of a new venture started by a family member.

Ms. Lin's authority as the family matriarch is highlighted in a decision to reject a nephew's request to rejoin the FT group. This nephew was an employee of FT but left to start his own business. He lost everything from the new business and was on the brink of bankruptcy. His grandmother (and Ms. Lin's mother) pleaded for her grandson with no success. Ms. Lin's nephew ended up filing bankruptcy. He eventually returned to FT and started over as an entry-level employee.

DISCUSSIONS AND CONCLUSION

While research on women's participation in family businesses has been on the rise, the impact of family roles on women's involvement has not received much attention in the field of family business. However, the individual's role in the family and its impact on the rest of the family have been important subjects in several social science disciplines such as anthropology, family studies, and history. Although the primary concerns of these disciplines are generally more on the family dynamics and the function of the family, rather than the economic activity committed by the family, some of their findings may inform business researchers to develop a better understanding of women's family business participation. This chapter explores the uniqueness of paternal aunts in family businesses by bridging the literature from both family business research and other social science traditions.

Previous family research of different societies at different time periods has produced a consistent finding that daughters are mostly secondary choices in family business succession decisions. Their male siblings, the sons, are often the preferred candidates to take over the family businesses founded by their parents. As women have been more empowered in the last decades, we are seeing more and more women executives and leaders in family businesses (Hall, 2019). However, the family's women, daughters and daughters-in-law, are still markedly underrepresented than their brothers in the C-suites of family businesses. Despite the overall underrepresentation of daughters in family business leadership positions, many daughters indeed have risen to become the matriarchs of the entire family.

We focus on paternal aunts, adult daughters, in this research because of their unique role in the family. Using the secondary data from the Taiwanese family business groups and an interview with a matriarch of a family business, this research explores the relationship between daughters and sons in family business participation. It appears that daughter participation increases as their brothers' family participation increases. This observation contradicts the notion that daughters are eligible to succeed in family businesses only when there are no eligible sons to take over the business. Our finding suggests that daughter participation in family businesses may be driven by other factors. One of the possible explanations may be how children are socialized in their upbringing. Hellerstein and Morrill (2011) analyzed labor data from 1909 to 1977 and concluded that fathers' specific human capital investment in their daughters explains a significant percentage of daughters' career choices. Similarly, Sandler and Morrill (2013) studied the labor participation of daughters and suggested a strong correlation between mothers and daughters' labor participation. These recent analyses point out that socialization may be a viable explanation to the daughter's family business participation. It is a topic to be examined in the future.

The case interview we conducted further illustrates the significance of the adult daughters' family role in a family business. Our interview clearly manifested the interviewee's intention to continue the family business legacy. According to Ms. Lin, the FT group will eventually be passed to her younger brother, the incumbent general manager, and to the younger generations of the Lin family. This statement, coupled with her relentless efforts to keep the family together, suggest a different type of "strictness" from "tiger mom" or simply strict parents. While a strict parent may be driven by maximizing his/ her children's potential to achieve personal success, the strict parental aunt may be aiming to help all of the children from her family of origin. In other words, a paternal aunt may have a broader scope of parenting towards her nieces and nephews. This practice is possible because a parental aunt is some- what close yet not too close to her nieces and nephews. This position allows her to claim the role of an unbiased and neutral family member. When this role is combined with another powerful position, such as the leader of the family business, the parental aunt may gain the legitimacy and power to serve the family as a matriarch. However, an alternative explanation is that the paternal aunt actually developed power and legitimacy from work or other external achievements then rose to the matriarchal position for the entire family. The emergence of a matriarch is another topic of future investigation.

This research is an exploratory effort to develop a better understanding of a relatively small yet growing practice in a family business. The findings have two major limitations. First, this study utilized data and interviews from Taiwan. While the qualitative interview reinforces the secondary data by providing more details about the matriarchal practice in a family business, it also reduces the generalizability of our findings. It is possible to have a very generalizable research based on data collected from a single country/region/culture, but it is necessary to control background variables to highlight the expected main effect. This task will require a different research design and is beyond the scope of the current project. Second, our data are collected from a narrow window (2009–14), but the primary goal of the family business is longevity. Additionally, it may take a long time to develop a matriarch or to finalize the succession decision. Our narrow window of data collection may have provided a current snapshot, but the data are much less effective in detecting long-term developments in family businesses.

The role of women can be quite ambiguous in their family of origin in Chinese society. They are delisted from the lineage when they get married but they continue to be a member of the family of origin even after marriage. Their relationship with parents, siblings, and families of siblings is close yet distant. This uniqueness enables the daughters (and later parental aunts) to participate in the family business as an enabler to family cohesion and business success. Our research provides some qualitative evidence to the implications of such uniqueness. Further studies are needed to understand the roles and impacts of daughters and even women in family businesses.

REFERENCES

Bettinelli, C., B. Del Bosco, and C. Giachino (2019), "Women on boards in family firms: what we know and what we need to know," in E. Memili and C. Dibrell (eds), *The Palgrave Handbook of Heterogeneity among Family Firms*, Cham: Palgrave Macmillan.

Bianco, M., A. Ciavarella, and R. Signoretti (2015), "Women on corporate boards in Italy: the role of family connections," *Corporate Governance: An International Review*, **23** (2), 129–44.

Bonner, B. and W. Bonner (2012), *Family Fortunes: How to Build Family Wealth and Hold on to It for 100 Years*, Hoboken, NJ: Wiley.

Campopiano, G., A. De Massis, F. Rinaldi, and S. Sciascia (2017), "Women's involvement in family firms: progress and challenges for future research," *Journal of Family Business Strategy*, **8**, 200–12.

Campopiano, G., F.R. Rinaldi, S. Sciascia, and A. De Massis (2019), "Family and non-family women on the board of directors: effects on corporate citizenship behavior in family-controlled fashion firm," *Journal of Cleaner Production*, **214** (20), 41–51.

Chen, X. (1985), "The one-child population policy, modernization, and the extended Chinese family," *Journal of Marriage and Family*, **47** (1), 193–202.

Cohen, M. (1976), *House United, House Divided: The Chinese Family in Taiwan*, New York: Columbia University Press.

China Credit Information Service (2014), *Business Group in Taiwan*. Taipei: China Credit InformationService, Ltd.

Curimbaba, F. (2002), "The dynamics of women's roles as family business managers," *Family Business Review*, **15** (3), 239–52.

Deng, X. (2015), "Father–daughter succession in China: facilitators and challenges," *Journal of Family Business Management*, **5** (1), 38–54.

Dumas, C. (1990), "Preparing the new CEO: managing the father–daughter succession in family business," *Family Business Review*, **30** (2), 169–81.

Ebrey, P. and J. Watson (1986), *Kinship Organization in Late Imperial China, 1000–1940*, Berkeley, CA: University of California Press.

Ernst & Young (2015), *Women in Leadership: The Family Business Advantage*. Retrieved from www.ey.com/Publication/vwLUAssets/ey-women-in-leadership-the -family-business-advantage/$FILE/ey-women-in-leadership-the-family-business -advantage.pdf

Fei, H.-T. (1939), *Peasant Life in China*, London: Routledge and Kegan Paul.

Fortes, M. (1969), *The Web of Kinship among the Tallensi*, London: Oxford University Press.

Freedman, M. (1965), *Lineage Organization in Southeastern China*, London: University of London, Athlone Press.

Freedman, M. (1966), *Chinese Lineage and Society: Fukien and Kuangtung*, New York: Humanities Press.

Friedman, S.L. (2006), *Intimate Politics: Marriage, Market, and State Power in Southeast China*, Cambridge, MA: Harvard University Press.

Fox, R. (1967), *Kinship and Marriage*, Harmondsworth: Pelican Books.

Hall, C.G. (2019), *How Family Businesses Are Embracing Women in Leadership*. Retrieved from www.ey.com/en_us/growth/how-family-businesses-are-embracing -women-in-leadership

Hellerstein, J.K. and M.S. Morrill (2011), "Dads and daughters: the changing impact of fathers on women's occupational choices," *Journal of Human Resources*, **46** (2), 333–72.

Hsu, F.L.K. (1965), "The effect of dominant kinship relationships on kin and non-kin behavior: a hypothesis," *American Anthropologist*, **67** (3), 638–61.

Huang, C.-W. (2016), *The Analysis of Ancestral Memorial Property Law and the Practice of Land Management*, Taipei: Wu-Nan Culture Enterprise.

Huber, B.R. and W.L. Breedlove (2007), "Evolutionary theory, kinship, and childbirth in cross-cultural perspective," *Cross-Cultural Research*, **41** (2), 196–219.

Hytti, Ulla, Alsos, Gry, Heinonen, Jarna, Ljunggren, E.(2017), "Navigating the family business: A gendered analysis of identity construction of daughters," *International Small Business Journal*, **35** (6), 665–86.

Jimenez, R.M. (2009), "Research on women in the business," *Family Business Review*, **22** (1), 53–64.

Johnson, K.A. (1983), *Women, the Family, and Peasant Revolution in China*, Chicago, IL: University of Chicago Press.

Kaslow, F.W. (1998), "Handling transitions from mother to son in the family business: the knotty issues," *Family Business Review*, **11** (3), 229.

Levi-Strauss, C. (1969), *The Elementary Structures of Kinship*, Boston, MA: Beacon Press.

Liu, F.-W. (2004), "From being to becoming: nüshu and sentiments in a Chinese rural community," *American Ethnologist*, **31** (3), 422–39.

Lyman, A.R. (1988), "Life in the family circle," *Family Business Review*, **1** (4), 383–98.

Marotz-Baden, R. and C. Mattheis (1994), "Daughters-in-law and stress in two-generation farm families," *Family Relations*, **43** (2), 132–7.

Martin, H.F. (2001), "Is family governance an oxymoron?," *Family Business Review*, **17** (1), 91–6.

Meyer, M.H. and A. Kandic (2017), "Grandparenting in the United States," *Innovation in Aging*, **1** (2), igx023.

Moran, G. (2015), "Exclusive: this is the type of business most likely to promote women leaders," *Fortune*, June 18.

Numazaki, I. (2000), "Chinese business enterprise as inter-family partnership: a comparison with the Japanese case," in C.K. Bun (ed.), *Chinese Business Network*, Singapore: Prentice Hall Asia.

Overbeke, K.K., D. Bilimoria, and S. Perelli (2013), "The dearth of daughter successors in family businesses: gendered norms, blindness to possibility and invisibility," *Journal of Family Business Strategy*, **4**, 201–12.

Overbeke, K.K., D. Bilimoria, and T. Somers (2015), "Shared vision between fathers and daughters in family businesses: the determining factor that transforms daughters into successors," *Frontiers of Psychology*, **6**, 625.

Overmyer, D.L. (2009), *Local Religion in North China in the Twentieth Century: The Structure and Organization of Community Rituals and Beliefs*, Leiden: Brill.

Radcliffe-Brown, A.R. (1971), *Structure and Function in Primitive Society*, London: Cohen and West.

Redding, G. (1991), "Weak organizations and strong linkages: managerial ideology and Chinese family business networks," in G. Hamilton (ed.), *Business Networks and Economic Development in East and South East Asia*, Hong Kong: University of Hong Kong, pp. 30–47.

Rowe, B.R. and G.S. Hong (2000), "The role of wives in family businesses: the paid and unpaid work of women," *Family Business Review*, **13**, 1–13.

Ruiz, S. and M. Silverstein (2007), "Relationships with grandparents and the emotional well-being of late adolescent and young adult grandchildren," *Journal of Social Issues*, **63** (10), 703–808.

Sanday, P.R. (1998), "Matriarchy as a sociocultural form: an old debate in a new light," Paper presented at the 16th Congress of the Indo Pacific Prehistory Association, Melaka.

Sanday, P.R. (2002), "Women at the center," in *Life in a Modern Matriarchy*, New York: Sage.

Sandler, M. and T. Morrill (2013), "Intergenerational links in female labor force participation," *Labour Economics*, **20**, 38–47.

Smith, R. (2014), "Assessing the contribution of the 'theory of matriarchy' to the entrepreneurship and family business literatures," *International Journal of Gender and Entrepreneurship*, **6**, 255–75.

Smythe, J. and S. Sardeshmukh (2014), "Fathers and daughters in family business," *Small Enterprise Research*, **20**, 98–109.

Straus, M.A. (2008), "Dominance and symmetry in partner violence by male and female university students in 32 nations," *Children and Youth Services Review*, **30** (3), 252–75.

Thomas, Bert J.T.J. (2001), *Constructing the Caribbean-American Family: The Influence of Middle Class Grandfathers over Their Grandsons*, Buffalo, NY: Afro-American Historical Association of the Niagara Frontier.

Topley, M. (1975), "Marriage resistance in rural Kwangtung," in M. Wolf and R. Witke (eds), *Women in Chinese Society*, Stanford, CA: Stanford University Press, pp. 67–88.

Wang, C. (2010), "Daughter exclusion in family business succession: a review of the literature," *Journal of Family and Economic Issues*, **31**, 475–84.

Ward, J.L. (1987), *Keeping the Family Business Healthy: How to Plan for Continuing Growth, Profitability, and Family Leadership*, San Francisco, CA: Jossey-Bass.

Welsh, D.H.B., E. Memili, E. Kaciak, and S. Ahmed (2013), "Sudanese women entrepreneurs," *Journal of Developmental Entrepreneurship*, **18** (2): 1–18.

Wolf, M. (1972), *Women and the Family in Rural Taiwan*, Stanford, CA: Stanford University Press.

Wright, M., J.J. Chrisman, J.H. Chua, and L.P. Steier (2014), "Family enterprise and context," *Entrepreneurship Theory and Practice*, **38** (6), 1247–60.

Wu, M., C.-C. Chang, and W.-L. Zhuang (2010), "Relationships of work–family conflict with business and marriage outcomes in Taiwanese copreneurial women," *International Journal of Human Resource Management*, **21**, 742–53.

Zhang, J., H. Zhu, and H.-B. Ding (2013), "Board composition and corporate social responsibility: an empirical investigation in the post Sarbanes-Oxley era," *Journal of Business Ethics*, **114**: 381–92.

Zheng, V. (2010), *Chinese Family Business and the Equal Inheritance System: Unravelling the Myth*, New York: Routledge.

9. Bifurcation bias and family compensation: The case of Dawu Group

Feihu Zheng and Hung-bin Ding

INTRODUCTION

A family firm is a business organization owned, controlled, and/or managed by a family. This type of business organization plays a vital role in the economic activities and the development of human society (Gomez-Mejia, Haynes, Núñez-Nickel, Jacobson, and Moyano-Fuentes, 2007; Shim and Okamuro, 2011). While some families may exercise strong influence on their businesses, others may be more passive and prefer delegating business decision making to non-family professionals. Despite the variations in family influence, many family firms hire non-family employees to satisfy the need of their business. While it has been widely acknowledged that family firms and non-family firms have different approaches in human resources (HR) management, the way a family firm recruits, manages, and retains non-family talent has not attracted much scholarly attention (Combs, Jaskiewicz, Shanine, and Balkin, 2018).

The need of non-family employees is a major management challenge to family firms for several reasons. First, family firms have their unique ideology which tends to value family control and long-term sustainability higher than short-term, quick growth (Johannisson, 2000; Gomez-Mejia et al., 2007). Although non-family employees may bring professional skills and experience to assist the growth and expansion of the family business, the ideological conflicts between family and non-family employees, especially executives, can be a source of internal conflict (Johannisson, 2000). Second, the emphasis on family control and long-term sustainability motivates family firms to develop managerial practices to support these organizational goals. For example, family firms favor hiring family employees (Jaskiewicz, Uhlenbruck, Balkin, and Reay, 2013). There are also differences in terms of the compensations received by family and non-family executives (Gomez-Mejia, Larraza-Kintana, and Makri, 2003). Additionally, family employees tend to have higher influence than non-family employees when the family firms' owners seek feedback from the employees (Huang, Ding, and Kao, 2009). These managerial practices are often viewed as unfair and form a foundation for the emergence of the bifurcation bias.

Bifurcation bias refers to the asymmetric treatment between family and non-family employees in the family firms (Verbeke and Kano, 2010, 2012; Daspit, Madison, Barnett, and Long, 2018). When the bifurcation bias is present, the family members receive preferred treatments regardless of their performance. On the other hand, the non-family employees receive lesser treatment which may include lower compensation and tougher evaluation in comparison to family employees. The presence of bifurcation bias there-fore changes the calculus of non-family employees because the non-family employees are passed over for promotions or are receiving fewer rewards than co-workers with family ties. The non-family workers are thus motivated to compensate their low rewards or loss of promotion with opportunistic behavior at the cost of their employers (Klein and Bell, 2007; Verbeke and Kano, 2010; Daspit et al., 2018). It is imperative for family firms to control bifurcation bias to minimize potential non-family employee opportunism.

One solution to the bifurcation bias problem can be to eliminate non-family employees. While many small family businesses have hired only family members and continue to do so, this "family-only" HR practice simply is not an option for many family firms. The non-family employees provide talent and manpower that are not available from within the family in many medium and large family firms. Hiring only family members would significantly reduce the family firm's ability to grow or even survive. Given the significance of non-family employees, another choice to address the bifurcation bias is to ensure fairness in management, especially HR management, thus eliminating bifurcation bias.

While identical and equal treatment between family and non-family employees can restore fairness in family firms, this practice can decrease the identification of family members in their business. This identification is a key intangible asset of family firms (Ding and Phan 2005; Ding and Lee 2008). When the family business is in crisis or is facing resource paucity, family members are willing to make greater sacrifices to save the family business if they perceive that the business is part of the family (Gomez-Mejia et al., 2007; Lee, Phan, and Ding, 2016). Eliminating the family identity can reduce the family members' devotion and willingness to sacrifice for the business when needed. In summary, the involvement of both family and non-family members improves the performance of family firms (Ding and Pukthuanthong-Le, 2012; Tabor, Chrisman, Madison, and Vardaman, 2018), maintaining fairness and controlling bifurcation bias within the family firms does not necessarily require the removal of either family employees or non-family employees from family firms altogether. The challenge is to create a system meeting the expectations of both groups.

As there are similarities and differences between the expectations of family and non-family employees, a growing number of family firms are addressing the needs of these two groups differently. Practices that enforce fair and equal treatment between family and non-family employees and within respective groups have been considered positive in reducing the negative effects of bifurcation bias (Samara and Arenas, 2017; Samara and Paul, 2018). Examples of fairness-ensuring practices include equal and fair hiring, promotion, and career development opportunities (Van der Heyden, Blondel, and Carlock, 2005), equal rewards (Fang, Memili, Chrisman, and Welsh, 2012), and equal opportunity to express concerns (Samara and Arenas, 2017). In addition to fairness-ensuring practices, family employees usually receive compensation independent from their employee performance. For instance, family employees can also be shareholders of the family business. The dividends distributed to families can be viewed as a unique, additional compensation only available to family employees. Making family members shareholders of the family business and compensating them with dividends separate from family employee compensation from the HR system of the family business is a practice that balances the needs for fairness and family relevance. However, determining the percentage of ownership can be a difficult process for many families. If family members have different assumptions about how many shares they own, this misconception can deeply divide a family and the family business (Baron and Lachenauer, 2016). The result of this divide can be devastating to a family business.

The Dawu Group, a major agricultural enterprise in China, experienced this shareholder challenge in the 1980s and 1990s, when the business was relatively small. As key family stakeholders held very different perspectives about share ownership, early discussions of share distribution fell apart. However, as the business grew and more non-family employees were hired, the Dawu Group faced mounting pressure to maintain fairness and family relevance. In order to address the expectations of stakeholders, the Dawu Group designed a system to ensure both fairness and family relevance without dividing shares among family members in 2005. The purpose of this case research is to look into the experience of Dawu Group and how it may inform practitioners when managing bifurcation bias and family compensation. We have selected Dawu Group for this research because there is a scarce supply of large family firms committed to disclosing their managerial practices over an extended period of time. Dawu Group has been publishing information about both since the mid-2000s. The documentation and interviews with key stakeholders allow us to develop a comprehensive understanding about the role of independent wealth management in the assurance of fairness in family firms.

While this chapter does not aim to develop new theories or to test existing theories, we intend to help practitioners develop appropriate systems to address bifurcation bias issues in their family business. More specifically, this case provides an example of family compensation without share division, thus avoiding the potential devastating discussions among family members regarding share ownership. In addition, Dawu Group's fairness-enhancing practices add to the discussions of bifurcation bias with new practice ideas. The rest of this chapter is organized as follows. The next section reviews the literature. The third section provides an overview of the Dawu Group and a brief description of its struggle to balance family relevance and professionalism over the years. The practical implications and the limitations of this case are discussed in the fourth section.

BIFURCATION BIAS AND FAIRNESS

Bifurcation bias (Verbeke and Kano, 2010, 2012) describes a state in which family firm employers apply different standards to family and non-family employees due to family firm owners' efforts to reduce transaction costs. When more non-family managers are hired to promote the professional management of enterprises, family employees and non-family employees will exist as two independent groups, who possibly have potential unequal employment status and a different understanding of enterprise leadership. The idea of bifurcation bias was inspired by "affect heuristic" in psychology, which can be explained as when decision makers make decisions based on their emotions and intuitions rather than messages from the objective characteristics of things. In family firms, such bias will lead to misjudgment in HR practices. Family employees are usually a reliable and stable source of labor and talent for the family firm because the family members are able to maximize their gains from the long-term success of the family business (Lee et al., 2016). Family firms are more likely to invest in family employees because family members are less likely to "betray" the family firm by taking the skills acquired from its family employer elsewhere. Additionally, family firm employers are less motivated to invest in the development of non-family employees because they are more likely to depart from the family firm for better opportunities (Verbeke and Kano, 2010). Because of the concern of transaction costs, family firms may save core positions and important decision-making power for family employees. The same consideration may also curtail professional managers' authorities and limit their promotions. The family dynamics of business owners may affect HR practice. Recent studies suggest that HR practice may be used to repair an unhealthy family condition by family firm owners. Although such a practice allows family business owners to leverage the positions in the business to improve family dynamics, the blurring of family dynamics and HR practice can create a sense of unfairness among non-family employees (Daspit et al., 2018). As a result, family firms with a high level of family involvement are more likely to be "unfair" to their non-family employees (Barnett and Kellermanns, 2006). These management practices facilitate the creation of bifurcation bias within a family firm. This bias arouses the profiteering attitudes of family employees and dampens the enthusiasm of professional managers to serve the company. If the bifurcation bias is extended, professional managers will be less motivated to invest in the specific human capital and the firm's absorbing of new management resources will encounter obstacles (Verbeke and Kano, 2010, 2012).

The negative effect can be managed through professional HR practice to instill justice or fairness[1] in an organization. Justice is defined as employees' perception of employers' consistency, equitability, respect, and truthfulness in decision making (Colquitt and Rodell, 2015). In short, justice is the conceptualization of fairness (Rawls, 2001). Organizational justice consists of four dimensions: procedural, distributive, interpersonal, and informational (Colquitt, 2001). Procedural justice refers to the fairness of procedures an employer uses to make salary, reward, evaluation, promotion, and assignment decisions. Distributive justice refers to the fairness of HR decisions including compensation, reward, evaluation, promotion, and assignment decisions. Interpersonal justice is defined as the interpersonal interactions between employees and employers in the HR decision procedure. Finally, information justice focuses on the diffusion of information and refers to the explanations the employer offers to the employee regarding HR decisions. Managerial practices to enforce all four dimensions of organizational justice may improve employees' sense of fairness and generate positive consequences for the family firm.

On the flip side, emphasis on fairness can weaken the family firm's ability and choices to financially compensate family members. Employers committed to fairness will strive to treat all employees equally. It implies that non-family members may receive higher compensation than family employees if the former outperforms the latter. Similarly, non-family employees may receive merit-based promotion or even obtain core decision-making power in the family firm. These consequences handicap the family owner's ability to create and distribute wealth to favor families through salary overpayment to family members. Family firms will not be able to hire or promote family members over more competent non-family employees. Family firms are also discouraged to overpay family employees over non-family employees.

In order to maintain a strong tie between the family employer and its business, many family firms have used dividend distribution to align the interests of families and the family firm. This common practice gives select family members shares of the business so that these individuals can benefit from the family business even if they do not have the professional skills needed to perform well as an employee in the family firm. While the dividend distribution can be set up as an entitlement to all family members or qualified family members, turning families into shareholders has its own challenges. This system has three common shortcomings. First, the dividends are tied to the earnings of the family firm. The dividends distributed to family members will be lower in a low-performing year. Second, as the shares are further divided among family members, the dividends received by each individual will become very modest in later generations. Third, unless the shares owned by the family founder have been determined from the beginning, the calculus of share division among family members can be a major challenge to the family. It is also a big challenge to determine which family members are eligible to receive shares of the family business and who deserves to be compensated. Given these concerns, many family firms have developed practices to compensate family members outside the family firm's salary payment.

THE DAWU GROUP

The researchers conducted a single case study at the Dawu Agriculture and Animal Husbandry Group (Dawu Group) in China to explore the impact of bifurcation bias on fairness and wealth management. Dawu Group's comprehensive services have covered three major industries with revenues over US$500 million and more than 5000 employees in 2017.[2] Apart from a financial loss due to an unexpected crisis in 2003, the corporation has had an average growth rate of over 30 percent per annum since its infancy (Du, 2011). This family business was chosen for our research for two reasons. First, Dawu Group is a family firm whose family owners insist on maintaining the family business identity. Second, the Dawu Group has been recognized by its provincial government as a leading brand and ranked nationally as a top 100 private company several times (Du, 2011). As this research focuses on the reduction of the bifurcation bias, a high-performing business is appropriate for this study.

We collected the case data mainly through interviews with key individuals from the Dawu Group. The authors visited Dawu Group three times in 2016 and 2017 to conduct multiple interviews. As displayed in Table 9.1, the research team interviewed the founder, chairman, vice president, division managers, and senior staff. The incumbent chairman, Meng Sun, is a second-generation member of the Sun family. His father, Dawu Sun, co-founded the Dawu Group with two younger brothers in 1985. Although Dawu Sun is no longer actively involved in daily business operations, he is still active in the family firm as the leader of the family. In addition to interviews, corporate records and internal education materials also play vital roles in this research.

Table 9.1   *Interviewees*

Interviewee	Number	Time	Interviewee	Number	Time
Chairman	1	3 h	Manager of Liquor Co.	1	1.5 h
Vice president	1	1 h	Manager of Food Co.	1	1.5 h
Assistant to chairman	1	2 h	Founder	1	3 h
Manager of Heritage Co.	2	2 h/person	Staff	2	1 h/person

OWNERSHIP AND COMPENSATION IN THE DAWU GROUP

There were two potential sources of bifurcation bias in the Dawu Group. The first source is the bias between the founder/owner Dawu Sun's family and members from other branches of the family. The second source is the bias between family and non-family employees. The Sun family has many relatives working in the business. But the relatives are far from adequate in terms of supplying the manpower needs of the large family firm. The sole owners of the Dawu Group, Dawu Sun and his wife, have recognized the need to manage the bifurcation bias since the inception of the business and have attempted to manage this challenge by sharing ownership of the firm.

Early Efforts to Align Stakeholder Interests

The present-day Dawu Group has only two shareholders, Dawu Sun and his wife. However, it was not this couple's original intention to keep the shares all to themselves. On the contrary, the Sun family had made two attempts to align the interests of stakeholders with shares, yet neither of them won target stakeholders' support.

Sun's first effort was to start a business with other co-founders/co-owners. It was 1984, shortly after the launch of the Chinese economic reform. The joint stock system was relatively new to Chinese society. Dawu Sun's wife started a farm business with four neighbors. There were five shareholders and each owned 20 percent of the farm at this point. All five co-founders also worked in the new farm business. However, this business lost all of its initial capital in the first year. All of the other four neighbors were determined to dissolve the business after taking the financial loss. Dawu Sun, then an employee at a local bank, helped to secure a small business loan to keep the farm alive. But the approval of the loan failed to persuade the other co-founders to stay with the business. Sun and his wife on the other hand saw the opportunity in the husbandry industry and decided to stay. The Suns purchased all of the shares from the other initial shareholders and bore all of the losses from year 1 to keep the business going. Since the other four co-founders had withdrawn from the business yet remained as employees, Sun and his wife became the only owner/shareholders in 1985. In 1992, Dawu Sun quit his bank job and invited his brothers to join the business to form the Dawu Group. Despite the addition of family members, Dawu Sun and his wife remained the sole shareholders of the family business.

Dawu Sun and his wife attempted to better align the interests of employees to the family firm through employee stock options in 1997. As the business had grown to become one of the largest agriculture businesses in the province, Sun was convinced that the joint stock system could better align the interests of employees and the business (Ji, 2015). His proposition was to give stock options to employees in lieu of cash bonuses. However, this idea was not well received by the employees because they preferred to be paid for labor rather than receiving dividends as shareholders (Ji, 2015).

The Grain Bank Crisis

The Dawu Group made another attempt to diversify ownership with family and non-family employees in the early 2000s, shortly after the Dawu Group survived the grain bank crisis in 2003. However, this effort also failed.

One of the main products of the Dawu Group is animal feed which is made from grain. The Chinese economic reform had provided incentives to farmers to grow more crops. However, the demand of the Chinese market did not catch up with the growth of supply in the mid- to late 1980s. Despite the oversupply of grain, Dawu Sun and his wife were short on cash to purchase the grain for animal feed production. The Suns therefore developed a deferred payment system to minimize the need for cash payment up front. This deferred payment system is the grain bank of the Dawu Group. Farmers can deposit their grain to the Dawu Group, which will use them to produce animal feed. The farmers can withdraw their grain deposits or equal value cash from the Dawu Group any time after the deposit. Dawu Group also encouraged the farmers to keep their grain deposit in Dawu Group by offering above-market interest rates.[3] If we simply see the deposited grain as a cash deposit, the Dawu Group is essentially running a banking operation to support its own business needs. In fact, this grain bank indeed allowed the family business to secure the supply of raw materials with delayed cash payments. This operation served the immediate needs of both the Dawu Group and local farmers.

Table 9.2   *Dawu family members in the grain bank crisis, 2003*

Name	Position
Dawu Sun (co-founder)	Director (in jail)
Erwu Sun (second brother)	Vice director (in jail)
Zhihua Sun (third brother)	General manager (in jail)
Huiru Liu (wife, co-founder)	Treasurer (fled)
Liuping (niece)	Vice general, then acting general manager
Sun Meng (eldest son)	Acting director

However, the success of the grain bank operation caught the attention of the government. Dawu Group was accused of illegal fundraising by the government (Table 9.2). The business was forced to cease most of the operations and all of the business assets were frozen. Dawu Sun and his two brothers, now also working in the family business, were arrested and detained for six months. Many executives were also arrested. Dawu Sun's son, newly graduated from college, was temporarily appointed as the chairman of the business group to oversee the contract fulfilment. Many employees were laid off and the business made significant losses during this period (Ji, 2015). It appeared to be a major crisis. In the end, the firm and its owner received a three-year sentence with probation and fines (Ji, 2015).

Upon surviving the legal crisis, the family and executives of the family business started discussions of ownership and compensation (Ji, 2015). These discussions were partially motivated by the Sun family's gratitude to the employees' loyalty during their most difficult time. It was also driven by heightened interests from families and non-family veterans for ownership and better compensation. Family employees generally demanded ownership of the business while non-family employees were more interested in salary raises. As the sole owner of the family business, Dawu Sun's initial reaction was to satisfy these demands by distributing shares to family and non-family employees. However, this idea soon proved to be far more difficult than anticipated. The family members and non-family employees were not able to come to an agreement on the distribution of shares. The discussion of share distribution was deeply dividing the family business and had become a major distraction to the business (Ji, 2015).

The Family Business Constitution

As the Dawu Group was unable to move the share distribution and employee ownership initiative forward, a different opinion, mainly from the family, emerged in the discussion. Instead of turning major stakeholders, including

family and non-family employees, to shareholders, would it be possible to suf-
ficiently compensate all of the stakeholders without dividing the ownership?
The stronger supporters for a non-dividing alternative were the parents of the
Sun brothers and Dawu Sun's wife. The suggestion for the non-dividing alternative quickly won the support of the majority of the stakeholders, especially
the family members. It was clear that the family members and relatives were
willing to accept reasonable financial compensation without equity ownership
as long as no one else owned equity of the family business (Du, 2011; Ji,
2015). As the family decided not to divide the ownership, the employee stock
option was also off the table. However, the family business still needed to
address the bifurcation bias concerns. All of the stakeholders eventually came
to agreement on two things. First, the Dawu Group needed to find a way to
fairly compensate both family and non-family employees without offering
its equities. Second, the owners, especially Dawu Sun and his direct family
members, deserved to be better compensated as they were the ones who took
the risk to start the business and were held legally accountable for business
practices. These two consensuses form the basis of a new system, which is
labeled as the Family Business Constitution of the Dawu Group.

The Constitution ensures fairness and family relevance with three key
elements. First, the Constitution regulates the salary raises of executives by
capping salaries to 15 times the salary of an entry-level position (Ji, 2015; Du
2011). The salary raises of mid-level managers and factory supervisors are
also subject to similar but smaller caps. Additionally, the employees of the
same pay scale receive basically the same base salary (Ji, 2015). The founders
of Dawu Group receive almost no bonus, leaving a large amount of profit in
the Group for rolling development, which provides a strong anti-risk ability
for long-term development and incentive design. In addition, the Group has
a normal performance bonus for its subordinate companies, thus the employees try to get a positive return – a cost incentive constraint (Ji, 2015). The
rigid compensation policy minimizes the compensation differences between
employees of the same pay scales and employees of different pay scales.
Second, the core members of the Sun family received monthly stipends from
the Group for their effort to start the business. This family-only compensation
also ensured that the Sun family was motivated to stay committed to the family
business. This stipend should not exceed three times the average salary of
employees. The family members also received lifelong free housing, medical
insurance, and tuition remission from the Group. Nevertheless, the family
members will not receive shares of the family business. The patriarch or the
designated family successor is the only shareholder of the Dawu Group.

Third, the Constitution introduced an election-based promotion policy. This
policy allows nearly all of the existing positions to be elected by employees.
Nowadays, most of the managerial promotions are now determined by election

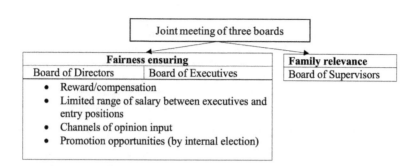

Figure 9.1   The structure of Dawu Group's family business constitution

(Ji, 2015; Du 2011). All employees who have worked in the business for a certain number of years are eligible to vote for their managers and executive team. Employees are also eligible to run for election-based promotions after a certain number of years of service. The Dawu Group elects its board of directors through this internal election. Regardless of their family affiliations, the executives and board members all receive extra benefits such as a free international family trip every year.

According to the Constitution, the Dawu Group is governed by three internal boards. These three boards are the board of supervisors (BOS), the board of directors (BOD), and the board of executives (BOE). The BOS represents the founder's family. It supervises the use of major corporate assets and the leaders of the other two boards. The BOD is similar to that of a typical corporate board in other organizations. What makes Dawu Group's BOD unique is that its members are determined by internal elections. As the Dawu Group has only one shareholder, the board is not representing the interests of the shareholders. However, the directors are elected by qualified employees and are responsible for the governing of the business. The BOE can be viewed as the executive team of the Dawu Group whose membership includes all of the executives and branch/division managers. The BOE is the one that carries out the strategic and operational plans. Although these three boards are trusted with different responsibilities, the final decision making occurs in the joint meeting of these three boards. The responsibilities and membership of the three boards are summarized in Table 9.3. We also summarize the timeline of the major events in Table 9.4. The structure of the Dawu Constitution is presented in Figure 9.1.

Table 9.3   The members and responsibilities of the three boards

Board of supervisors (BOS)	The BOS mainly consisted of the Sun family members and advisors.
	The duty of BOS is to draft and revise general rules and regulations, as well as to monitor the BOD and the BOE from legal, institutional, and moral perspectives.
	The supervisors are also responsible for overseeing finance and equities. The board has ownership of the business, yet has no control over decision making and operations.
	The general elections of the supervisors are held every three years by members of the Sun family.
Board of directors (BOD)	The BOD is composed of directors elected by employees of the company.
	All directors are responsible for developing the strategic goals and direction of the Group, as well as making investment decisions of subsidiary companies. They are also responsible for selecting the top leaders for each subsidiary company, deciding on annual profit targets and making bonus allocation plans.
	Members can enjoy director subsidies as well as use both public and private cars.
	A chief executive officer holding the position for more than two terms consecutively or accumulatively, and other directors holding the position for more than eight terms, is entitled to retirement benefits.
	Dawu Group also encourages the children of the directors to study abroad and to start their own business.
	The BOD can make administrative and strategic decisions, but do not have any ownership or operational power.
Board of Executives (BOE)	The BOE is made up of the top leaders of subsidiary companies and office directors.
	All executive board members are to coordinate in raising and using funds and ensure the efficient implementation of projects and tasks, all in compliance with the decisions made by the BOD.
	The executives on the board are entitled to performance-based bonuses and year-end bonuses. At retirement, a general manager who has held the position for more than three terms is able to enjoy the same benefits after retirement.
	Board members who have made great contributions can also enjoy the pay level of directors.
	The BOE only has power in operational issues with no ownership or administrative rights.

Source: Compiled by the authors based on information provided by Du (2011) and Ji (2015).

DISCUSSIONS AND IMPLICATIONS

The Sun family of the Dawu Group made two attempts to address the issues of fairness and family relevance by using shares as a means of reward and family compensation before the 2003 crisis. Both attempts failed. These experiences, coupled with the 2003 crisis, motivated the Dawu Group to design a system (i.e. the Dawu Constitution) that ensures fairness in terms of reward, promotion, and access to information while maintaining family relevance. Since the inception of the new system in 2005, the Dawu Group has seen significant

Table 9.4   *Major events of Dawu Group*

Year	Major events
1984	Ms. Hui-ru Liu invited four neighbors to start a farming business in her town. There were five families altogether. Each family owned 20 percent of the shares of the business by contributing RMB$2000.
1985*	The business lost 16,000 after one year. Ms. Liu's husband, Mr. Dawu Sun, was an employee of a local bank. Mr. Sun engineered a small business loan to his wife's business. This loan paid off the debt. However, the co-founders wanted to exit the farm business so Mr. Sun and his wife assumed full responsibility of the debt and became the sole shareholders of the business.
1992	Mr. Sun's two younger brothers quit their jobs and joined the business.
1995	The Dawu Group was recognized as a top 500 largest business in China by the National Industry and Business Bureau of China.
1997*	The Dawu Group planned to offer stock options to employees but this proposal was declined by employees. The employees preferred to receive a fixed salary and merit-based bonuses rather than shares.
2003	The crisis of the grain bank.
2004	Trial implementation of the Dawu Constitution.
2005	Formal implementation of Dawu Constitution.

Note: * These were the failed efforts to make employees and other families shareholders.

growth without major disputes between family and non-family employees. This system generally minimizes bifurcation bias in terms of reward, compensation, promotion, and channels of input while keeping the family relevant. Its effectiveness in reducing family conflict has also been considered by other Chinese family businesses as a successful model.

As a family business, it is not surprising that the Sun family of the Dawu Group works hard to maintain family relevance in their business. Their commitment to control bifurcation bias is extraordinary. Based on our interviews and the corporate documents (Ji, 2015), it appears that the experience of the grain bank crisis of 2003 played a big role in shaping the perspectives of the Sun family.

The 2003 grain bank crisis was a shock to the Dawu Group and its employees. Our interviewees recalled that the local government formed a taskforce to take over Dawu Group during the grain bank crisis and almost all of the executives were arrested. This government team demanded all the transactions to be reported to them, otherwise the employees involved would be punished. But the employees of Dawu Group, behind the back of the takeover team, secretly worked together to keep the business alive. They not only kept a day-to-day account but also made an inspection tour by themselves in the factories. All they wanted to do was to protect the firm from falling apart. The Sun brothers were arrested and imprisoned for half a year, but not a single mid-level manager left their post and many employees continued to give support and protection to the corporate property secretly. It is clear that the survival of the Dawu Group was largely dependent on the commitment of the employees. As most of the executives and key family leaders were in jail, the non-family employees manifested a strong commitment to their employers and to keeping the business alive. It is a fair statement to say that the "lessons learned" from this crisis motivated the Sun family to review and to think through its relationship with employees and families. The result of this reflection is Dawu Group's Family Business Constitution.

Dawu Group's system addressed two seemingly conflicting forces in a family business: fairness assurance and family relevance. This business has a unique ownership model since all of the shares are controlled by the patriarch and his wife. Although the concentration of ownership is common among small and young family firms, it is unusual to have one couple controlling all of the shares of a large organization. Dawu's high ownership concentration may be unique, but it does highlight an option to resolve the share division issue among families. The discussions of share distribution can be sensitive and difficult because the distribution of shares has a direct impact on how much wealth a family member will receive in the long run. Nevertheless, by offering all of the family members the same benefits, just like an equal shareholder, a resolution was made without a debate or conflict of share distribution discussions.

The second implication of the Dawu case is the role of the BOS in family wealth management. Since no one except the patriarch owns shares of the family business, the Sun family has to create a separate mechanism to distribute wealth among families. This arrangement is similar to the increasingly popular practice adopted by families to diversify sources of family financial income. An affluent family can create an independent administrative mechanism to create, manage, and distribute family wealth without relying on dividend and salary payments. An example of such an administrative design is the single-family office (SFO). An SFO is an independent organizational entity tasked to manage the wealth of the family (Rosplock, 2014). The wealth management side of an SFO can be very active, including investors engaged in wealth creating through active investments (Rosplock, 2014; Wilson, 2012). The focus of an SFO is clearly on serving the entire family, not just the family members who work in the family business, so there are no bifurcation bias concerns on the treatment of non-family employees. An SFO may or may not be incorporated, but an SFO represents a family's effort to separate their business and family wealth management regardless of the organizational form. It is estimated that there are more than 10,000 active SFOs in the world (Wilson, 2012), but this number is a small fraction of the global family business population. While an SFO is a more formalized design of family wealth management and independence, there are other less formal practices designed to separate family wealth management from corporate HR practices. In summary, an independent administrative mechanism of family wealth distribution allows families to provide family entitlements without compromising fairness within the business.

In addition to practice, the Dawu case also has a theoretical implication. Similar to the comparative advantage based on "labor" productivities, there also lies the comparative advantage based on "ownership" productivities, which involve interpersonal differences of abilities, knowledge, or attitudes toward risk (Alchian, 1965). For the former two, if ownership rights are transferable, then specialization of ownership in those areas in which people believe they have a comparative advantage will yield gains (we call it the comparative advantage effects of specialized application of knowledge in control). For the latter, the exchange of ownership will enable a reallocation of risks among people (risk bearing), leading to greater utility in the same sense that exchange of goods does. In this way, Alchian found that a person can separate the productivity of knowledge and effort in what he owns from the risk bearing. According to Alchian (1965), the owner's "knowledge" difference is not only shown in the productivity, but also a powerful tool for the resource allocation decision in different risk situations. Thus, some people choose to hold shares to reflect their "risk preference" knowledge, and some choose to be professional managers or decision makers to highlight their comparative advantage in capacity and knowledge (productivity). In the case of the Dawu Group, we have learned that shares are not always desirable for all stakeholders. It is likely that shares are more desirable for individuals who hold "ownership productivity." This will be a subject for future studies.

This research has several limitations. First, we were not able to empirically test the relationship between the financial performances of the Dawu Group and the Constitution. The business has certainly been doing very well since its survival of the grain bank crisis in 2003, but the availability of the data does not allow us to have a meaningful analysis to assess the contributions of the new system to the performances of the business.

Second, the Dawu Group is relatively young, and the Sun family is still small. If there are many family stakeholders making claims of the family business ownership, it may be more difficult to satisfy these claims with the system developed after the 2003 grain bank crisis. In addition, our interviews do not provide much information about the dynamics of the Sun family. A clearer picture of the family dynamics may better inform us about the effects of the Constitution.

NOTES

1. Although justice and fairness have subtle differences when applied in a legal context, these two terms are used interchangeably in the literature of management and business ethics (Samara and Paul, 2018).
2. Information accessed from the corporate website of the Dawu Group (August 1, 2019).
3. The "interest" of grain deposit is calculated based on the market value of the deposited grains.

REFERENCES

Alchian, A. A. (1965), Some economics of property rights, in *Economic Forces at Work*. Indianapolis, IN: Liberty Press.

Barnett, T. and Kellermanns, F. W. (2006), Are we family and are we treated as family? Nonfamily employees' perceptions of justice in the family firm. *Entrepreneurship Theory and Practice*, 30, 837–54.

Baron, J. and Lachenauer, R. (2016), The 5 models of family business ownership. *Harvard Business Review*, September 20.

Colquitt, J. A. (2001), On the dimensionality of organizational justice: A construct validation of a measure. *Journal of Applied Psychology*, 86, 386–400.

China Credit Information Service (2014), Business Group in Taiwan. Taipei: China Credit InformationService, Ltd.

Colquitt, J. A. and Rodell, J. B. (2015), Measuring justice and fairness, in R. S. Cropanzano and M. L. Ambrose (Eds), *Oxford Handbook of Justice in the Workplace* (pp. 187–202). Oxford: Oxford University Press.

Combs, J., Jaskiewicz, P., Shanine, K. K., and Balkin, D. B. (2018), Making sense of HR in family firms: Antecedents, moderators, and outcomes. Human Resource Management Review, 28(1), 1–4.

Daspit, J., Madison, K., Barnett, T., and Long, R. (2018), The emergence of bifurcation bias from unbalanced families: Examining HR practices in the family firm using circumplex theory. *Human Resource Management Review*, 28(1), 18–32.

Ding, H. B. and Lee, H. S. (2008), Make or buy? The invisible hand behind of the hiring decisions of family firms, in J. Butler (Ed.), *Theoretical Developments and Future Research in Family Business* (pp. 195–211). Charlotte, NC: Information Age Publishing.

Ding, H. B. and Phan, P. (2005), Family member employment and the formation of family business networks. *Journal of Business and Entrepreneurship*, 17(2), 24–38.

Ding, H. B. and Pukthuanthong-Le, K. (2012), Organizational legitimacy and the performance of family firm IPOs. *Journal of Business Economics and Management*, 14(1), 156–81.

Du, Y. (2011), Hebei Dawu Group: Building the first "Family Business Constitution" in China. Barcelona: IESE Publishing.

Fang, H., Memili, E., Chrisman, J. J., and Welsh, D. H. B. (2012), Family firms' professionalization: Institutional theory and resource-based view perspectives. *Small Business Institute Journal*, 8(2), 12–34.

Gomez-Mejia, L., Haynes, K., Núñez-Nickel, M., Jacobson, K. J. L., and Moyano-Fuentes, J. (2007), Socioemotional wealth and business risks in family-controlled firms: Evidence from Spanish olive oil mills. *Administrative Science Quarterly*, 52, 106–37.

Gomez-Mejia, L., Larraza-Kintana, M., & Makri, M. (2003). The determinants of executive compensation in family-controlled public corporations. *Academy of Management Journal*, 46(2), 226–37.

Huang, Y. C., Ding, H. B., and Kao, M. R. (2009), Salient stakeholder voices: Family business and green innovation adoption. *Journal of Management and Organization*, 15(3), 309–26.

Hytti, Ulla, Alsos, Gry, Heinonen, Jarna, Ljunggren, E. (2017), Navigating the family business: A gendered analysis of identity construction of daughters. *International Small Business Journal*, 35(6), 665–86.

Jaskiewicz, P., Uhlenbruck, K., Balkin, D., and Reay, T. (2013), Is nepotism good or bad? Types of nepotism and implications for knowledge management. *Family Business Review*, 26, 121–39.

Ji, W.-L. (2015), Family business constitution of Dawu Group. Dawu Group.

Johannisson, B. (2000), Modernising the industrial district: Rejuvenation or managerial colonisation, in M. Taylor and E. Vatne (Eds), The Networked Firm in a Global World: Small Firms in New Environments (pp. 283–308). Abingdon: Routledge.

Klein, S. B. and Bell, F. A. (2007), Nonfamily executives in family businesses: A literature review. *Electronic Journal of Family Business Studies*, 1(1), 19–37.

Lee, S., Phan, P., and Ding, H. (2016), A theory of family employee involvement during resource paucity. *Journal of Family Business Strategy*, 7(3), 160–6.

Rawls, J. (2001), *Justice as Fairness: A Restatement*. Cambridge, MA: Harvard University Press.

Rosplock, K. (2014), *The Complete Family Office Handbook: A Guide for Affluent Families and the Advisors Who Serve Them*. New York: Bloomberg Press.

Samara, G. and Arenas, D. (2017), Practicing fairness in the family business workplace. *Business Horizons*, 60(5), 647–55.

Samara, G. and Paul, K. (2018), Justice versus fairness in the family business workplace: A socioemotional wealth approach. *Business Ethics: A European Review*, 28(2), 175–84.

Shim, J. and Okamuro, H. (2011), Does ownership matter in mergers? A comparative study of the causes and consequences of mergers by family and non-family firms. *Journal of Banking and Finance*, 35(1), 193–203.

Tabor, W., Chrisman, J.J., Madison, K., &Vardaman, J.M. (2018). Nonfamily members in family firms: A review and future research agenda. *Family Business Review*, 31(1), 54–79.

Van der Heyden, L., Blondel, C., and Carlock, R. S. (2005), Fair process: Striving for justice in family business. *Family Business Review*, 18(1), 1–21.

Verbeke, A. and Kano, L. (2010), Transaction cost economics (TCE) and the family firm. *Entrepreneurship Theory and Practice*, 34(6), 1173–82.

Verbeke, A. and Kano, L. (2012), The transaction cost economics theory of the family firm: Family-based human asset specificity and the bifurcation bias. *Entrepreneurship Theory and Practice*, 36(6), 1183–205.

Wilson, R. C. (2012), *The Family Office Book: Investing Capital for the Ultra-Affluent*. Chichester: Wiley.

Index